Dialogue and Discourse

Dialogue and Discourse

*A sociolinguistic approach to modern
drama dialogue and naturally occurring
conversation*

Deirdre Burton
Department of English, University of Birmingham

ROUTLEDGE & KEGAN PAUL
London, Boston and Henley

First published in 1980
by Routledge & Kegan Paul Ltd
39 Store Street,
London WC1E 7DD,
9 Park Street,
Boston, Mass. 02108, USA and
Broadway House,
Newtown Road,
Henley-on-Thames,
Oxon RG9 1EN
Set in 10 on 12 Journal by
Hope Services, Abingdon
and printed in Great Britain by
Biddles Ltd Guildford

British Library Cataloguing in Publication Data

Burton, Deirdre
Dialogue and discourse.
1. Dialogue   2. English drama — 20th century
— History and criticism   3. Speech acts
(Linguistics)   4. Sociolinguistics
I. Title
822'.9'140926   PR739.D/   80–49961

ISBN 0 7100 0560 1

Contents

Acknowledgments

Grateful acknowledgment is made for permission to quote from the following copyright sources: the entire text of 'Last to go' from *A Slight Ache and Other Plays*, copyright © 1961 by Harold Pinter; from *The Dumb Waiter*, copyright © 1961 by Harold Pinter; from *Towards an Analysis of Discourse* by J. McH. Sinclair and R.M. Coulthard, © Oxford University Press 1975, reprinted by permission of Oxford University Press. The analysis of 'Last to go' in chapter 1 is an adapted version of an article entitled 'Making conversation' in *Language and Style*. The discussion of Sinclair and Coulthard's descriptive apparatus is printed in a slightly different form in a collection of conference papers edited by Margaret McLure and Peter French (1980) as *The Sociolinguistics of Children's Conversations* (Croom Helm).

Personal acknowledgments are many, and a pleasure to make. I am very grateful indeed for the interest, encouragement and advice I have received from colleagues in the English Language Research Unit at Birmingham University, but in particular I would like to thank John Sinclair and Malcolm Coulthard whose comments, criticism and ideas I have always valued highly. The work offered here would have been unthinkable but for their own. A similar central and pervasive influence has been Mike Stubbs, linguist extraordinary of the Linguistics department at the University of Nottingham. I am especially indebted to him for his many helpful suggestions (some of which I stubbornly ignored), his relentless clarity in thinking through any interesting academic problems, and for the uncanny way in which he remembers ideas I produce in casual conversation, but neglect to write down, and which would otherwise be forgotten entirely.

The English department at Birmingham University is a stimulating environment in which to be teaching, writing and having conversations. I owe a great deal to colleagues like David Lodge, Tom Davis, Mark

Storey and the inimitable Mr Faulkes. The work I do with my post-graduate students, listed here in alphabetical order (for reasons they will appreciate) as Gill Alexander, Liz Bangs, Sue Broughton, Ron Carter, Susi Höbel, Kay Richardson, and Val Webb, is my pleasure and my benefit. I have also learned a great deal from the undergraduate students who took a course with me during 1978–9 on 'Linguistic approaches to literature'. Richard Mead shouts questions about my method for analysing discourse from twelfth-floor windows.

Cheryl Evans has worked efficiently and impressively, producing a typescript at great speed, and correcting me on many details I had overlooked.

I owe a strange, special and old debt to the talents of Gess Banks of the French department in Birmingham, and Peter Davison, now of the English department at the University of Kent, but erstwhile white tornado of the English department at Birmingham. They first introduced me to Pinter's 'Last to go', which is discussed here in chapter 1, in a course of undergraduate lectures on modern drama. Superb teachers, both of them, they had the audience rolling in the aisles (which is no mean achievement at 9 a.m. on cold Tuesday mornings in the middle of winter) whilst never selling us short on intellectual matters. I am not the only person to have benefited from their teaching.

Introduction

This book is organized in two distinct but essentially complementary parts. The first is called 'Dialogue', and the second 'Discourse'. To me these represent two closely related focuses within current sociolinguistics (understanding that term in its widest sense), but then these are ideas I have been working with for some time now, and I am sure I need to spend time and space here making clear how I understand these terms, and what aspects of these areas the reader may expect to find in the following chapters.

'Dialogue' contains studies of specific modern drama texts, and is basically an exercise in a new area of literary-linguistic stylistics. Chapters 1, 2 and 3 demonstrate how recent advances in the sociolinguistic description of spoken discourse, or conversational analysis, can be drawn on to account for reader and audience intuitions about the dialogue in those texts. The links between topics covered in the sociolinguistics literature and speech events in the plays are surprisingly easy to find. The results are rich, varied and temporarily satisfying, for, although much more practical work on dialogue can and should be undertaken in this way, from the point of view of linguistic-stylistics theory, this approach can only be a starting-point. It is argued in chapter 4 that a rigorous and comprehensive analysis of dialogue style must be able to draw on a rigorous and coherent theoretical and descriptive framework for the analysis of all naturally occurring conversation. It is the design of such a framework that is the focus of part 2.

'Discourse' is an attempt to expand one powerful linguistic theory of naturally occurring talk. This model (Sinclair and Coulthard, 1975), is only one of the many linguistic, sociolinguistic, ethnomethodological and philosophy of language frameworks available for the analysis of stretches of language more than one sentence or one utterance long. Its various advantages and shortcomings are detailed in chapter 6. In chapter 7, another model, based on similar principles, is offered for the analysis of all conversational data. This was devised using the dialogue of the texts discussed in part 1 as a heuristic device, and the warrant for this is given in chapter 5. Suggestions for further research are given in chapter 8.

There are several standard pieces of work that I have specifically not undertaken, since they have been done so many times before: justifying a linguistic-stylistic approach to a literary text, and comparing literary-critical statements with linguistic ones; justifying the study of connected discourse; justifying the study of 'language-used-in-context'. One reason for this was purely practical, in that I was reluctant to take up valuable space with arguments already competently presented elsewhere. Another, much more important reason is to do with the state and status of these various arts. As Kuhn (1962) points out, one way of distinguishing dominant academic paradigms at any given time is to observe what kinds of concessions and apologies are made in the opening chapters of works in related subject areas. To take a simple example, in current introductions to systemic grammar, the reader can find frequent explanations of how it is that this model differs from a transformational-generative model (see Berry, 1976, for example), whereas, as far as I am aware, no work on transformational-generative grammar would carry an explanation of how its own model differed from the systemic one. Since linguists have been writing clearly-defined stylistics for some four decades now, I think it is inappropriate to continue justifying the case for this work according to the implicitly dominant literary-critical paradigm. Any reader unfamiliar with these arguments and demonstrations is directed towards the following: Halliday (1966), McIntosh (1966), Jakobson (1960), Uitti (1969), Freeman (1970), Sinclair (1966a), Fowler (1971), Widdowson (1975). Similarly, see the following works on the value of the linguist studying connected discourse: Firth (1935), Halliday (1964), Dressler (1970), Ballard *et al.* (1971), Hendricks (1972), Pike (1964), van Dijk (1970, 1972), Widdowson (1976). And again, see the following for the importance (for some linguistic goals within some theoretical frameworks) of studying language in context: Firth (1935), Weinreich (1966), Hymes (1972a and b, 1977), Labov (1970), Halliday (1971), Lakoff (1972), Haberland and Mey (1977).

Whilst it will, I imagine, be obvious that this work is not intended as literary criticism, I hope it might be useful to any critic with an appropriate theoretical framework in which to accommodate my descriptive work. My choice of plays and playwrights is dictated entirely by their relevance to the topic of the book as given in the opening paragraphs above, and makes no concessions to literary history, movements or other such respectable literary criteria. Similarly I make no claims to have studied Pinter or Ionesco in depth, although again I hope that anyone who is engaged in such an activity might find my descriptive work useful.

To sociologists, and particularly sociologists of literature and drama, I will have produced what must appear to be a mysterious and eclectic set of cited references. I am very much aware of theoretical debates that would have been aired, and contrastive positions that would have been located, had there been world enough and time. But again, I hope that the analytical work as such might be of interest to specialists in this area too.

As this introduction suggests, I anticipate readers from various backgrounds making use of this book. Thus, whilst my primary audience has been conceptualized in terms of those already interested in language and style, stylistics and discourse analysis, I have also designed explanatory passages throughout for others with complementary background knowledge and interests. These will be over-explicit for some readers, but will, I hope, enable any reader to make sense of my discussions and arguments.

Part One: Dialogue

Chapter 1

The stylistic analysis of modern drama texts: some background remarks and a practical example

It is an interesting fact that stylisticians do not write about modern dramatists or modern drama texts. By this, I do not mean to imply that they deal with them inadequately, but — much more simply — that they appear not to study them at all. There is a very clear demonstration of this fact in Bailey and Burton (1968), the only comprehensive bibliography to date. Firstly, in their index of 'Styles under scrutiny' there are no modern dramatists listed at all. Secondly, and much more significantly, in their major divisions of the book as a whole they present a large section entitled 'English stylistics in the twentieth century', which, after general theoretical studies, lists of statistical studies and entries on translation problems, is subdivided into only two substantial sections: 'Prose stylistics' and 'Style in poetry'. Drama stylistics has no place at all. In the light of this phenomenon, Halliday (1964) is worth considering:

> It is part of the task of linguistics to describe texts; and all texts, including those, prose and verse, which fall within any definition of 'literature', are accessible to analysis by the existing methods of linguistics.

Since any unusual definition of literature would surely include three genres, I think the continued exclusion of dramatic language from modern stylistic analysis deserves some investigation.

The first and most obvious reason for the bipartite and not tripartite categorization, is the fact that non-poetic dramatic dialogue may sometimes be classified as merely another type of prose. Abercrombie certainly makes this point clearly enough (Abercrombie, 1959):

> Most people believe that *spoken prose,* as I would call what we normally hear on the stage or screen, is at least not far removed,

when well done, from the conversation of real life. Writers of novels are sometimes praised for 'naturalistic dialogue', others such as Miss Ivy Compton Burnett, are criticized because nobody speaks like the characters in their books.

But the truth is that nobody speaks at all like the characters in any novel, play, or film. Life would be intolerable if they did; and novels, plays or films would be intolerable if the characters spoke as people do in life. Spoken prose is far more different from conversation than is normally realised.

Since this passage was intended for a linguistically naive audience, these are sound and necessary statements — making the sorts of distinctions it would be both proper and essential to make in such a pedagogical context. Page (1973), writing on speech in the novel, makes a particular point — incorporating in his text, for comparison with fictional speech, a short piece of transcript of naturally occurring conversation — complete with the hesitation-phenomena, repetitions, false starts and stammers that characterize almost any transcript of naturally occurring talk. Also, he provides actual, literary-critical examples of Abercrombie's 'most people':

A familiar kind of tribute to such mimetic writing is to praise it for its closeness to real speech. We are told, for instance, that 'dialogue. . .consistently echoes the speech of the day', that 'there is no line of dialogue from a novel that could not easily be imagined proceeding from the mouth of an actual person', and, of a modern novel, that 'the dialogues. . .could not reproduce actual speech more faithfully, and more unselectively, if they had been transcribed from a tape-recorder'. These are striking claims from impressive sources. But it seems probable that the whole concept of realism as applied to fictional speech is often based on an inadequate or inaccurate notion of what spontaneous speech is really like.

Certainly, a linguist with even minimal experience of naturally occurring speech, either on tape or in the inevitably tidied-up representation of a transcript, would have to agree. On the other hand, in the context of linguistic stylistics, the very point that Abercrombie and Page are dismissing, the fact that readers have the definite impression that fictional speech or spoken prose seems to be like or unlike naturally occurring conversation, is extremely interesting and relevant. Here, surely, is evidence of what we normally use as the starting point of a stylistic analysis;

the fact that the analyst, as reader, has certain intuitive impressions of a set of stylistic effects – intuitions which should be open to linguistic justification on a closer study of the text.

If we accept that there is an interesting relationship between play dialogue and real conversation, and if we agree that it might be linguistically interesting to consider the language used in dialogue specifically in the light of this relationship, then the stylistician has an immediate problem in deciding how to conceptualize the underlying linguistic mechanisms that are, in some way, being used and exploited by the writer of dialogue, and reacted to by the reader of dialogue. For, despite the many quibbles in aspects of stylistics writing, such as which syntactic paradigm to use, what constitutes 'style', the goals and focuses of stylistic analyses, the relevance of different linguistic features and so on, there is never any real doubt expressed about the fact that, in order to write about style in a linguistically justifiable way, we must be able to relate the language used in a text, or by an author, to the conventions of the language as a whole. All practical stylistics papers carry this assumption. For one example among many, Benamou (1963) presents a theory suggesting that style results from deviations from linguistic conventions, and analyses thus a sentence from Proust, connectives in Voltaire, adjectives in Colette and verbs in Camus. (See also Gorny, 1961; Ohmann, 1964; Greenfield, 1967; Hill, 1967; Jakobson, 1968; Enkvist, 1971; Fowler, 1972; Quirk, 1972; Widdowson, 1972).

This underlying methodological principle is explicitly reinforced in more theoretical papers too. Thus Mukařovský (1932) makes a comparatively early statement on the idea of norm and deviation with relation to poetry, 'The distortion of the norm of the standard is. . .of the very essence of poetry', whilst Bloch (1953) states that this comparison between the norm of the language used and the language as used in the text is a basic parameter for stylistics: 'The style of a discourse is the message carried by the frequency distributions, and transitional probabilities of its linguistic features, especially as they differ from those same features in the language as a whole.' Similarly, and more recently, Stankiewicz (1960), in his discussion of poets as innovators – in this context, writers using familiar words in unusual syntactic structures – makes a statement about stylistics procedure which is applicable to all varieties of language-in-use: 'The student of poetry is in no position to describe and explain the nature of poetic language unless he takes into account the rules of the language which determine its organisation.'

5

Of McIntosh's proposed four stylistic modes (1961) — normal collocations and normal grammar, unusual collocations and normal grammar, normal collocations and unusual grammar, unusual collocations and unusual grammar — it is interesting, though not perhaps surprising, that it is the more noticeably 'deviant' texts that attract the attention of most stylisticians. Thus, much of the impetus behind the transformational-generative approach to work in stylistics lies with those texts which exploit most fully potential deviance from linguistic norms of the everyday, familiar, automatized language. Levin, for example (1963, 1964, 1965), uses the grammar to define differences in poetic language, with the explicit underlying hypothesis that deviancy, in itself, is a marker of poeticalness, and the more measurably deviant a text can be shown to be, the more 'poetic' it is in its effect. Similarly Thorne's (1965) notion of constructing micro-grammars for individual poetic works assumes that there are noticeable points of similarity and dissimilarity between the grammar of the piece being studied and the grammar of the underlying language as a whole. From the latter, the poet selects some features and rules, but not others. Both Saporta (1960) and Rifaterre, the latter working in an information-theory context, would support these ideas. For example (Rifaterre, 1960), 'The stylistic context is a linguistic pattern broken by an element which was unpredictable.'

There is, of course, a symbiotic relationship between stylistic analysis and syntactic theory. The sort of reciprocal relationship between study of the text and study of the syntax of the language, where knowledge of one is enhanced by study of the other, is brought out particularly well by Franges (1961), who points out that our concept of the underlying norm can only be taken for granted in some areas, and that continual modifications must be carried out. I take it that this underlies all the statements quoted here, and the many others that could be drawn on to illustrate the arguments about the norm–deviation relationship as a focal issue for practical and theoretical stylistics:

> Ainsi norme et déviation ne doivent être prises qu'en tant que
> termes appartenant à la stylistique descriptive ne pouvant avoir
> ni valeur esthétique ni critique. Il va de soi qu'il reste encore
> beaucoup à faire pour déterminer ce qu'est la norme. [So norm
> and deviation should only be taken as terms appropriate to de-
> scriptive stylistics — having neither aesthetic nor critical value.
> It goes without saying that there is still much work to be done in
> determining the norm.]

I find Halliday's (1964) brief résumé of the norm and deviation question particularly sensible – his conclusion being that the analyst needs to consider both the norm of the underlying language, in so far as he knows it, and the norm set up by patterns in the text itself.

From all this, it follows that in order to talk about style linguistically, we need to have access to an accumulation of linguistic information about the standard language (using that term in a common-sense way here), and information which is working towards theoretical coherence and is descriptively adequate at all the linguistic levels that are to be considered in any text which is to be studied. If, therefore, we are interested in the norm–deviation relationship realized in the micro-conversations of a drama dialogue, it similarly follows that we need a relevant set of linguistic materials with which to describe this relationship. Clearly, the sorts of features traditionally used in stylistic analysis (phonological, lexical, syntactical) will not, on their own, be sufficient. It is particularly interesting to consider the only linguistic analysis which is clearly related to my interests here: Page's work on speech as represented in the novel (Page, 1973). He certainly does raise some of 'the fundamental questions of the nature of fictional speech, its role as one of the elements of the novel, and its relationship to other elements and to the speech of real life.' When it comes to actual concrete analyses of text, however, he concentrates exclusively on represented speech as an element of the prose, and emphasizes its formal relationships with the other prose elements of the novel rather than its relationship with the 'speech of real life'. Accordingly, he analyses it in terms of lexis, syntax and orthographic conventions, as this very typical quotation demonstrates clearly:

> There is a sense in which, in such speeches as these, lexical and syntactic features are made to correspond to qualities of moral character. The formal syntax of Fellmar, remote from the structures of spontaneous speech, suggests the artificiality and unreliability of his behaviour as well as his social status; at the other extreme, the blunt declarations of Western, who prefers short sentences and has a marked distrust of subordinate clauses, are consistent with his impetuous manner and his indifference to canons of polite behaviour. His vocabulary relies heavily on short, concrete words, in contrast to the more morally unsound characters for abstractions.

Given that Page is writing about speech as part of a novel, as opposed to dialogue written to be spoken by real human beings in a tangible, visible theatrical set of some kind, there is some justification for this sort of approach, although I consider it a shortcoming in the study that he did not consider the fictional–real relationship more thoroughly. However, consider also this extract from John Russell Brown (1972), where the topic is indeed theatre-talk:

> The short second sentence — 'Well, why don't you?' — points attention at Cliff's inability to reply, but, because it is in two phrases, it also sharpens the rhythm and so reveals a quicker attention under Jimmy's opening gambit. Then, the phrase lengthens until the unexpected 'New Economics', which is punched home with a rounder, polysyllabic and partly repetitive phrase. The growth of power is further shown by the assurance of the following, almost throw-away sentence, with neat, running alliteration, at the end: 'It's all a matter of payments and penalties'. This relaxed verbal tension is offset by a growing physical exertion as Jimmy 'Rises', and then the climax of this part of the speech can come freely in its longest and its largest single phrase, 'those apocalyptic share pushers'.

It is, I think, fairly obvious that if we want to consider play-talk and its degree of similarity to real-talk, then discussing sentences, phrases, alliteration, polysyllabic words and so on, is not going to tell us a great deal.

The only possible linguistic level to use as a basis for such analysis is *discourse*, or, even more specifically, *conversation* – as an aspect of discourse. A work by Larthomas (1972) which considers many interesting features of French classical and modern drama texts, and which is certainly aware of some of the problems of discussing drama dialogue as written language rather than as written-to-be-spoken language, justifies a purely syntactical approach by the following statement (p. 332):

> L'analyse en ce domaine est difficile parce que si nous connaissons bien la langue écrite, nous connaissons très mal la langue parlé.
> [Analysis in this area is difficult, because although we understand written language well, we know little about spoken language.]

As yet, of course, conversational analysis is uncollected, only partially adequate theoretically, sporadically insightful, occasionally misguided. Nevertheless, there is now a substantial body of descriptive linguistic work on conversational analysis available, and if we are ever going to progress beyond mere intuition and assumption in this very interesting potential area for stylistic analysis, then we must surely use this type of linguistics for our information about the norm.

So, as a brief illustration of the type of stylistic work I envisage in this area, I will discuss here a short Pinter sketch: 'Last to go' (1961a). As all analysts know, analysis expands to fit the time available (see Pittenger *et al.*, 1960). The present analysis is an attempt to make clear the methodological approach to be taken up at length in chapters 2 and 3, where the main texts are discussed in lengthier detail. I find a certain sympathy with Longacre here, who, in reviewing van Dijk (1972) in the *Journal of Linguistics* (March 1976), says the following:

> I have worked enough on this problem [a generative grammar of discourse] in relation to a specific text to know that (1) it can be done, and (2) the resultant formal structure is so intricate, involved and lengthy that perhaps no-one will be interested in looking it over when one is through.

This shorter piece of analysis is offered in the hope of demonstrating, quite simply and quickly, the way in which conversational analysis can and does prove useful in the stylistic analysis of drama text.

Firstly, I shall give the text of the sketch, to consider as data. Secondly, I shall articulate what I feel to be some effects created by the text. Thirdly, I shall specify some relevant rules of conversational structure, as observed and specified by analysts of naturally occurring conversations, and show how these are used and exploited in the text to create the effects that I notice intuitively. Like Sacks (1972), I feel confident that some of my intuitions about a text will be markedly similar to those of other readers of the same text. With the present text I feel secure on two counts. Firstly, having used it as a teaching text, I know that a substantial number of my students have 'read it the same way', and I have not as yet come across anyone who disagrees with the type of intuitions I state here. Secondly, by stating clearly what (some of) my impressions are, and demonstrating features of the text that ground these impressions, I assume I am 'proving the possibility' (Sacks, 1970) of my reading the text that way. Any other reader or analyst who understood the text differently would of course be free to offer and justify an alternative set of observations.

LAST TO GO

A coffee stall. A BARMAN and an old NEWSPAPER SELLER. The BARMAN leans on his counter, the OLD MAN stands with tea. Silence.

MAN	You was a bit busier earlier.	1
BARMAN	Ah.	2
MAN	Round about ten.	3
BARMAN	Ten, was it?	4
MAN	About then.	5
	(*Pause*)	
	I passed by here about then.	5a
BARMAN	Oh yes?	6
MAN	I noticed you were doing a bit of trade.	7
	(*Pause*)	
BARMAN	Yes, trade was very brisk here about ten.	8
MAN	Yes, I noticed.	9
	(*Pause*)	
	I sold my last one about then. Yes. About nine forty-five.	9a
BARMAN	Sold your last then, did you?	10
MAN	Yes, my last 'Evening News' it was. Went about twenty to ten.	11
	(*Pause*)	
BARMAN	'Evening News', was it?	12
MAN	Yes.	13
	(*Pause*)	
	Sometimes it's the 'Star' is the last to go.	13a
BARMAN	Ah.	14
MAN	Or the . . . whatsisname.	15
BARMAN	'Standard'.	16
MAN	Yes.	17
	(*Pause*)	
	All I had left tonight was the 'Evening News'.	17a
	(*Pause*)	
BARMAN	Then that went, did it?	18
MAN	Yes.	19
	(*Pause*)	
	Like a shot.	19a
	(*Pause*)	

BARMAN	You didn't have any left, eh?	20
MAN	No. Not after I sold that one.	21
	(*Pause*)	
BARMAN	It was after that you must have come by here then, was it?	22
MAN	Yes, I come by here after that, see, after I packed up.	23
BARMAN	You didn't stop here though, did you?	24
MAN	When?	25
BARMAN	I mean, you didn't stop here and have a cup of tea then, did you?	26
MAN	What, about ten?	27
BARMAN	Yes.	28
MAN	No, I went up to Victoria.	29
BARMAN	No, I thought I didn't see you.	30
MAN	I had to go to Victoria.	31
	(*Pause*)	
BARMAN	Yes, trade was very brisk here about then.	32
	(*Pause*)	
MAN	I went to see if I could get hold of George.	33
BARMAN	Who?	34
MAN	George.	35
	(*Pause*)	
BARMAN	George who?	36
MAN	George . . . whatsisname.	37
BARMAN	Oh.	38
	(*Pause*)	
	Did you get hold of him?	38a
MAN	No. No, I couldn't get hold of him. I couldn't locate him.	39
BARMAN	He's not much about now, is he?	40
	(*Pause*)	
MAN	When did you last see him then?	41
BARMAN	Oh, I haven't seen him for years.	42
MAN	No, nor me.	43
	(*Pause*)	
BARMAN	Used to suffer very bad from arthritis.	44
MAN	Arthritis?	45
BARMAN	Yes.	46
MAN	He never suffered from arthritis.	47

BARMAN	Suffered very bad.	48
	(*Pause*)	
MAN	Not when I knew him.	49
	(*Pause*)	
BARMAN	I think he must have left the area.	50
	(*Pause*)	
MAN	Yes, it was the 'Evening News' was the last to go tonight.	51
BARMAN	Not always the last though, is it, though?	52
MAN	No. Oh no. I mean sometimes it's the 'News'. Other times it's one of the others. No way of telling beforehand. Until you've got your last one left, of course. Then you can tell which one it's going to be.	53
BARMAN	Yes.	54
	(*Pause*)	
MAN	Oh yes.	55
	(*Pause*)	
	I think he must have left the area.	55a

It seems to me that there are two different categories of 'effects' worth considering in this text. Firstly, we intuitively feel that this is very like 'real' conversation. Of course, the fact that Pinter often (though not, note, always) writes realistic-sounding dialogue is not surprising news for anyone. What would, however, be news would be to specify how a given dialogue is like a naturally occurring conversation, and to do this in ways that are not merely impressionistic, nor superficial, but which relate to specifically linguistic mechanisms discovered in use in naturalistic data, and for which there is a set of formal rules governing production, realization and structure.

Secondly, within the confines of this 'realistic conversation' we are able to make intuitive statements about the interactive characters of the conversationalists. Thus it is quite clear that they are 'making conversation'; that the Man is more eager and more competent in this than the Barman; that it is a difficult and uncomfortable situation for both of them; that they are trying to be friendly without having too much to say to one another; that all this is rather comic; that the conversation has not finished when the curtain falls; that the unseen George takes on a rather special significance, reminiscent of many other unseen people and places in Pinter plays. The interesting problem, again, for the linguistic-stylistician is to specify how we know all this, and to specify it in a way that is linguistically interesting. Since our data is in some way an exploitation of overheard conversation, it seems feasible that conversational analysis would have something particularly relevant to contribute to this specification.

So I want to consider two problems. Firstly, why does this dialogue sound or read something like a real conversation? Secondly, how do we know so much about the interactants in the dialogue? Whilst it would be misleading to claim that discourse analysis is in any way complete in either its theoretical or descriptive adequacy, there is nevertheless a substantial body of linguistic writing that presents aspects of the rule-governed behaviour of conversationalists — some of which I shall draw on here. Three pieces which seem particularly apposite are William Labov's work on shared knowledge (Labov, 1970), Gail Jefferson's work on repetition (Jefferson, 1972) and John Laver's work on phatic communion (Laver, 1974). Whilst most of this section will be concerned with considering those works in particular, I shall indicate at the end of it how other major research papers might profitably further the analysis of the sketch in question.

Labov makes a small but crucial and exact point concerning 'shared knowledge'. He classifies, quite simply, all reported events in a two-party conversation as A-events (known to speaker A), B-events (known to speaker B) and AB-events (known to both A and B). From this he derives a simple but invariant rule of interpretation of discourse (Labov, 1970, p.124): 'If A makes a statement about a B event, it is heard as a request for confirmation.' A recurrent feature of the Pinter text is statements that are indeed heard as requests for confirmation — in the sense that they get confirmation. It is a simple matter for the analyst to pick out two-part exchanges that follow this pattern: 1/2, 10/11, 12/13, 18/19, 20/21, 22/23, 24/side-sequence/29, 52/53. The first of these is initiated by the Man, and all others by the Barman. There are several interesting points to be made here.

Firstly, it is important to notice that the actual referents for all these paired utterances are, in fact, not B-events but AB-events. Thus the characters are continually questioning and confirming matters that they both already know, that they must surely know that they both know, and that the audience certainly knows that they know. This is made quite clear, in that all but one of the requests for confirmation are re-statements of an earlier statement easily located in the text, for example:

MAN	I sold my last one about then. Yes. About nine forty-five.
BARMAN	Sold your last then, did you?
MAN	Yes, my last 'Evening News' it was. Went about twenty to ten.
	(*Pause*)
BARMAN	'Evening News', was it?
MAN	Yes.

This is surely where much of the humour of the piece lies. Here the mechanism of the talk, whilst extremely effective in continuing the talk *per se*, is incongruous in terms of our understanding of the more usual conventions of shared knowledge. As well as being humorous, though, it is important to notice that this is by no means an impossible feature to use in naturally occurring conversation. It is essential to realize that it is a very specific type of conversation that Pinter is recognized as writing. A simple verification of this is that, every now and then, it is quite acceptable for people engaged in a conversation — or listening to one — to stand back from it, in an analytic role, and remark that it is 'Pinteresque'. One noticeable feature of such noteworthy conversations is their too-frequent-to-ignore use of AB-events as items for confirmation by A to B, or vice versa.

There will be more to say about this mechanism of talk when we come to discuss phatic communion in its own right. At this stage it is worth pointing out that one way of doing phatic communion is to refer to AB-events. And one way of making phatic communion into on-going conversation is to refer to AB-events as if they were B-events for confirmation — thus ensuring a reply from your co-conversationalist. So, if the characters are willing to talk as a social activity, but have very little to talk about, it is entirely consistent that the Man should open the talk in this form. It is also, structurally at least, consistent with the rules of naturally occurring conversation.

If we also consider the intuition that the Barman is, of the two speakers, the one who is more at a loss for conversational topics, it is interesting to notice that it is he and not the Man, who, after the opening utterance, makes exclusive use of this strategy — almost as if he takes a conversational cue from the initial successful utterance. It is interesting, too, that he reinforces the interactive potential of these statements with suffixed tags — a sort of belt-and-braces security to further his desire to continue the talk and receive answers. Notice, too, all is well as long as the Man not only confirms in the right place (which he does, reliably), but also expands his contributions sufficiently to allow more talk to be built on this simple model. When he does not, one of two things happens often enough to be worth commenting on. Either the Man is constrained to expand after an ensuing pause (5/5a, 9/9a, 17/17a, 19/19a), or the Barman breaks the pause himself with an utterance that once again repeats the statement-for-confirmation model (11 pause 12, 17a pause 18, 19a pause 20, 21 pause 22).

It is important, once we have noticed the foregrounding of this pattern through its frequent occurrence, to notice where the pattern changes. It changes significantly at utterance 33, where 'George' is introduced as a topic, and the characters orient their talk towards a third person, rather than themselves. The change in conversational pattern lends the absent George a peculiar significance in his own right – as a less obviously phatic referent. He is reminiscent of the many other people and places which Pinter characters refer to, but which are never seen by the audience, and, again, repeated reference to the Christian name of an absent person is a typical feature of real-life conversations which participants realize are Pinteresque. Notice that the pattern of AB-statement-as-request-for-confirmation returns once George and his whereabouts and arthritis are exhausted. In terms of the text, however, this promotes the George section as a particularly noticeable deviation from a norm that the text itself sets up. We are thus led to believe that this is an important piece of reference.

The repeated pattern itself lends humour to the piece – simply by virtue of its repetition. Here we see mechanical elements of the conversation strictly as formal devices, and, as Bergson (1911, p.87) suggests, points where the mechanical nature of human activity is foregrounded are always amusing:

> The comic is that side of a person which reveals his likeness to a thing, that aspect of human events which, through its peculiar in-elasticity, conveys the impression of pure mechanism, of auto-matism, of movement without life.

It is noticeable that there is usually laughter from an audience at line 55, where they are led to believe that the preceding passage was going to branch out into referentially interesting material, but which at 55 returns to the mechanistic transference of speaker-turns and AB-events as topic.

Now that we are considering repetition as a feature of the text, it is

15

relevent to consider what Jefferson has to say on the topic. It is a commonly stated observation in literary criticism that talk is 'repetitive' in Pinter's plays, and that in some vague, intuitive way this makes it conversation-like. Jefferson, in her work on side-sequences, offers a clarification of this rather unspecific category of 'repetition', which is useful here — particularly as she identifies 'repeats' as a strictly functional item in talk.

Firstly, she distinguishes between a repeat as a functional item — which is used to produce more talk on the referent to that item — and a 'replication', which may have a functional load, such as 'framing' or 'locating' a focus item, but which may have no prospective structural purpose in the interaction, acting instead as a cohesive device. Notice that a 'repeat' need not replicate, but may well reformulate a preceding item. Notice also that a speaker may 'repeat' on himself.

Her data makes this rather more clear. She cites a stretch of children's talk, where the youngest is supposed to be counting to ten at the start of a game of tag, but makes a formal mistake:

STEVEN   One, two, three, ((pause)) four, five, six ((pause))
          eleven, eight, nine, ten.
SUSAN   'Eleven'? — eight, nine, ten?
STEVEN   Eleven, eight, nine, ten.
NANCY   'Eleven'?
STEVEN   Seven, eight, nine, ten.
NANCY   That's better.

From this she presents the following observations and working definitions:

> A 'repeat' is differentiable from such a similar object as a 'frame' or a 'locator', which may also be replicating that which has been said before. That is to say, in 'Eleven'? — eight, nine, ten?' it is 'eleven' which is being 'repeated', and the 'repeat' is 'framed' by replications of the digits 'eight, nine, ten'.

She also indicates here the distinctive work of a repeat:

> The differentiability of a 'repeat' from other replications derives from the distinctive work that they do; repeats have as a specific consequence of their occurrence and recognition that, for example, further work will be done.

This is one area where Jefferson's clarification of the function of repeats is useful in considering the Pinter text. It is a simple matter for the analyst to go through the text and pick out repeats and replications. What is interesting is to notice just how much the repeat is used to ensure that 'further work will be done', that is, that the conversation will keep going.

Taking a few lines at random, we can mark out the pattern shown in Figure 1.1. Particular repeats are performed on the 'about ten', 'sold my last' and 'Evening News'. As an interactional resource, these items

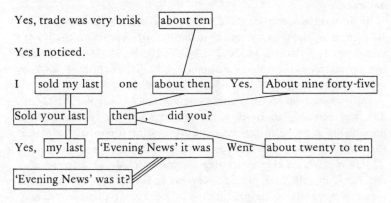

Figure 1.1

are 'repeated' right through the text. Thus, reference to the situation of the characters and their work and possessions 'about ten' are to be found in lines 1, 3, 4, 5, 5a, 8, 9, 9a, 10, 11, 18, 21, 22, 23, 25, 27, 28, 32. Similarly, 'Selling my/your last' repeats are to be found in lines 9a, 10, 11, 13a, 17a, 18, 19, 19a, 20, 21, 51, 52, 53 (expanded). And references to the 'Evening News' in comparison with other papers may be found at 11, 12, 13, 13a, 15, 16, 17, 17a, 18, 19, 21, 51, 52, 53 (expanded). It is relevant to point out that these last two repeats are dropped for some thirty lines and are brought in again at line 51, towards the close of the sketch.

There are also some much more localized 'repeating' sequences, particularly lines 33-8 (about George), lines 38a-43 (getting hold of George) and 44-9 (George and his arthritis). These George-oriented sequences, whilst they alter the topic of the characters' talk, do not alter the repeating mechanism – in that the way the talk proceeds is

17

quite simply by using repeats for further work; either confirmation or negation by the other party. The end of the sketch presents the two topics intermeshed, though again the mechanism itself still remains intact. And, as mentioned above in the remarks on shared knowledge, this marks George out for special attention. Notice particularly the set-up joke at 37/38. Here, the ostensive purpose of the 'George' repeats, is to clarify exactly who George is. The fact that the Barman accepts George Whatsisname after all this work seldom fails to raise a laugh from the audience.

If we want to compare the conversational styles of the Man and the Barman, it is useful to observe that the Barman repeats on the other's talk (lines 4, 8, 10, 12, 18, 20, 22, 24, 26, 30, 34, 36, 38a, 42, 48, 52), but on his own talk only at a distance — that is, when there has been intervening talk (lines 32, 48, 50). The Man, on the other hand, frequently repeats on himself within one utterance (lines 9a, 21, 23, 39, 53), and certainly to break a silence (lines 17/17a, 19/19a). This is presumably a strong formal criterion for our intuition that the Man is the more eager and competent conversationalist of the two.

Jefferson also makes interesting comments about 'product-items' — the items in talk that precede repeats, and are the justification or reason for repeats to be produced. She points out that the product-item will occur in the utterance immediately preceding the utterance containing the repeat, and that the utterance with the product-item will be permitted to be completed. For the most part, this standard procedure is strictly followed by the conversationalists in the text. Where the juxtaposition norm is broken (lines 50, 51, 55a) at the end of the sketch, it is noticeably comic. And again, because the structure is not quite 'as it should be', the mechanism of the talk becomes particularly obtrusive, and humorous in the Bergsonian paradigm.

Much of what has already been said concerns the fact that the two characters are 'making conversation' about very little. It has frequently been observed that Pinter's characters are 'talking about nothing in particular', are 'making conversation for the sake of it' or are 'indulging in phatic communion'. Where John Laver's paper is extremely useful is in his reassessment of the term 'phatic communion' itself, and his demonstration of the different types, functions and realizations of the phenomenon. It would probably be most helpful to begin by summarizing his general points, and to continue by focusing on specific details which are relevant to the style of this Pinter sketch.

In general, then, Laver very sensibly remarks that earlier definitions of phatic communion are useful for pointing out that there is indeed a category of talk that is not particularly important for its referential content but more for its social function, but he stresses that these definitions are vague and generally descriptive, and do not acknowledge the very precise set of parameters that may be observed in the use of phatic communion in social interaction. It is these rules which an analyst of interaction wants to specify.

He cites Malinowski (in Ogden and Richards, 1923, p.315), and his classic definition of phatic communion as 'a type of speech in which ties of union are created by a mere exchange of words', and John Lyons (Lyons, 1968, p.417), who says that phatic communion 'serves to establish and maintain a feeling of social solidarity and well being.' Laver's argument is that we can say much more about these 'ties of union', and, indeed about 'solidarity'. Specifically, we can say more about the mechanisms for 'establishment' and the mechanisms for 'maintenance', and we can certainly be much more precise about the 'exchange of words'. Laver explains this succinctly:

> Phatic communion is not a simple phenomenon . . . its function
> of creating ties of union, if that is indeed its principal function, is
> achieved by subtle and intricate means whose complexity does
> not deserve to be minimised by the use of such phrases as 'a mere
> exchange of words'

and he formulates a set of specific questions to which we need answers, and for which some answers are certainly available:

> What are the actual phenomena of phatic communion? When do
> these phenomena occur within the scope of a given interaction and
> in what type of interaction? . . . What is the functional significance
> of a speaker's choice of indulging in one type of phatic communion
> rather than another?

Laver begins to clarify his material by suggesting that we consider three phases of an interaction — opening, medial, closing. In this his observations tally with writers like Goffman (1971) and Schegloff and Sacks (1973), which suggests that there is a strong warrant for regarding such phases in an interaction. Interestingly, though, these writers all concentrate more on the first and third phases, thus also suggesting that more analytical work needs to be done on the rather vague notion of 'medial'. Laver's point here is that it is in the opening and closing phases of an interaction that most phatic communion is seen to be done, and that, note, these are points of psychological insecurity of differing kinds and degree. Similarly, he maintains that the different realizations of phatic communion that can be observed at these two points are functionally related to the stage in the interaction:

> The point I would like to reach at the end of the paper is that the fundamental social function of the multi-stranded behaviour that accompanies and includes phatic communion is the detailed management of inter-personal relationships during the psychologically crucial margins of interaction.

He goes into considerable detail about the different kinesic, proxemic and linguistic patterns of phatic communion to be observed at openings or closings. I shall concentrate here, however, on those details that are specifically relevant to the style and effect of our Pinter text.

One very obvious area of relevance is the opening utterance and its reply. Laver underlines the importance of territoriality as a constraint on who speaks first:

> When one participant is static in space and the other is moving towards him, in whatever type of physical locale, then, unless there are overriding special reasons, there seems to be a strong tendency, both in Britain and America, for the incomer to initiate the exchange of phatic communion . . . the speaker realises that in some sense the static listener can be acknowledged as the owner of the territory . . . he acknowledges his own awareness of his invasion of the listener's territory . . . he declares in effect that his intentions are pacific, and offers a propitiatory token.

In passing I should perhaps point out that 'overriding special reasons', as well as referring to particularly odd events, also refer to encounters where role positions are previously clearly known to the participants — thus these generalizations do not hold for many cases in our experience like doctor–patient interviews, beginning tutorials etc. I point this out merely to avoid confusion.

In the Pinter text, it is relevant that the Man opens the talk. The coffee stall is markedly the Barman's territory. Given the time of night, and the place of the encounter, a demonstration of pacificity is doubtless doubly obligatory, and the Man seems to acknowledge this by doing the opening. In order for this happy state of affairs to continue, the Barman is then constrained to reply. This connects with our observation that the Barman is the more forced of the two speakers — the point here being that not to reply at this specific point of the encounter is to be hostile. Laver underlines this:

> By conceding the initiative to the listener, to accept or reject the token (by replying or declining to reply) the speaker puts himself momentarily in the power of the listener . . . the speaker asserts a claim to sociolinguistic solidarity with the listener. If the listener accepts the invitation he gives the speaker safe-conduct to enter his territory without making him suffer a counter-display of hostility.

Thus, the Man ensures at least the opening of the interaction in a straightforward, orderly, rule-governed way. Significant also is the choice of the kind of realization of his phatic-communion token that he uses. For opening phases, Laver proposes a limited set of possibilities acceptable to speakers: formulaic greetings; reference to factors specific to the context of situation of the two speakers, with past, present or future reference like 'foggy this morning'/'nice day'/'going to clear up this afternoon, they say'. Another possible feature of the opening is a direct reference to either self-oriented or other-oriented topics like 'gosh I'm hot'/'you look cool' and so on. And yet another feature relevant here is a reference to ongoing work — particularly as a claim to equal status. Thus, 'this is too much like hard work for my liking'. So, on three counts — the reference to context of situation (past), other-orientation and reference to ongoing work, the Man makes what we must, as competent conversationalists, intuitively recognize as an appropriate opening to the talk. His reference to earlier business of the Barman is, as a claim to equal status, a handy way into his later talk of his own activity.

In a sense, the sketch never really progresses from this type of 'opening' strategy. There are two related points to be made here. Firstly, as we discussed above, as a recurrent strategy for making more conversation the Barman uses AB-events which are, by definition, phatic, in that they are not referentially interesting or important in anything other than the social-solidarity sense. And similarly, both participants repeat on each other and on themselves, again, not adding to the referential material significantly. Thus each character is continually offering more tokens of phatic-communion openings, and, equally continually, the other speaker has to offer demonstrations of non-hostility by conceding replies. It is interesting that when they realize they are beginning to disagree, and display hostility, over George and his arthritis, they switch the conversation back again to the non-hostile talk of the newspapers and the agreed fact that 'he must have left the area'. Secondly, the fact that we know that phatic communion co-occurs with psychological insecurity gives us the strong impression that the whole interaction is an uncomfortable event for the participants.

It is interesting that nowhere in the sketch do we see any of the features that co-occur with the closing phase and its rather different tokens of phatic communion, as observed and described by Laver. These would include, for example, tokens with explicit reference to the psychological and social relationship of the participants, reference to external forces inhibiting the continuation of the talk, consolidation, reference to future encounters and so on. This lack of final-stage tokens contributes to our feeling that the conversation is still under way at the final curtain. And again, this is a comic effect. The characters are managing to 'make conversation' for a considerable, and as far as we can tell, indefinite time – and still without going beyond the opening stages of phatic communion.

A word or two here about the silences. Pinter is notorious for his use of silence. And it is an obviously recurrent feature of this particular text. In talking of the psychological insecurity of opening conversations Laver refers again to Malinowski (Ogden and Richards, 1923, p. 314):

> speech is the intimate correlate of [man's gregarious nature] , for, to
> natural man, another man's silence is not a reassuring factor, but, on
> the contrary, something alarming and dangerous. . . . The breaking
> of silence, the communion of words, is the first act to establish
> links of fellowship. . . . The modern English phrase 'Nice day
> today' or the Melanesian phrase 'Whence comest thou' are needed
> to get over the strange and unpleasant tension which men feel when
> facing each other in silence.

I must underline the culture-specific quality of these remarks, as borne out by ethnographic studies of silence and its meaning and function in different societies (see, for example, Basso, 1970; Mowrer, 1970). However, given our society, and, of course, Pinter's society, these observations are certainly valid. In the text, the pauses are certainly seen as intolerable, and I have shown above how the Barman and the Man have mechanical devices for getting round them – so that, in effect, after each pause, the opening statement is yet another example of an opening token in phatic communion. Hayakawa comments very usefully (Hayakawa, 1952, p.70):

It is possible to state as a general principle, that the prevention of silence is itself an important function of speech, and that it is completely impossible for us in society to talk only 'when we have something to say'.

What Pinter is doing in this sketch is demonstrating this observation in an extreme case. And I hope to have shown that by using discovered rules of conversational analysis, we may begin to understand just how it is that we realize the complexities of this underlying observation, and indeed just how much Pinter is pointing out to us.

The possibilities inherent in this small text are by no means exhausted by this short discussion. There are other relevant articles that might have been drawn on here. For example, Schegloff and Sacks (1973) consider how closings are made by speakers, and how silences are interpreted as 'belonging' to one or other speaker — and both these ideas could be explored in relation to the text. Sinclair and Coulthard's work on discourse structure (1975) could be useful to clarify what happens in the text both within and across the exchange boundaries that both speakers recognize. The possibilities are enormous. What I have tried to do, however, is to demonstrate how an analyst of play-talk can benefit from linguistic analyses of real talk. And how, in fact, he must draw on this now substantial body of material if he is to make relevant, non-casual statements.

Chapter 2

A stylistic study of Ionesco's 'The Bald Prima Donna'

Given the lack of existing work in stylistics and modern drama, *The Bald Prima Donna* seemed an obvious and useful choice of text to start with, in that it is most usually known as a play specifically about, let us say, communicative incompetence. One only has to read some of the early reviews to see this view repeatedly expressed, as in Kenneth Tynan's very typical comments, for example (1958):

> Here was a writer ready to declare that words are meaningless and that all communication between human beings was impossible.
> . . . Ionesco's is a world of isolated robots, conversing in cartoon-strip balloons of dialogue that are sometimes hilarious, sometimes evocative, and sometimes neither, on which occasion they become profoundly tiresome.

Ionesco himself, whilst stressing that, for him, the point of the play is an expression of the human condition and its implicit anguish, which he attempts to convey by breaking down cliché-ridden and formulaic 'social language' (his phrase), explains his strategies and results thus (1956):

> One fine day, some years ago now, I had the idea of making a dialogue by stringing together the most commonplace phrases, consisting of the most meaningless words and the most worn out clichés that I could find in my own or my friends' vocabulary — and to a lesser extent in foreign language manuals.
>   My initiative was ill-rewarded: overcome by a proliferation of corpse-like words, stunned by the automatism of conversation, I almost gave way to disgust, unspeakable misery, nervous depression. . . . The play caused a great deal of laughter. I was utterly amazed, for I thought I had written 'The Tragedy of Language!'

Whichever of the various interpretive views one sympathizes with here, it remains clear that the dialogue of the text is strikingly interesting for our purposes, since it seems to be simultaneously presenting and implicitly commenting on features of both dramatic dialogue and everyday conversation. The overwhelming simple impression I take from the text is that the dialogue teases out the conventions of both stage interaction and real interaction, making strange the machinery of both. There is neither plot development nor character development in any straightforward sense. Episodes follow each other with little sequential motivation. Referential material is continually proposed and then contradicted – often in the immediately next utterance – and then finally dropped. Apart from the occasional utterance connected with an individual character's occupation, or sex stereotype, there seems no discernible rationale for the allocation of particular utterances to particular characters. In successive episodes, the point of the interactions as shown seems to be the demonstration and observation of general principles of either stage or everyday interaction. These too are brought into focus and exploited, often only to be neglected as the next episode and the next set of interactive principles are brought in.

Against this general background effect, there are of course more specific, precise and localized effects created in the text. I shall structure this study around these episodes, taking each separately, discussing my impressions of these localized effects, and adducing linguistic evidence to account for them.

The text is most simply divisible into episodes according to the grouping of sets of participant characters on stage. For the most part this happens to correspond with sharply differentiated shifts in both style and topic, that is, in what the episode is about, what the characters are doing and how they are behaving and talking. Using this convenient method of dividing the text, occasionally edges are blurred. However, simply for convenience I shall use this method for sectionalizing the play quite strictly, and will comment where necessary on the few problems that arise. The sections can be glossed as follows:

1 Mr and Mrs Smith's evening at home
2 Mr and Mrs Smith with Mary
3 Mary with Mr and Mrs Martin
4 Mr and Mrs Martin discover they are man and wife
5 Mary sums up the situation
6 The Smiths and the Martins

Within several of these sections there are stylistically discrete sub-sections, which again for simplicity, convenience and clarity I shall specify more precisely as I come to discuss each of the eleven main sections.

I am, in fact, describing only the English translation of this play (by Watson, published in 1959), but for simplicity will refer to it as Ionesco's text throughout. Clearly, this is not exactly the same activity as describing the original play, but, as I have stressed earlier, this is not a study of individual authors but a description of particular texts. Given this, I see no immediate problem in studying the English translation of the play from the point of view of the English-speaking analyst.

One very general and simple point, that is worth stating here as a preface to the more detailed discussion of the play, is this: whilst Ionesco's play is one of many that are called 'absurd', the use of that label, although a useful aid to the memory, is no more than that. It hides precisely those features that it might be interesting to describe and consider. One very general attempt in this chapter, then, is to specify in exactly what ways the text achieves its varying types of absurdity.

1 Mr and Mrs Smith's evening at home

Mrs Smith's opening monologue

from: MRS SMITH   Goodness! Nine o'clock!
  to: MRS SMITH   There was nothing wrong with him at the time.

The opening of the play creates several impressions and effects that need to be accounted for. Firstly, it is clear that Ionesco is presenting us with some sort of parody of the openings to traditional, fourth-wall bourgeois theatre-plays, and at the same time, by doing this, is warning us that his play can not be heard or read in this way. Secondly, he presents an extended version of an equally well known clichéd verbal situation which focuses on the trivia of wife-to-husband domestic small-talk. In fact, as we shall see below, this aspect of the opening is linked with the stage-talk parody in terms of plot exposition. As well as these general effects, we also begin to build up impressions of the interactants. Mrs Smith is both unreliable and boring. Mr Smith is rude or bored or both.

I want to begin by considering the parody of bourgeois stage-talk. Firstly, to describe how it works, and secondly, to estimate its implications in terms of the information it offers the audience.

The opening sentence, 'Goodness! Nine o'clock!' is a very obvious adaptation of the well-worn cliché used by stereotypical maids, dusting the furniture as the curtain rises, as in, for example, 'Six o'clock, the master will soon be home', where the audience is unsubtly given situational information that it either needs or wants. The formula is a well-known one, of course. It is important here to notice that it is produced immediately following the stage clock striking only three, so that the audience is at once offered two pieces of conflicting information, one of which must be false. Any momentary confusion an audience might have as to which item is unreliable — given that the stage-effects staff might perhaps have made a simple mistake, or given that the clock in the fictional microcosm might later turn out to be routinely six hours fast or six hours slow — is swiftly resolved by the oddities in the rest of the utterance, and we shall consider these in due course. For the time being, however, notice that this simple sentence ties in very neatly with a notion that is frequently repeated in classic articles in the philosophy of language. For example, Austin (1958), in writing about the claimed differences, yet underlying similarities, between constatives and performatives (which will be given in detail below), points out the over-simplistic approach of formal logicians to the truth values of statements, and, talking of real-life conversations, says, 'In reality nothing is more common than to find that one can state absolutely nothing on a given subject because one is simply not in a position to state whatever it may be.' He then suggests that stating something without just cause or appropriate knowledge is analogous to the more easily seen infelicity of giving an order when you have no right to do so. Thus, in his argument, the rather neat and precise formulations about performatives can usefully throw light on the more traditionally familiar notions of constatives.

Grice (1967) turns this very sensible observation around, and presents it more forcefully in the form of a conversationalist's maxim:

Do not say that for which you lack adequate evidence

Clearly, even in terms of the minimal events of the play so far, Mrs Smith, as far as the audience is concerned, is breaking that maxim. She is thus instantly and blatantly established as an unreliable commentator. I take it that, in ordinary realistic theatre, one of the jobs the audience is involved in is processing various clues, including misleading ones, so as to establish for itself who is a trustworthy speaker and who is not. There is sufficient evidence in Mrs Smith's first sentence, given the preceding stage effect, for the audience to make a quick and easy decision here.

The classic article by Grice, from which the above maxim is taken, is surprisingly useful for making several points with regard to this first section, and is worth a quick summary at this point.

Briefly, he is writing within the framework of a general attempt to consider natural language within the philosophy of language, but not merely in established formalistic terms of 'its ability to serve the needs of science', and its inevitable inadequacies in that respect as compared with an ideal constructed language, 'the sentences of which will be clear, determinate in truth value and certifiably free from metaphysical implications'. He works towards a categorization and explanation of non-conventional implicatures, here described as 'conversational implicatures. . .essentially connected with certain general features of discourse'. He begins, therefore, by trying to describe some of these features.

An important point to notice is that, like many other writers considering conversation in general terms, rather than analysing conversational data, he sees conversation as a tidy, co-operative and purposeful (in the simplest sense of the word) construct:

> Our talk-exchanges do not normally consist of a succession of disconnected remarks, and would not be rational if they did. They are, characteristically, to some degree at least, co-operative efforts; and each participant recognises in them, to some extent, a common purpose or set of purposes, or at least a mutually accepted direction.

I have no doubt that Grice was able to see the problems and limitations of this extremely orderly and essentially end-product model of conversation. Comparison with Garfinkel (1967) or Cicourel (1973) or any of the ethnomethodologists (see, for example, Sudnow, 1972) proves revealing here. However, it is a convenient simplification for the sorts of proposals he wishes to offer. Given this perspective, then, he suggests a 'rough general principle' that participants may be expected to observe, which he labels the 'Co-operative Principle': 'Make your conversational contribution such as is required, at the stage at which it occurs, by the accepted purpose or direction of the talk exchange in which you are engaged.' Under this general principle, he distinguishes four super-maxims, with more specific observations, which are labelled for convenience as Quantity, Quality, Relation and Manner. They can be briefly formulated thus:

Quantity: 1 Make your contribution as informative as is required (for the current purposes of the exchange)
2 Do not make your contribution more informative than is required
Quality: Try to make your contribution one that is true, and more specifically
1 Do not say that which you believe to be false
2 Do not say that for which you lack adequate evidence
Relation: Be relevant
Manner: Be perspicuous
1 Avoid obscurity of expression
2 Avoid ambiguity
3 Be brief (avoid unnecessary prolixity)
4 Be orderly

Grice himself points out many of the shortcomings in this approach that later critics have picked up in detail (see for example Lewis, 1969; Lakoff, 1973; Strawson, 1974; Walker, 1975; Parrett, 1976; Lyons, 1977). The most important of these seem to be that, firstly, these maxims may themselves be ordered in terms of their importance, particularly in terms of what Schegloff (1968) calls the allowance of 'strong inferences' about a participant breaking one or another maxim. Secondly, there is doubtless a need for other maxims: aesthetic, social and moral (see Hudson, 1975, for example). Thirdly, there is this crucial caveat:

I have stated my maxims as if the purpose of a talk exchange were a maximally effective exchange of information; this specification is of course too narrow and the scheme needs to be generalized to allow for such general purposes as influencing and directing the actions of others.

Grice also points out ways in which a participant may fail to fulfil a maxim: he may quietly violate it; he may opt out of the Co-operative

Principle; he may be faced with a clash between two maxims which can only be resolved by violating one of them (compare recurrent ethical problems as experienced by Asimov's positronic robots (Asimov, 1973); or he may deliberately flout a maxim. This last choice is a powerful exploitation of the system. His examples concerning conversational implicatures are given in three groups: firstly, where no maxim is flouted; secondly, where a maxim is flouted but is interpretable by the supposition that one maxim clashed with another; and thirdly, where maxims are ostentatiously flouted, generating linguistic items traditionally glossed as figures of speech.

We have, above, accounted for a problem in Mrs Smith's first sentence, by saying that she seems to be violating the maxim of Quality. As the utterance continues it remains problematic, in that, since we assume that the couple have had supper together (and if we are in any doubt about the reference of 'we' in this utterance, our doubt is dismissed later when Mrs Smith discusses how many helpings of fish had been taken), then it is strangely inappropriate for Mrs Smith to tell her husband what he must already know about the menu, and what she must know that he knows. She here violates the maxim of Quantity, for her utterance in the microcosm is surely more informative than is required. The same observation applies to her telling Mr Smith where they live, what their name is, and the name of their two-year-old child.

This, I take it, foregrounds a central and continual problem with regard to plot exposition within the confines of more traditional, realistic theatre. The fundamental problem in plot exposition can be described borrowing Labov's terminology (1970; and see discussion of 'Last to Go'). If the characters in a play are designated as A and B, and their audience as C, then the most basic problem is this:

> How can A or B recount AB-events to each other, for C to overhear, in such a way that C knows what he needs to know in order to follow the significance of events on stage, but so that the mechanism of the recounting is not obviously incompatible with the ostensible realism?

In other words, the recounting must not violate the maxim of Quantity, in terms of the microcosmic conversation. As Sacks, talking of naturalistic, everyday conversation, more casually puts it (1970), 'You don't tell people what they know already'.

Of course, the ultimate joke in this Ionesco parody is that the audience does not need the information that is portrayed at length and so unsubtly. At this point in the play it is not, of course, possible to be sure that one will never meet, nor hear further reference to the little boy, Helen, Peggy, Mrs Parker, the Doctor, the Johns family and the yoghourtician from Constantinople. Nor is it obvious that the picture of Mr and Mrs Smith as parents is totally unnecessary to anything that later occurs. We can, perhaps, suppose that the details of who ate most at dinner, and which local mayonnaise is the best in quality are un-likely to be of vital importance. It is an important issue for any theatre audience to decide whether this sort of writing is 'badly written plot exposition' or a parody of that sort of writing, and a foregrounding of constraints on writers in certain dramatic genres. The extremely blatant nature of the bad writing makes it likely that we are hearing or reading the latter.

In the light of this, notice that Austin (1958), in his discussion of performatives and constatives (to be discussed more fully below), describes the very general ways in which any utterance can be 'un-happy': 'it may be issued under duress, or by accident; it may suffer from defective grammar or from misunderstanding; it may figure in a context not wholly 'serious', in a *play*, perhaps, or in a poem' (my emphasis). Similarly, Searle (1969), in his elaboration of the speech act of 'promising' (again to be discussed below), gives as his very first and most general condition for the successful utterance of this illocutionary act that 'normal input and output conditions obtain'. This he glosses as follows:

> I use the terms 'input' and 'output' to cover the large and in-definite range of conditions under which any serious linguistic communication is possible. 'Output' covers the conditions for intelligible speaking, and 'input' covers the conditions for under-standing. Together they include such things as that the speaker and the hearer know how to speak the language; both are conscious of what they are doing; the speaker is not acting under duress or threats; they have no physical impediments to communication such as deafness, aphasia or laryngitis, *they are not acting in a play* or telling jokes etc. [My emphasis.]

Similar points are found in Turner (1970) and Labov (1970), citing Sacks. In a sense, what Ionesco is doing here, in making his play so obviously a play parody, and in foregrounding the staginess of it, is surely to point out to us quite clearly that normal input and output certainly do not apply. To any sophisticated post-Brechtian audience

31

(or any Jacobean audience, for that matter), this might be entirely matter-of-fact. Nevertheless, we know, in common-sense terms, that there are audiences for bourgeois realistic theatre who do empathize with events and characters on stage and in fiction, taking the events on stage as, in a crude way, events in life. If it is the case that soap-opera audiences might still believe in the fictions presented to them, this seems a timely and sure way of reminding the audience that the play is only a play.

To turn now to the extended presentation of wife-to-husband small talk, Ionesco uses what Schegloff (1968) calls a 'standard joke of the society':

> A tired husband returns from the office, sinks gratefully into his
> easy chair and opens the evening paper to the sports page. His
> nagging wife, however, wishes to unburden herself of the accumu-
> lated troubles of the day and begins an extended monologue.
> Routinely she leaves a slot of silence and he dutifully inserts
> 'Yes dear', until, dimly aware that all is not as it appears to be,
> she says, 'Are you ignoring me?' and he replies 'Yes dear'.

I would want to argue with the notion of 'leaving a slot' in ordinary, everyday conversation, though the way in which Schegloff continues this notion does indeed sound like the material in the Ionesco opening: 'Speakers with extended things to say may routinely leave slots open for the other to insert an 'uh uh' thereby recalling them to the continuing course of the activity.' Since this is what seems to be happening in the text, and since it also sounds rather odd, and works well in terms of the stage joke, this would seem to suggest that this type of behaviour is not the norm in ordinary interaction. I particularly take issue with Schegloff's concept of one person being in control of slot-silence and forcing the other participant to fill it. Strangely enough, Yngve (1970), in writing about the distinction between actually taking a speaking turn and 'backchannelling' in someone else's turn (compare Duncan, 1972, here), draws on exactly the same stereotypical domestic situation, but casts it in what seems to me, in discourse terms, to be far more appropriate and naturalistic:

> The husband who buries his head in the newspaper and carefully
> listens to what his wife has to say, while he neglects to send any
> messages in the backchannel will soon find himself accused of not
> paying attention to what his wife is saying although he has heard
> and understood every word.

In terms of the layout of the play, there is some confusion over whether Mr Smith is to be seen as taking turns in the talk, or merely doing backchannel work. On the one hand his contributions are not presented, as, for example, 'MR SMITH (*clicks his tongue*)', so that in terms of the stage directions, at least, he appears to be backchannelling. On the other hand, for the most part his clicks occur at strict structural breaks in Mrs Smith's monologue (with the possible exception of the break in the talk about mayonnaise). So that in some sense he could be described as taking a turn, if only in the sense that Mrs Smith might be said to modify her flow after his contributions. Notice, though, that he does not appear to be listening. In particular, he does not respond to her direct question, 'How did that come about?' Schegloff (1968) writes appositely here on 'conditional relevance' and 'noticeable absences', where, given a first-pair-part like, say, an initial greeting, a summons or a question, then we can in most cases expect to hear a corresponding second-pair-part appropriately following:

> When we say that an answer is conditionally relevant upon a
> summons, it is to be understood that the behaviours referred to
> are not 'casual options' for the persons involved. A member of
> the society may not naively choose not to answer a summons. The
> culture provides that a number of strong inferences can be drawn
> from the fact of the official absence of an answer, and any member
> who does not answer does so at the peril of those inferences being
> made.

Thus, although Mr Smith is covered in terms of the points made by Yngve and the earlier Schegloff quotation, he nevertheless falls prey to certain strong inferences here. Without evidence suggesting any alternative interpretation, we might infer that he is angry or sulking, etc. Our simplest assumption must be that he is rudely ignoring his wife, and hardly listening at all.

However, we feel some sympathy in this, for, as suggested above, we certainly feel that Mrs Smith is extremely boring. Turner (1972) has some interesting observations to make about successful small-talk that are relevant here too. He is writing about encounters between strangers, but nevertheless the rules he formulates hold good for this situation too, though they are admittedly overbuilt for persons in a 'continuing state of incipient talk' (Schegloff and Sacks, 1973). Turner says:

I take it that when persons are thrown together in a situation where they can see they have time to get through, it can be a problem 'what to talk about'. And one way of solving the problem could be expressed as a procedural recommendation as follows: provide a topic that selects a membership categorization device embracing the maximum number of participants, and one for which any category member will have a value.

The term 'membership categorization device' is borrowed from Sacks (1972), and can be understood in a common-sense way here. In fact, Mrs Smith has chosen topics of a singular lack of interest in the microcosm, since for the most part she is merely telling her husband what he knows already. Except, perhaps, in the sequence concerning mayonnaise and yoghourt. Here, if she has membershiped him at all it appears to be as 'housekeeper' – a categorization which he does not seem to accept. Notice, too, that her topic is inept in terms of the macrocosm as well. Whilst, just conceivably, there might be members of the audience willing to listen to such topics, if they were playing a constructive interactive part, and if the references were to their own, non-fictional world, it is more likely that the majority of the audience will find these topics highly tedious.

Finally, Reisman (1974), in his description of talk in an Antiguan village, has a surprising point of correspondence here. I write 'surprising' because, for the most part, the interactive patterns reported in his paper seem remarkably different to our own (see particularly remarks on turn-taking and greeting rituals). However, there is a nice point of comparison in the following item:

To have something to say that is worth hearing and also repeatable implies that it is fairly short, and as a result, there is a process of condensation and allusion at work all the time. One is expected in many contexts to 'catch' the meaning. And conversely there is a feeling that undue explicitness implies a dull person.

The conversation about doctors

| *from*: | MR SMITH | Then how was it that the doctor came through it? |
| *to*: | MRS SMITH | It's never struck me before. |

This section is 'absurd' in quite a different dimension. Firstly, Mrs Smith sets up Dr Mackenzie-King as a 'fine doctor', and justifies this by pointing out that he never prescribes anything for a patient that he has not tried out himself first. This rapidly expands to include the rather gruesome notion of operations. The doctor survives, but the patient does not, and this leads Mr Smith to complain that, in that case, Mackenzie-King is not a good doctor – and that either the operation should have been successful on them both, or both should have died. In a sense, this all follows quite logically once one accepts the original premise that a good doctor treats himself in exactly the same way as his ailing patient, and certainly, apart from a brief protest at her husband's choice of metaphor, comparing a patient to a boat, Mrs Smith can see that the argument is logical enough.

Again, a reference to the philosophy of language is useful for explaining this particular absurdity. In our actual world, doctors do not of course take unnecessary medicine, nor do they undergo unnecessary operations. However, in a *possible* world (see Lyons, 1977, or Anderson, Allwood and Dahl, 1977), such as can be set up to deal with, among other things, problems for generative semantics, if it were the case that it was this feature that distinguished a good doctor, then the discussion that follows is quite legitimately entailed.

Notice the similarity here to data used in classic generative semantics, where, in order to make points about what real-world semantics must exclude, similarly bizarre propositions are produced, for example:

John kills his neighbour every Xmas.

Notice also that this sort of problematic possible-world proposition is at the root of the argument about grammaticality, well-formedness and cultural beliefs (Lakoff, 1971b). It is important here, I think, that Mr and Mrs Smith share this possible world. Thus Ionesco creates a very different effect from that of, say, a scene where only one of them had this set of cultural beliefs. Here we cannot support one character and consider the other as crazy. The entire stage world as presented thus far seems only to be a possible world.

Grice is also useful for commenting on the initial utterances in this sub-section, where Mrs Smith's reply, 'Because the operation was successful on the doctor, and on Parker it wasn't', is clearly tautologous. In the framework of Grice's Co-operative Principle, this counts as flouting the Quantity maxim:

Extreme examples of a flouting of the first maxim of Quantity are provided by utterances of patent tautologies. . . . I would wish to maintain that at the level of what is said, in my favoured sense, such remarks are totally non-informative, and so, at that level cannot but infringe the first maxim of Quantity in any conversational context.

Notice, as Grice goes to some lengths to point out, this does not mean that the tautology has no function in the discourse. He would argue that it is informative at the level of what is thereby implicated, which means that a hearer must be able to explain the speaker's choice of a particular tautology. I would argue here that the reason for this particular choice is not immediately obvious. I hear Mrs Smith as either avoiding giving a more informative answer, or possibly not knowing a more informative answer. She also simultaneously seems to suggest that Mr Smith's question was not in any case a reasonable contribution.

Another feature of their possible world is an unusual vocabulary structure, where, in the sense of Lyons's structural semantics (1968 and 1977), 'sailors' are not subordinates of 'the Royal Navy'. 'The only respectable thing left in England is the Royal Navy,' 'But not sailors,' 'No, of course not.' This, is, of course, not impossible even in the usual possible world: it is quite permissible for Mr Smith here to be referring to the institution of the Royal Navy, as an entity quite distinct from the human components of that institution. Nevertheless, the utterances about sailors have at least a double-think quality to them, that is easily explained by the mismatch in vocabulary structure.

The conversation about the Watsons

from: MR SMITH   Well, well, well!
to: MRS SMITH   I can't answer all your silly questions.

Mr. Smith introduces this overall topic by a misplacement marker, which, as it turns out, is highly misleading. Schegloff and Sacks (1973) comment on the misplacement marker thus:

> Misplacement markers. . .display an orientation by their user to
> the proper sequential-organization character of a particular place in
> a conversation, and a recognition that an utterance that is thereby
> prefaced may not fit, and that the recipient should not attempt to
> use this placement in understanding their occurrence.

Thus in the text Mr Smith can be heard to indicate to Mrs Smith that she should not look to the previous talk for the relevance of this contribution about the death of Bobby Watson, as, ostensibly at least, it is announced in his newspaper. He thus generates the confusion about whether or not the information was in fact located in the newspaper, and whether or not the information was surprising, and should properly be treated with surprise, as befits new information from such a source.

A routinely disruptive feature of the whole section relates again to work in the philosophy of language. And again, Austin is specifically helpful here. In comparing relatively clear-cut notions about performatives to the often muddled assumptions that cluster around constatives, he makes some very useful points. Essentially he is demonstrating the similarity between performatives and constatives, with a view to describing constatives as speech acts with an underlying form 'I assert that X.'

He considers the following examples of 'trouble', and accounts for the unhappiness in terms of presupposition, implication and entailment. For convenience, I shall alter the layout, and shorten the examples:

Constatives

1 All John's children are bald, but [*or* and] John has no children

2 The cat is on the mat, but [*or* and] I don't believe it is

3 All the guests are French, but [*or* and] some of them aren't

Performatives

1 I bequeath my watch to you, but [*or* and] I have no watch

2 I promise to be there, but [*or* and] I have no intention of being there

3 I say 'I welcome you', and then treat you as an enemy or an intruder

The two examples under (1) are unhappy in terms of presupposition. That is, the reference to John's children presupposes that they exist, and similarly, the reference to the watch in (1b) presupposes the existence of the watch, and both are made void for lack of reference. The examples under (2) are unhappy in terms of implication, that is, as Austin puts it:

> The procedure for stating is designed for those who honestly believe what they say, exactly as the procedure for promising is designed for those who have a certain intention, namely the intention to do whatever it may be that they promise. Without these appropriate beliefs or intentions appropriate to the content of the utterance, there is lack of sincerity, and abuse of the procedure. In the troubled examples, both are self-voiding and hence our sense of outrage.

The examples given under (3) are slightly more problematic, but Austin suggests that in making a statement like 'all the guests are French,' the speaker commits himself in some way to behaving appropriately in respect of the statement once it has been made:

> If in the sequel I state things incompatible with my utterance. . .
> there will be a breach of commitment that one might well compare
> with that of the case in which I say 'I welcome you' and then pro-
> ceed to treat you as an enemy or an intruder.

In juxtaposing and comparing these examples, he does, I think, show very clearly that the constative utterance is every bit as liable to un-happiness as the performative. And it is precisely this sort of unhappiness that prompts 'our sense of outrage' in this passage about the Watsons. So that, for example, the utterance, 'She has regular features, but you can't call her beautiful. She's too tall and too well-built. Her features are rather irregular, but everyone calls her beautiful. A trifle too short and too slight, perhaps,' is clearly unhappy in terms of entailment, and the confusion between utterances (1), 'MRS SMITH "Lucky they didn't have any children"' and (2), 'MRS SMITH "But who will take care of the children?"' can be explained in terms of presupposition. In a sense, of course, it would be possible to gloss both these and similar examples in the text in terms of 'contradiction' or by using similar lay terminology. However, when it is possible to make finer distinctions, and distinctions which depend on observations made by studies of general principles of language use and conventions, then it would be perverse to take the less delicate description as sufficient.

[margin note: aah, but cf Wittg. on over-precise 'definitions']

Notice, also, an interesting problem in utterances made after the clock strikes five, concerning the marriage of the Watsons, who have just been established as dead. It is not difficult to think of other stage plays where the framing of these particular utterances by the striking clock would indicate something like a flash backwards or forwards in time, which would then suggest a disjunction between the references before and after the striking of the clock. A particularly interesting example of this occurs in Tom Stoppard's *Travesties*, where he uses a cuckoo-clock for just this purpose and effect. Notice though his ex-planatory gloss and warning:

> This scene has several of these 'time slips'. . . . It may be desirable
> to mark these moments more heavily by using an extraneous sound
> or a light effect, or both. The sound of a cuckoo-clock, artificially
> amplified, would be appropriate. . . . At any rate the effect of these

time-slips is not meant to be bewildering, and it should be made
clear what is happening.

In the case of the Ionesco play, this sort of 'time slip' interpretation of
the wedding-discussion section would enable us to make sense of the
talk, since 'they' and 'them' need not refer back to the dead Watsons.
There are two things which prevent us from that easy interpretive procedure. Firstly, the clock has, by this stage of the play, been securely
established as unreliable, idiosyncratic in the extreme, and without a
tidy, formal relationship with the dialogue. Notice particularly the stage
directions immediately following this section of talk: *'There is a
moment's silence. The clock strikes six. There is a pause. The clock
strikes two. There is a pause. The clock strikes fifteen. There is a pause.'*
The second and more important point is that, by this stage, the text itself has trained us to accept absurdities *per se*, and to hear them as
absurd rather than to formulate rational resolutions. Halliday (1973)
discusses a very similar point in considering the problem areas of so-
called norm and deviation. He points out that the text itself leads the
reader to expect certain types of pattern which are the 'norm' of the
text, and that it is not only in terms of whatever we think we know
about norms of the language in general that we react to any text. This
particular example seems to display this feature rather well: for an
audience it has very practical and, I think, unproblematic consequences.
In this context, see also de Camp (1976), on the ease with which
informants are trained into making grammaticality judgments.

One final point here is again to do with plot exposition. If we were
to need all this information about the intricacies of the Watson family,
we should be hard put to it to recall all these strange details. I take it
that unless a plot trick is involved (compare Anthony Schaffer's *Sleuth*,
1973), dramatists take care not to duplicate names of characters, so as
not to confuse the audience. Along with the low-information names
like Smith and Mary, Ionesco is making it quite clear here that this is
not necessary information for the audience to retain.

The argument

from: MRS SMITH   You said that just to upset me.
  to: MR SMITH   . . .put the lights out and go bye-byes.

The argument is both silly and childlike. At a simple level, this is owing
partly to the way in which the two characters misuse stereotypical

category-bound activities as terms of abuse. 'Category-bound activities' are discussed in Sacks (1972); they are activities that are appropriate to, and done by, particularly designated categories of people – as in, for example, 'the baby cried'. Again, this is a very simple, ritualistic exploitation (compare Labov, 1972a).

The childish quality of the talk also accords well with findings by Brenneis and Lein (1977). Their work involved collecting and analysing children's arguments and quarrels, and considering these as speech events with characteristic patterns of content and style. It is important to realize that for the analyst of naturally-occurring conversation these materials are somewhat misleading, because the authors persuaded the children to simulate disputes. They do of course admit that their data are 'not representative of spontaneous verbal exchange', and claim that the same sorts of technique can be observed in both simulated and spontaneous disputes, although they evidence no data on the latter to support this. Given, however, that children in simulated argument will presumably be enacting stereotypical assumptions about the verbal nature of disputes, then the findings here are still relevant to the highly stylized argument in the Ionesco text.

Firstly, as Brenneis and Lein point out, it is interesting that the children use absurd propositions and accusations so outlandish that both speaker and hearer know that these are not true in any simple sense. They are spoken in seriousness, as if they were true. Secondly, the authors argue that semantic continuity is the most important organizational feature in the argument data, whilst counter-patterns provide rules for follow-up utterances following an initial accusation or assertion, for example:

ANN   I could lift up a boulder with one toenail.
JOEY   I could lift up a boulder with nothing.

The data also show the children using other-sex categorization as a means of abuse and counter-abuse, though the authors do not comment here. They do suggest that the only routinely used way out of an argument is via the sort of move glossed in a common-sense way by Sinclair (Sinclair and Coulthard, 1975) as 'plane change'. The argument here in the play follows all these strategies very neatly and closely, and if it is true that the Brenneis and Lein data represent the speech event 'children's dispute', then this marked similarity between their data and Mr and Mrs Smith's utterances at this point will help account for the intuition that their argument sounds childish.

2 Mr and Mrs Smith with Mary

from: MARY I am the maid.
  to: MRS SMITH We'll go and get dressed quickly.

This section begins with a similar problem to the one in the earliest section, for Mary's entrance line, 'I am the maid,' is a piece of information that the audience must know that the Smiths already know. In a very quick and simple way, Ionesco is parodying conventions of plot exposition. There is little more of interest here, except to notice the repetition of the device with the entrance of this new character.

The rest of Mary's utterance, taken with the two that follow it, sounds distinctly odd:

MARY   I am the maid. I have just spent a very pleasant after-
         noon. I went to the pictures with a man and saw a
         film with some women. When we came out of the
         cinema we went and drank some brandy and some
         milk, and afterwards we read the newspaper.
MRS SMITH I hope you spent a pleasant afternoon. I hope you
         went to the pictures with a man and drank some
         brandy and some milk.
MR SMITH   And the newspaper.

A simple way of explaining this can be found with reference to Keenan (1977). Here, drawing on her data of children's talk, she is writing about the function of repetitions in discourse, very sensibly arguing that this is a far more complex area than common notions about imitation would admit. She points out specifically that writers on children's repetitions tend to ignore the illocutionary character of the product utterance to which a child might be responding. The following observation is of particular relevance to the problem at hand:

> Repetition with omissions are appropriate in responses other than
> information questions as well. For both adults and children alike it
> is appropriate to repeat just one or two words from the utterance of
> a conversational partner to comment attitudinally. . .to agree with
> . . .to self-inform. . .to query.

Whatever the illocutionary character of the utterances just quoted (and I would tend to assess them as some sort of greeting routine), the odd-ness stems, I think, from the fact that the reciprocating utterances do not repeat just one or two words, but overmuch of the product utterance, and thus sound highly formal, stilted and more than a little bizarre. If we do see this as a greeting routine, then this highly formal yet unfamiliar sequence is a way of making strange the ritualistic nature of everyday, taken-for-granted greeting routines in general (see Goffman, 1971).

Other items of particular interest in this section cluster around these utterances:

MRS SMITH   . . .We'd had nothing to eat all day long. You shouldn't
             have gone off like that, Mary.
MARY   But you gave me your permission!
MR SMITH   We didn't do it on purpose.

Here again, the peculiarity inherent in these utterances can be explained in relation to classic papers in the philosophy of language, drawing particularly on Austin's work on performatives (1958, 1961, 1965), and Searle's later elaboration of this in terms in his consideration of speech acts (1969).

The most obvious impression created by Mr Smith's utterance is that he is talking nonsense. In common-sense terms we know that if you give someone permission then you have to do it on purpose. The classic works by Austin and Searle on performatives and the conditions for the production of felicitous speech acts allow us to ground this common-sense knowledge more securely. And these particular works, together with a critique of Austin by Turner (1970), allow us access to strangely precise insights about the text.

Perhaps the quickest way to describe Austin's very rich notion of performative utterances is to give his own description of them in contrast with constatives:

> The constative utterance, under the name so dear to philosophers
> of statement, has the property of being true or false. The performative utterance, by contrast, can never be either: it has its own
> special job, it is used to perform an action. To issue such an utterance is to perform the action — an action perhaps which one
> scarcely could perform, at least with so much precision, in any
> other way. Here are some examples:
>   I name this ship Liberté
>   I apologise
>   I welcome you
>   I advise you to do it.

Later in the same paper he adds a further helpful discrimination. Given that there exist – as he himself puts it – two 'normal' forms in which the performative finds expression; one as above, for example, where the utterance may begin with the performative verb in the first-person singular present indicative active, and the other as one might find in formal written language, having a verb in the passive and second- or third-person present indicative, for example, 'Passengers are requested to cross the line by the footbridge only'; he then very usefully and precisely points out:

> If we ask ourselves as we sometimes may, whether a given utterance
> of this form is performative or constative, we may settle the
> question by asking whether it would be possible to insert in it the
> word 'hereby' or some such equivalent – as, in French, the phrase
> 'par ces mots-ci'.

I take it that 'I give you permission to do X' would be a very clear and obvious example of an explicit performative verb. And, in the Ionesco text Mary is (amongst other things) describing a previously issued performative, whilst Mr Smith is commenting on that performative. That is, they express no disagreement over the status of that earlier utterance, and we can assume that some sort of recognizably explicit performative utterance was both given and taken.

In pointing out that a performative may be criticized on quite different dimensions from the truth–falsity criteria usually applied to constatives, Austin states that a performative, to be successful, must be issued in a situation appropriate in all respects for the act in question, and suggests that there might be three possible ways in which a performative might be infelicitous: depending on nullity, abuse (insincerity) and breach of commitment. Some expansion of this might be helpful:

1 Nullity. The act is null and void if the speaker is not in a position to perform the act in question. Thus the bigamist cannot, by saying the appropriate words in the marriage ceremony, get married a second time. A person cannot name a ship if he is not the designated person for the official job.

2 Insincerity. The act is unhappy on this dimension if, say, a person promises to do X without intending to carry out X. The *formula* is thus absurd.

3 Breach of commitment. This refers to the possible events that might

follow in consequence of a certain speech act, where one event, if it happens, will be in order and where another event, if it takes place, will not be in order. For example, if someone has said 'I promise' he will not be in order if he then breaks his word. Similarly, if someone says 'I welcome you' and then treats the welcomed person as an enemy or an intruder he will not be in order either.

Using these more precise distinctions than our common-sense knowledge would allow us, it is possible to see that Mr Smith is guilty of the second type of unhappiness listed above. He has, in the utterance quoted (in terms of the microcosmic fictional world only, of course), explicitly and verbally abused the formula that, as far as we can tell, he has earlier used to Mary. It is interesting that Ionesco has singled out the most blatant and unsubtle of possible unhappinesses, and makes the infelicity so explicit that it cannot pass unnoticed. Similarly, if we use Searle's (1969) formulation of sincerity conditions in order to locate this unhappiness in the text, we find it is created by an explicit breach of the central sincerity condition, and an implicit breach of the essential condition. Again, the unsubtlety of the absurdity is the prominent conclusion to be taken from this. This unsubtlety is reminiscent of many of the mechanisms working in the play so far.

Roy Turner's very useful paper (Turner, 1970), which criticizes aspects of the work in speech-act theory from the standpoint of the practical analyst (see also Hirsch, 1976), contains some observations that are particularly relevant to the way we hear Mary's utterance. For the most part I find myself very sympathetic to Turner's comments. He faults Austin's work on performatives by pointing out some intractable problems for the analyst of naturally occurring conversations. He demonstrates (with data) the impossibility of any mechanical recognition-procedures for performatives in context, arguing that, even if it were possible to construct some sort of dictionary list of explicit performative verbs, the analyst (and, of course, co-conversationalists) can only understand what sort of work any utterance is doing with reference to fine details of the interactional location of the utterance in question. Thus, in his data, we hear one participant as 'doing complaining' with reference to a fine network of criteria, and not by any simple matching of form and function. However, there is one rather small point in the article which had not, in fact, ever struck me as problematic until I realized the way in which it matches up with these utterances in the play. The point centres upon the possibility of recognizing an act such as excusing or justifying by the fact that it occurs in the context 'following an accusation'. Turner poses his problem with this possibility in the following way:

> Suppose then, that in the face of an accusation, a person answers, 'He ordered me to do it'. Austinian logic would require us to treat such an activity as *doing* the activity, 'excusing' or 'justifying'. What then of his treatment of utterances like 'He ordered me to do it', as derived from, dependent upon, and reporting on an earlier employment of a performative? In looking at some piece of talk as the 'later' report which serves as evidence for the 'earlier' existence of a performative utterance, Austin appears to claim that utterances can be treated as reports or descriptions without reference to the interactional location of the utterance in question.
>
> Consider then the following difficulty that seems to be entailed by Austin's treatment of performatives.
>
> We should find it odd to say that Jones had 'uttered a few words' in the circumstances that what Jones did could be seen as 'getting married'. Should we not also find it odd to say that A was 'describing' some earlier talk of B's as a performative in the circumstances that what A was doing was 'providing an excuse'?

Whilst I do not wish to quibble with the detailed argument of which this is but one stage, I do want to point out something that becomes obvious when looking at the text; simply that one routine way of doing excusing following an accusation is to report or refer to an earlier performative issued by the other speaker, for the benefit of the present speaker, in such a way that the act which is being excused can be seen to be one part of the range of rights and obligations set up by the use of that performative in the first place.

To mention Mary's utterance 'I've bought myself a chamber-pot' very briefly: its bizarre quality can be explained in terms of Grice's very terse maxim (which leaves a multitude of problems unasked), 'Be relevant'. Easy as it usually is to construct contexts of relevance for oddly sounding successive utterances (see Burton and Stubbs, 1976), there seems to be no easy remedy here. Notice that Mr and Mrs Smith take no notice of it, and thus do not appear to hear it as relevant either, though we have no substantial evidence of this. In a sense it appears that, although they do themselves share a strange possible world, Mary does not seem to be in exactly the same world at this point.

3 Mary with Mr and Mrs Martin

from: MARY   What do you mean?
to: MARY   Sit down and wait.

This very short encounter shows the maid simultaneously welcoming the guests and treating them as intruders (see the infelicity examples from Austin above). It seems at first surprising that the aspects of conversation that Ionesco chooses to highlight should match so neatly with those chosen as examples in the philosophy of language. And yet, on further consideration, this is hardly surprising at all. The philosopher of language attempts to find clear, simple and blatant examples from our experience of language in use, and Ionesco similarly is choosing very obvious and unsubtle examples of interactional behaviour in order to make his attitude towards social language similarly clear and unequivocal.

This tiny section is, then, an extreme distortion of a highly ritualized interactional norm; that of initial greetings used as a type of phatic communion, used to display non-hostility (see Malinowski in Ogden and Richards, 1923; Lyons, 1968; Laver, 1974; Schegloff, 1968; Schegloff and Sacks, 1973; Goffman, 1971; and so on). Sociolinguists have spent considerable time and effort on these openings to conversations, for as Schegloff says (1968):

> The opening segment of conversation is perhaps everywhere especially advantageous for sociolinguistic research. What one can say to anyone and how one must deal with anyone with whom one speaks, may imply fundamental assumptions about the rights and obligations mutually felt by members of a society — perhaps any human beings — are felt to owe to each other.

Here, of course, Mary simply denies the politeness behaviour expected in any greeting, but most particularly in that of a servant doing the surrogate welcome for her employers. In chastising the Martins for being late, she is of course contradicting the information and the sympathy expressed by her (to Mr and Mrs Smith) in the previous section, which is again a breach in entailment in Austin's terms. She also sounds like, say, a cross authority figure, and, with regard to what Schegloff above calls 'rights and obligations', she is undoubtedly asserting her rights and not accepting many obligations. Notice, though, that she does not entirely deny these obligations, for she does let the Martins into the room, she does speak, she does grudgingly let them sit down. How she achieves this grudging aspect is in itself quite interesting. She uses that checking structure, 'What do you mean. . .', which, as Garfinkel and his students have shown (1967), is very easily taken up as a demonstration of hostility. Also, she both comments disapprovingly on the others' behaviour, and gives them alternative rules for behaviour in terms of society's politeness conventions. She is here using specifically superior-to-inferior talk: teacher–pupil, mother–child (see chapter 3 for a fuller discussion of this). And bluntly checking for understanding, as she does, is a dominant interactant's prerogative, and her choice of means here is reminiscent of situations where the addressee is in some way considered an incompetent interactant, in that it suggests she is addressing a small child, a foreign language speaker or a person with some physical impediment to understanding.

Equally noticeable, however, is the lack of any response from the Martins. Had they regarded this turn of Mary's as a greeting, then a reciprocal greeting would have been in order (see Schegloff, 1968, discussed more fully below). If on the other hand they had heard it as a reprimand, then some sort of apology or excuse might have been in order (see Austin, 1961). One might, I suppose, take it that since they produce neither, they might well be confused about whether they are being welcomed or treated as intruders. However, such real-world judgments do not really seem applicable in this particular context. What we can say is that they refuse to acknowledge Mary's claim for superior status, and, in opting out of the Co-operative Principle, in fact make a claim for the maintenance of superior status still.

4 Mr and Mrs Martin discover they are man and wife

from: MR MARTIN   I beg pardon, madam.
   to: MRS MARTIN   Donald darling, it's really you.

In this strange dialogue, Mr and Mrs Martin discover that they are man and wife. This odd procedure is made even more strange by the means in which they reach the discovery. Notice that Ionesco's clues for the paralinguistic features of the episode at once distance the interaction from any conceivably realistic representation: *'The following dialogue is spoken in a drawling monotonous voice, rather sing-song, without light and shade.'* However, even without these instructions to the players, the very blatantly repetitive poetic structuring of the piece would render it highly improbable as dialogue in any case (see Burton, 1977).

As well as this focus on the poetic function, there are several effects that seem worth special consideration. These are: the extreme politeness of this talk between man and wife; the length of the episode; and the high redundancy load. In a sense these three features are interrelated, and are perhaps most economically approached from a consideration of the first.

The impression of high formality is achieved in several ways. Firstly, there is a very strict procedure for turn-taking (compare Sacks, Schegloff and Jefferson 1974, and their naturalistic data), with Mr Martin taking the lead, as it were, in initiating items of information for confirmation by Mrs Martin. Notice that Mrs Martin's cohesive repetitions are overdone (see remarks by Keenan above), but in looking at these alone, it is obvious that they are in some sense 'second parts' in relation to fairly easily deducible 'first parts' (compare Sacks, 1970, on the third-part quality of the utterance preface 'I still say though that. . .'). For the most part, these initiations by Mr Martin are merely mundane, and, in their slow-moving precision, reminiscent of interactive computer programmes that refuse to allow any short-cuts in the interactive dialogue. However, the utterances about travelling third class are violations of presupposition rules (see Austin above), and the descriptions of Alice sound unlikely, to say the least.

The formality of the talk is also created by the use of over-formal (for English culture) address terms throughout, and the equally consistent and repetitive use of politeness prefaces by each party. Considering the address terms first, there are some relevant observations to be found in Ervin-Tripp's work on the systematic description of address-term usage in American English (1972). In considering socialization, she points out that adults entering a new culture may well have to learn new sociolinguistic rules. In demonstrating some of the problems and probable solutions for speakers in this situation she draws an interesting comparison between English and French address-term rules:

A Frenchman in the United States might start out by assuming that monsieur = Mr, madame = Mrs, and so on.

However, the rules for occurrences of these forms are different in France. In polite discourse, routines like 'merci', 'au revoir', 'bonjour', and 'pardon' do not occur without an address form in France, although they may in the United States. One always uses 'Au revoir Madame' or some alternative address form. Madame differs from 'Mrs' in at least two ways. Unknown female addressees of a certain age are normally called madame, regardless of marital

status. Further Mrs $+ \theta = \theta$, madame $+ \theta =$ madame. As a matter
of fact, the rule requiring address with routines implies that when
L[ast] N[ame] is not known, there cannot be a 'zero alternant'
— some form of address must be used anyway, like the English
'sir'.

By looking at the English text of the Ionesco play, one might assume
that the French text would have *monsieur* and *madame* where the
English text has 'sir' and 'madam'. In this case the English text emerges
as far more formal with respect to this item than the French, for, as
Ervin-Tripp has pointed out, the use of *monsieur* and *madame* is routine, whilst, as she implies, the use of 'sir' is unusual, and, as we know,
the use of 'madam' is most unusual, except in highly formal service
encounters between strangers with a deference relationship between
addresser and addressee. In English, the text has an almost archaic air.
What the English text cannot represent, however, is the distinction
between the formal second-person address pronoun and the informal,
that would be easily differentiated in the French (see Brown and
Gilman, 1960). So, in part, this use of formal address terms compen-
sates for this. However, since the T[u] and V[ous] distinction is also
a normal feature of everyday interaction, and the French text would
not be particularly marked except for the fact that the audience assumes
Mr and Mrs Martin to be husband and wife and on T[u] terms, then the
English text undoubtedly over-compensates.

The lengthy and formulaic politeness prefaces are reminiscent of the
data discussed in Stubbs (1973). It is perhaps interesting to recall that
in his committee data, prefaces and similar padding accounted for
approximately 40 per cent of the actual talk. Certainly here they
account in part for the length of the episode, and another interesting
point of reference here is Geertz (1960) on Javanese, where he suggests
that politeness markers are universally time-consuming. Notice, too,
that the prefaces account for the obvious redundancy of the text.
Firstly, because they are drawn from a very small repertoire of items
which in themselves become tedious with repetition, but also because
(like personal-points-of-view prefaces in Stubbs's data) they tell the
audience what propositional content will be following in the rest of
the utterance. In other words, even before Mrs Martin produces her
over-long repetitions for confirmations, the prefaces she uses tell us that
she will in fact be confirming.

5 Mary sums up the situation

from: MARY   Elizabeth and Donald.
to: MARY   My real name is Sherlock Holmes.

This section seems fairly clear and consistent, and I can find little of interest to write about it other than the description of its function already given above. However, it is reminiscent of Abercrombie's 'spoken prose' (see chapter 1). The information is densely packed and confusing, involving complex alternative paired variables; the left eye, the right eye, the red eye, the white eye and so on. The argument that Donald and Elizabeth are not Donald and Elizabeth because the child they are referring to is not the same child, whilst in a sense plausible, sounds highly coincidental, and the overall impression is of Mary summing up in the manner of a legal barrister, or — as the last sentence suggests — in the manner of an authoritative sleuth. The repeated first names of the characters involved also make this summing-up very much like a plot summary, thus enhancing the notion of the detective-fiction style of the monologue.

6 The Smiths and the Martins

The Smiths greet the Martins

from: MRS SMITH   Good evening.
to: MR SMITH   Why have you come so late?

This is very similar in both effect and means used for that effect, as already discussed with reference to Mary's 'welcome' above (in section 3), particularly in Mr Smith's expressions. But notice that, with regard to the quotation from Schegloff given in that discussion, there is an explicit reference in Mrs Smith's greeting to the notion of rights. Also, whilst there seems to be a very clear distinction between Mrs Smith's polite greeting and Mr Smith's rude greeting (see Schegloff on strong inferences to be taken from deviant interactive behaviour, 1968), the audience can see through her ostensible politeness, for, as the stage directions indicate, the couple has not in fact changed into its 'glad rags'. Similarly, we must assume that in the microcosm the phrase 'without announcing your intended visit' must be heard as an implicit criticism, from the way in which it is phrased (see Hudson, 1975, on socially motivated conversational implicature). It is of course contradicted in Mr Smith's follow-up utterance. Notice again, there is no reciprocal response from the Martins. It is a 'noticeable absence', in Schegloff's terms.

The Smiths and the Martins make extremely small talk

from: MR SMITH Hm!
to: MR MARTIN That's true, too.

Again, much of the point of this episode has been covered above in considerations of phatic communion. Like the husband–wife newspaper situation, the grunts and talk about the weather are simple societal stereotypes that Ionesco chooses. The extreme formality of the ascending-frequency use of 'Hm!' and the use of the clock as a participant accentuates the emptiness of the talk. The evident fatuousness of the concluding compromises emphasizes precisely those qualities, which are presumably what Ionesco meant when commenting on social language. The point is, of course, that as audience we are presumably still listening carefully to the talk; there would be no reason for being in the theatre if we were not doing so. In some theatre the use of small talk provides information other than the immediately referential; say about the attitudes of the interactants (see, for example, Wilde, 1895, or Stoppard, 1975). Ionesco is able to make use of extreme situations and extreme effects simply because he must assume that the audience is listening carefully to this very banal conversation.

Story-telling

from: MRS SMITH You two are always travelling around.
to: MR SMITH Perhaps it was the same gentleman.

Up until this point in the play, Ionesco has been using and re-using a small repertoire of his observations about interaction, as will perhaps have become obvious from repeated frames of descriptive reference used to account for text effects. However, at this point he introduces a new type of speech event: social story telling. Notice though, the text presents us with stories that sound odd in various different ways. Describing these oddities is by no means a simple matter, but two sets of work in conversational analysis are helpful here: Labov and Waletzky's tightly argued and rigorous descriptive work in the structure of narrative as a means of encapsulating personal experience (Labov and Waletzky, 1967; Labov, 1972b); and Sacks's much looser yet most insightful

51

observations about story-telling in an interactional context, and the relationship between the interactive features of the talk and the structuring of stories (1968, 1970).

Mrs Martin's story about the man tying his shoe-laces, given a stimulus by Mrs Smith, though given appreciation on completion by the microcosmic audience, fails for the macrocosmic audience, as a well-formed and well-functioning narrative, on several counts. Firstly, despite its several claims to tellability, and its eager acceptance as a reportable event by the microcosmic audience, it does not appear to the macrocosmic audience as a story worth the telling. Labov and Waletzky (1967) stress the crucial contribution of what they term the evaluative function of a narrative:

> Narrative will be considered as one verbal technique for re-
> capitulating experience, in particular, a technique of constructing
> narrative units which match the temporal sequence of that ex-
> perience. Furthermore, we will find that narrative which serves
> this function alone is abnormal: it may be considered empty or
> pointless narrative. Normally narrative serves an additional function
> of personal interest determined by a stimulus in the social context
> in which the narrative occurs.

We certainly do hear Mrs Martin's story as empty and pointless, though yet again we are at odds with the other, fictional, interactants, who apparently hear, and certainly react to, the story as fitting the stimulus provided in the text, both by Mrs Smith's prompt, and also by Mrs Martin's claimed evaluations of the narrative. Labov (1972b) modifies the claims of the earlier work on narrative, by expanding considerations of this evaluative function, indicating that this particular function permeates the narrative in a complex way, and is of a different level of ordering from the other semantic rhetorical units of normal narrative: the Abstract, the Orientation, the Complicating Action, the Result and the Coda (see below). This later discussion of evaluation suggests it is a permanent counter to the possible question from the audience, 'So what?'. Labov thus extends and exemplifies the notion of reportability, highly relevant to Mrs Martin's story topic here:

> If the event becomes common enough, it is no longer a violation of
> an expected rule of behaviour, and it is not reportable. . . .
> Evaluative devices say this to us: this was terrifying, dangerous,
> weird, wild, crazy, or amusing, hilarious, wonderful, more generally

that it was strange, uncommon, or unusual — that is, worth reporting. It was not ordinary, plain, humdrum, everyday or run-of-
the-mill.

And, of course, it is precisely on this dimension that Mrs Martin's story
is unsuccessful for us. Whilst her external evaluations tell us that the
story is worth reporting, we can find nothing worth hearing in narrative
terms in this very run-of-the-mill event. Mr Martin's follow-up story,
whilst it fits Sacks's criteria for a second story very nicely (Sacks, 1970),
also fails for exactly the same reasons.

Notice, though, that there is a superficial difference between the
structure of the two stories that makes Mrs Martin's story at least
sound, at first, more like a proper narrative than her husband's offering.
Labov and Waletzky, in their concentration on the fine details of the
structure of the narrative in terms of the clauses used, and their relationship with the temporal sequence of the events they are encapsulating,
define the minimal narrative: 'We can define a minimal narrative as a
sequence of two clauses which are temporally ordered: that is, a change
in their order will result in a change in the temporal sequence of the
original semantic interpretation.' They refer to this elsewhere as the
presence of at least one temporal juncture, or the establishment of at
least one a-then-b sequence of events. Now, in Mr Martin's story there is
no evidence of any temporal juncture whatsoever. In Mrs Martin's
story, however, the clauses in the nub of her story — 'His shoe-laces
had come undone and he was tying them up' — appear to exhibit just
this relationship, and it takes a moment's thought to realize the absurdity of this illusion, in that, outside a looking-glass world, this is the
only possible order for the particular events specified. It is only in a
quick hearing that the impression of a narrative is given.

Labov clarifies his subsections for normal narrative structure at its
fullest, by suggesting underlying questions appropriate to each section:

Abstract:	What was this about?
Orientation:	Who, what, when, where?
Complicating Action:	Then what happened? (the essential section)
Evaluation:	So what?
Result:	What finally happened?

In terms of the microcosm, Mrs Martin's story is accepted as one containing that essential Complicating Action. As macrocosmic audience
we are left asking the question 'Then what happened?'; in other words

we hear a substantial amount of Orientation and claimed Evaluation, but not the essential narrative kernel.

When Mr Smith suggests that perhaps the gentleman that Mr and Mrs Martin separately refer to might in fact have been the same gentleman, he moves towards another aspect of reportability that Sacks describes thus:

> There are people who are entitled to have their lives be an epic.
> We have assigned a series of storyable people, places and objects
> and they stand as something different from us. . . .there are for the
> society in general a collection of people about whom detailed
> reports – that would never, not merely be ventured about others,
> would never be thought about others. The way in which Elizabeth
> Taylor turned around is a something noticeable, reportable. The
> way in which your mother turned around is something unseeable,
> much less tellable.

In other words, if only the anonymous gentleman of the two stories had in fact had an interesting identity, then the stories would have been justifiably tellable. Mr Smith's suggestion that the two tellers might be talking about the same person, whilst not really a sufficient reason for these stories, at least approaches a feasible criterion.

A few other features in this section seem worth comment. For example, the highly stylized chorus contributions, such as 'Oh!', 'It can't be true', 'What? What?', 'Fantastic!', break that absolutely fundamental rule of conversation given repeatedly in the work of Sacks and his followers that 'one party speaks at a time'. Schegloff (1972, p. 350) points to the strength of this rule, and certainly here it foregrounds the artificiality and scripted nature of the dialogue – most particularly because the speakers not only speak simultaneously, but manage to say the same thing simultaneously.

Also, the frequent interruptions to Mrs Martin's story are interesting. Sacks (1968, 1970, 1974) points out that given the other fundamental rule, 'speaker change recurs', there is a special problem for the person who wishes to tell a story in a social setting, in that (as Labov also indicates above) narratives routinely take more than one utterance to produce, and the hopeful story-teller has to indicate to the other potential turn-takers that he intends to take the floor until they can hear that his story has finished. In the text the floor is given to the Martins, they do the necessary work to claim the floor for Mrs Martin, and provide an adequate story preface for the listeners to recognize when the story has finished, which, despite premature reactions, they confidently do identify at an appropriate point. Thus, the other participants are definitely rule-breaking when they hold the story up. There is a nice problem when Mr Smith says 'Mustn't interrupt, my dear, it's disgraceful of you' and, in pointing out this rule, quite explicitly is seen as doing the same perverse action.

The ringing at the door

from: MR SMITH   Listen there's a ring at the door.
   to: MR SMITH   It's the Captain of the Fire Brigade.

This section plays with a notion that there can be a ring at the door without anyone being there to ring it — again, a looking-glass-world comment on simple philosophical problems — and parodies the empirical investigations of such situations and the trustworthiness of inductive logic. As far as the talk is concerned there are only a few foregrounded effects in the language that I want to consider here.

In response to the sound of the bell, Mr Smith produces an identical utterance each time. I assume that Ionesco is also commenting here on simple behaviourist notions of stimulus and response. I take it that as Mr Smith's repeatedly identical utterances sound bizarre, this is a criticism of oversimple notions of these relationships, stressing the automaton aspects of the theory.

The simple alignment of the two women against the two men recalls the equally simple argument between Mr and Mrs Smith earlier in the play, except that here the conversation is, because of the four participants, able to split into two sets of two-party conversations. Notice, though, that the conversations are not confused with each other in any way. The clarity of who speaks what to whom is left intact.

7 The Fire Chief joins the party

The Fire Chief settles the problem

from: FIRE CHIEF   Good day all.
   to: MR MARTIN   They've all the time in the world.

This is a very simple extension of the problems in the preceding scene, and given the principles suggested in the introduction, does not seem worth pursuing here.

The Fire Chief announces the reason for his visit

from: MRS SMITH   Please make yourself comfortable.
  to: MR SMITH   Neither am I.

Clearly there is a problem here, for had the Fire Chief come on such important business as 'Have you by any chance a fire in the house?' suggests, then he should properly have announced it immediately, and not have taken up time with sorting out the Smiths' domestic argument, and other polite niceties. Sacks (1972), in discussing speakers' rights in more general terms, makes this point far more strongly:

> Suppose two adults are copresent and lack rights to talk to each other, e.g. they have never been introduced or whatever. For any two such persons there are conditions under which one can begin to talk to the other. And that those conditions are the conditions used in fact to begin talk is something which can be shown via a first piece of talk. Where that is done we will say that talk is begun with a ticket. That is, the item used to begin talk is an item which, rights not otherwise existing, serves to warrant one having begun to talk. For example one turns to the other and says, 'Your pants are on fire'; it is not just any opening but an opening which tells why it is that one has breached the correct silence, which warrants one having spoken. Tickets then are items specially usable as first items in talk by one who has restricted rights to talk to another. And the most prototypical class of tickets are 'announcements of trouble relevant to the other'.

In the text, the Fire Chief, by virtue of his occupation, his acceptance into the house, his welcome and so on, does not have these sorts of restrictions. And certainly, since his reason-for-calling is specifically connected with trouble relevant to the others, then his self-effacing mitigating sheepishness in for example 'I'm terribly sorry, but I must ask you first if you would be so kind as to be willing to excuse. . .', is most inappropriate verbal behaviour.

The story-telling round

from: MRS SMITH   As you're in no hurry.
  to: MR SMITH   It always strikes the contrary to the right time.

In this section, the Fire Chief tells four stories, and Mr and Mrs Smith tell one each. They none of them seem adequate, and their inadequacies can again be discussed in terms of the work partly described above in relation to earlier stories in the text.

The Fire Chief's first story shares some of the features that clustered around Mrs Martin's earlier story. Again, the stated evaluation before the event — the fact that his stories are drawn from life — is not compatible with the story when it occurs, for it is a surreal fable with bizarre components. Again too, the other participants chorus their approval and encouragement. The minimal narrative requirement is met this time in the irreversible nature of the question and answer, 'Why haven't you swallowed your trunk?' and 'I always thought I was an elephant', though again the nonsensical referential material militates against this structural feature, and must make the utterance only sound like a narrative without it being one. The Orientation is strangely realized, but sufficient, and includes the traditional and formulaic 'Once upon a time', so that it does sound like the start of a proper story. Mrs Martin's question 'Wh-what is the moral?' is like Labov's 'So what?' in paraphrase, and shows for once a degree of agreement between the response in the microcosm and the response in the macrocosm; but notice that Mr Smith endorses the Fire Chief's suggestion that there is a deducible point for those sensitive enough to find it, and Mrs Smith, in asking the man to tell another story, perhaps suggests that the performance was acceptable to her too.

The second story about the young calf certainly has a series of a-then-b clauses, and yet the ostensible causal connections between these clauses are both contradictory and nonsensical. Again, we have the impression of a narrative in the Orientation, Complicating Action (though no Evaluation) and Result, but clearly, the narrative is totally unbelievable. Notice that the others claim that they have heard it as a true story before, since it both appeared in the newspapers and is supposed to have taken place near where they live.

The third story, though singularly uninteresting, has at least the bare bones of a narrative fable, whilst Mrs Smith's follow-up story, which plays with the pun on 'ape', adds a further two clauses to the same story.

Mr Smith's contribution, full of bizarre elements, is rather well made in narrative terms, containing two narrative cycles complete with Orientation, Complicating Action, Results and a final Resolution — though no Evaluation, which means in Labov's terms that it is inadequate in terms of usual stories in interaction. The contradictory responses to the story are a familiar routine by now.

Mrs Smith's story, interrupted with a cyclical ritual between the claiming of the floor the first time and the claiming of the floor the second time, begins with a sensible Orientation, a pseudo-complicating action that reverses the presuppositions of the Orientation, and ends with another surreal nonsense totally at odds with the very sensible and prosaic opening.

The Fire Chief's final story about the cold — which turns out to be a simple statement about a character catching a cold — is really simply a highly complex Orientation, with thirty-eight clauses. Again the event is truly non-reportable, as even the story-teller admits in 'just like everyone else'. It has no a-then-b sequence, and it contains much information that the audience may assume it needs to retain, in order to understand the story, but which it does not in fact need at all (see Sacks, 1968). And once more, responses are contradictory: Mrs Smith reacts to it as an acceptable strange story, Mrs Martin again 'fails to see the point'.

8 Mary joins the party

from: MARY   Sir-madam.
  to: MARY   . . .Caught fire —

Mary enters as her deferential self once more, and her employers re-inforce this notion by pointing out that her presence is not acceptable. Ward (1971) comments on this with reference to black children in the domestic setting, where the rule seems to be 'be silent or be absent'. The play takes on the nature of a parody of melodrama, where long-lost loves come together. An interesting sequence showing the two men fumbling for words, 'a little — er — a little — er. . .', is an unusual item in any script, though compare, for example, Edward in Pinter's *A Slight Ache* (1961b).

9 The party after Mary has left

from: MRS MARTIN   That gave me the shivers.
  to: FIRE CHIEF   Let's hope so. For everyone's sake.

In taking his leave, the Fire Chief follows patterns observed by Schegloff and Sacks (1973) for leave-taking in telephone conversations. They set up the features of a 'proper closing' thus:

> The two crucial components for the achievement of a proper closing
> . . .are the terminal exchange which achieves the collaborative termi-
> nation of the transition rule, and the proper initiation of the closing
> section which warrants the undertaking of the routine whose
> termination in the terminal exchange properly closes the conversation.

They point to the specific problems that require, for their solution, the
proper initiation of a closing sequence. Firstly, there is the formulaic
close ordering of adjacency pairs in the actual terminal exchange.
Secondly, there may be some topics or 'mentionables' which, if they
are not to appear inappropriately important, must be held back either
until they occur 'relevantly' or as a last item of talk. This means that
there must be advance notice given of the potential end of the conversation, so that mentionables not yet brought into the conversation
by means of tied relevance may here be introduced conveniently.
Following the usual patterns then, the Fire Chief gives an excuse for
going — 'Well I must be going. . . .I have a fire to attend to' — thus
opening up a pre-closing section of the talk. This is taken up by the
others, and, with a blatant misplacement marker, 'By the way', he then
brings in his as yet unmentioned mentionable — knowing the encounter
is about to close. Interestingly enough, there is scarcely any conceivable
way in which the bald prima donna topic could have arisen naturally,
and so it has to be asked thus if it is to be asked at all. Similarly, it is
of course the most obvious question from the macrocosmic audience,
in the sense of 'What is the meaning of this title and this play?'. We
gather from the horrified reactions of the other microcosmic interactants, that the Fire Chief's question is, to use another and lay terminology, an unmentionable. Mrs Smith's angry rejoinder, 'She always
wears her hair the same way', leaves us all no wiser at all, and, as so
often before, contradicts one of the givens in the preceding utterance;
the prima donna's baldness.

10 The verbal whist game

from: MRS MARTIN   I can buy a pocket-knife for my brother.
  to: ALL   . . .thatter way, thisser way.

This large section subdivides in a common-sense way into three stylistically differentiated sub-sections. With some overlap between them,
these can be crudely categorized as (1) pseudo-proverbs and epigrams
(up to 'I'd rather slaughter a rabbit than whistle in the garden'), (2)

tongue twisters (up to 'Don't flip her. She's fallen to pieces') and (3) shared utterances and systematized patterns (from 'Alfred' to '. . .thatter way, thisser way'). I want to discuss features of the section in relation to two sets of ideas in the discourse literature. The first concerns the literature on speech play that examines the developmental aspects of play with speech and sound in small children. The second concerns the literature on speech play that considers epigrams and gnomic utterances. But first, consider this extract from Halliday and Hasan (1976) which, I would think, must refer to this section of the play rather than any earlier section:

> A set of sentences that in any other environment would not constitute a text is admissible as such in a book about language. . . . the effects of their occurrence in a situation to which they are inappropriate can be seen in Ionesco's play the *Bald-Headed Prima-donna*. But they illustrate the general principle that the hearer or reader when he is determining consciously or unconsciously the status of a specimen of language, invokes two kinds of evidence, the external as well as the internal; he uses not only linguistic clues but also situational ones. Linguistically he responds to specific features which bind the passage together, the patterns of connection, independent of structure that we are referring to as cohesion. Situationally he takes into account all he knows of the environment; what is going on, what part the language is playing, and who are involved.

Now whilst I would agree wholeheartedly with the main point of the paragraph — that the reader takes into account the internal linguistic features of the text he reads or hears, and also the situational external features — and whilst, in a simple sense, I can see the point of using Ionesco's text as an example of deviance, it seems to me that in using *The Bald Prima Donna* as this example of inappropriateness, Halliday and Hasan have completely ignored essential external features of both the macrocosm and the microcosm. To take the macrocosm first; by this stage in the play, it must surely be obvious to any reader or hearer that the text is 'a book about language', rather than an attempt at a text in the traditional theatrical paradigm. In this context, the set of sentences in this section are thus entirely appropriate. With respect to the microcosm; if we do take into account all we know of the environment, 'what is going on, what part the language is playing, and who are involved', then similarly we should have enough knowledge of the microcosmic interaction to accept the set of sentences as appropriate again. The characters, who we know by this stage do not follow anything like the normal rules of discourse, are depicted as playing a game of verbal whist (see the stage directions), offering pseudo-proverbs as 'turns' in rounds of play, so that if we really do take into account 'what part the language is playing and who are involved' then the language here is perfectly acceptable and appropriate.

The pseudo-epigram section

from: MRS MARTIN I can buy a pocket-knife.
   to: MR MARTIN . . .whistle in the garden.

This first part of section 10 is constructed using utterances that sound very much like idiomatic proverbs and epigrams, but which are, for the most part, noticeably deviant. They are produced as tokens in a verbal game of whist, although the speakers do not take strict turns at contributing to the game, and I can discern no consistent pattern in the types of pseudo-proverb used by any individual character. I am interested in the following aspects: how is it that we recognize deviant epigrams as epigrams? Can we be any more precise in describing ways in which utterances are deviant with respect to the traditional notion of the epigram? How does the cyclical and repetitive use of these epigrams in extended rounds of talk relate and compare with their use in ordinary conversation, and what overall points can we draw from the episode?

Several ethnographers and sociolinguists have written about epigrams and proverbs (see, for example, Rothstein, 1968; Seitel, 1969; Milner, 1971; Kuusi, 1972; Dundes, 1975). Of these, a work by Dina Sherzer, although discussing their use in a literary context (a Beckett novel), seems to be the most useful for my purposes here. Her 1976 article appears in the context of Kirschenblatt-Gimblett's collection of work on artistically oriented aspects of speech play in interaction. Sherzer focuses on Beckett's *Molloy* (1951), and shows how Beckett exploits and violates the reader's expectations of gnomic statements. In suggesting a typology of gnomic expressions in Beckett, she considers the general nature of such expressions, and draws some useful general observations together. Her overall point is that Beckett is 'putting language on display' (the same can, of course, be said for Ionesco), foregrounding the art of writing both overtly, as when his gnomic expressions actually refer to writing, but also more covertly, when the manipulation of the form *per se* draws attention to the creative process. She emphasizes the playful nature of such expressions, which is certainly consistent with the game-playing impression created in Ionesco's text (though one has the impression that the competitive aspect of the game takes over at certain tense points). Where I find her work most useful, however, is in her discussion of what she calls 'the gnomic code', and the constituent elements of gnomic expressions. And, as she says: 'Because of their semantic, phonological, lexical and syntactic properties, gnomic expressions are immediately recognizable in written texts and oral discourse.' This is certainly the case in the Ionesco text. Although we have heard very few of these epigrams previously, we are in no doubt that they are exponents of this gnomic code, though minimally deviant. What we cannot know without a careful consideration of the properties of that underlying code is precisely how they are deviant, how many different types Ionesco uses and whether it would make sense to talk of some as 'more deviant' than others. I want here to work towards a typology, in order to come to grips with the data in an interesting way, and also to consider the interactive properties and consequences of their use.

Sherzer collects together properties of gnomic utterances which may be summarized as follows. Note that I have reorganized, simplified and abstracted here in order to clarify the most useful parts of the paper:

Semantic properties:
1 They deal with basic aspects of life — love, health, age, poverty, riches, work, and so on — and must be non-trivial.
2 They are concerned with expressions of general opinion, rather than personal opinion, and imply that the society in general would endorse the sentiments proposed.
3 They can often be taken metaphorically rather than (or sometimes as well as) literally.
4 They advocate strategies or give advice.
5 They state a general truth in contrast with the specificity of the context in which they appear, often by referring to a range of broad and general experience outside that context of use.

Syntactic properties:
1 Present tense, suggesting a-temporality, or references to any time. Again, this is often in contrast to the situation and context in which they occur.

2 Characteristically symmetry is highlighted: parallelisms, repetition
devices, bipartite structures.
3 Frequent use of the copula.
4 Frequent use of impersonal pronouns and nouns: 'we' 'one' 'people'.
5 Imperatives may be used.

Phonological properties:
1 They often make use of alliteration, assonance and rhyme.

Lexical properties:
1 They may make use of archaisms, but in any case are not colloquial.

Her remarks on function and contexts, although not heavily stressed in
the paper, are obviously extremely important for our purposes here.
Of function she writes: 'The ultimate function of gnomic expressions
is to manipulate language, to create a striking disposition of verbal
forms in order to teach, to convey wisdom or to express a particular
philosophy.' (Compare Kirschenblatt-Gimblett (1974) on Eastern-
European Jewish folk-narrative.) For context, she points out four
characteristics, all of which can be seen not to be in force in Ionesco's
scene:

1 The form is differentiated from surrounding speech (see above).
2 They sum up what has been said before and generalize about it.
3 They may be codas to particular scenes.
4 They do not follow trivial stimuli.

In terms of context then, Ionesco is again making strange a particular
type of language use. Whilst in terms of function the utterances do
create this striking disposition of verbal forms, we cannot be sure just
what philosophy or wisdom they are meant to convey or teach. Ionesco
himself puts it mystically, somewhat characteristically, thus (1956):

A work of art is the expression of an incommunicable reality that
one tries to communicate — and which sometimes can be communi-
cated. That is its paradox and its truth. . . .Unfortunately, the wise
and elementary truths they [the characters] exchanged, when
strung together had gone mad, the language had become disjointed;
words now absurd, had been emptied of their content and it all
ended in a quarrel the cause of which was impossible to discover.

When it comes to the manipulation of formal properties *per se*, the
following table (Table 2.1) indicates crudely the types of exploitation

Table 2.1.

	Recall	Phonology	Lexis	Syntax	Semantics	Function	Context
Lundi, mardi, mercredi, jeudi, vendredi, samedi, dimanche	✓						
Edouard a la plume de ma tante, sa soeur Odette va à l'école, et moi je suis Anglais							2
What a funny family				2			
I'd rather see a bird in a field than a marrow in a wheelbarrow				1/2/3			
A haddock in a paddock is better than a crab in a lab		1		1/2/3			
A Englishman's home is his castle	✓		1				
I don't know enough Spanish to make myself understood							
I would give you the slippers of my mother-in-law, if you gave me the coffin of your husband				2			
I am looking for a monogamist to marry our maidservant		1	1	1/3			
The pine is a tree, whereas the pine is also a tree, and an oak breeds an oak every morning at dawn				1/2/3			
My uncle lives in the country, but that's none of the midwife's business				1/2			
Paper is for rationing and the cat's for the rat.							
Cheese is for rationing				1/2/3			
A motor car travels very fast, but I'd rather have a cook to cook the dinner				1/2			

	Recall	Phonology	Lexis	Syntax	Semantics	Function	Context
Don't be a silly goose, kiss the conspirator instead	✓			5			
Honi soit qui mal y pense	X	1					
I'm waiting for Mahomet to come to my mountain				1/3			
Social progress is much better coated with sugar		1		5			
Down with polishing							
You can't polish your spectacles with black boot-polish				1/4			
Yes, but when you've got money you can buy everything you want							2
I'd rather slaughter a rabbit than whistle in the garden				1/2			

Dialogue

that Ionesco employs, with reference to the classifications given above and drawn from Sherzer's work. Though this is a fairly indelicate analysis, it indicates that, like the story types used earlier, whilst the epigrams sound acceptable they are being used inappropriately with reference to semantics, conversational function and context. Given the formal criteria, though, it is tempting to read and understand these pseudo-epigrams as non-trivial, stating general truths, expressing general opinions and so on.

The entire verbal whist game
I want now to consider developmental aspects of speech play in relation to this section. A paper by Catherine Garvey (1977) presents a survey of work on developmental aspects of features of language in children in the pre-school period, focusing on speech play in the context of inter-active play. (The scope seems to be from children of 2:10 to 5:7.) A quick summary of her findings should prove useful in discussing this section as a whole. The overall point that I want to make is that as the section progresses, the talk gets more and more childlike. If the characters' play-talk is compared with Garvey's account, then the characters can be seen to be regressing in a fairly simple way. Notice that the comparison, whilst not of course exact, is strikingly similar. Notice too this comment of Elinor Keenan's (1975) in discussing how and when her own children resort to 'sound play' that is, talk with no literal referential meaning: 'It is tempting to say that sound play occurs when a topic or set of topics have been exhausted by the speakers.' It is interesting that, apart from the cyclical re-start, the repeat of the beginning of the whole play that follows this section, this is Ionesco's final constructive contribution to his play about disintegrating language. It is as if all other topics have been exhausted, and sound play is the only possibility left to him.

Garvey presents the most primitive level of all in verbal play as babbling (0:6–0:10), which develops into repetitive rhythmic vocal-ization (Stern, 1974) and then play with syllable shapes, prosodic features, either for the pleasure inherent in the noise itself, or as an accompaniment to other play: 'Vocalizations as accompaniments to motor activities move from hums, squeals, shrieks and bellows to repetitions, often melodic strings of syllables.' In this context, consider the utterances right at the close of the section which accompany train imitations.

Between two and three years, children start using the conventionalized 'beep-beep' or 'vroom-vroom' noises to accompany play where relevant. They may sometimes use lexical rather than onomatopoeic represent- ations, as in for example, 'cut cut cut' or 'sew sew sew'. And in this context consider Mrs Smith's utterance, 'Choo, choo, choo, choo. . .'

Children then move into a phase which is transitional between play with sound and play with the features of the linguistic system. Garvey cites children of 3:0 taking words apart syllabically and putting them together again, and calls them

> Instances of the nonliteral and nonsocial exploitations of the
> sound properties of language for their own intrinsic interest. They
> exhibit a focus on the form and structure of speech particularly
> on the phonological subsystems of syllable structure and pitch. . . .
> Further, the meaning properties of the phrases appear to have
> evaporated with repetition, much as in the process called verbal
> satiation.

In the text, the utterances 'Pistletoe, pistletoe. . .' onwards seem to display these sorts of features, although the participants do appear to be taking account of each other's contributions in the making of their own. Garvey instances Keenan (1975) as the only account of social verbal play between young children (see the discussion of this in chapter 3), and suggests this was only possible because the children knew each other so well. If we take it that the Smiths and the Martins knew each other well enough, then their social play along the same nonsense (yet structured nonsense) lines seems appropriate enough. Garvey also instances at this stage children playing with 'building blocks' of sequences, repetitions of newly-learned structures; and much of the play from ' "Alfred!" "Tennyson!" ' onwards, and in par- ticular from ' "Business, Bosnia, Buster!" ' to ' "Do re mi fa sol la si do" ', seems to have this character, albeit with reference to quite sophis- ticated, culturally learned patterns and structures.

Finally, Garvey comes to talk of genuine shared play, and suggests that for the older children she studies there are three different, and often simultaneously used, types of play: (1) spontaneous rhythm and word play (compare the second section of the game), (2) play with fantasy and nonsense (compare the first and second sections of the game) and (3) play with speech acts and discourse (compare the first section of the game). Any episode in her data might contain all three.

In many ways, then, the progression of the three sub-sequences in the context of the overall verbal whist competition matches a regressive patterning deduced from Garvey's suggestions.

11 The recycled start to the play

from: MRS MARTIN   Goodness! Nine o'clock!
to: MRS MARTIN   . . .his mayonnaise is bad. . .

There is very little to be said about this recycling to the beginning of the play, except that it reinforces the anonymity of the various individual, named characters we have been considering during the course of the text. By this final device, Ionesco confirms that any attempt on the hearer's part to ascribe characteristics or character development to any of the people portrayed on stage, must have been self-defeating. It also suggests to me, that as there has been no progression in the play, there can similarly be no simple way to end, except by a series of dots.

This study of *The Bald Prima Donna* has drawn on a broad range of work in discourse analysis, in order to account for a variety of effects created in the dialogue of the text. In particular this has focused on selecting different types of 'absurdities' that emerge as the play progresses but other interesting and accountable features have been discussed where appropriate. Whilst many of the play's effects are rather neatly accounted for in this way, this selective approach is highly problematic in terms of theory and methodology. There is a fuller discussion of this in chapter 4, since similar problems arise in discussing effects in *The Dumb Waiter*. Notice, however, that both chapters 2 and 3 are called 'studies' rather than 'analyses' precisely in relation to the problematic status of any such selective procedure.

A notable feature of this study has been the use made of apposite work in the philosophy of language as well as work on naturally occurring conversations. As suggested earlier, this was something of a surprise. The original assumption had been that, despite the inherent fascination and useful heuristic qualities of this work, any practical use of the ideas and findings applied to data would be highly limited. (See, for example, Hirsch, 1976.) However, the Ionesco text, in that it does not attempt to simulate naturalistic talk, but is concerned with presenting general philosophical problems inherent in generalized notions of communication, is certainly amenable to discussion in terms of the philosophy of language. A disturbing corollary to this, particularly with regard to the almost uncanny specific similarity between this dialogue and many of the examples used in the philosophical literature, is a reinforcement of the now common suspicion that work in the philosophy of language, though rich, insightful and powerful in its own terms, bears very little relation to everyday talk.

Chapter 3

A stylistic study of Pinter's 'The Dumb Waiter'

There are several straightforward reasons for choosing to study this text here. Firstly, and most generally, since it is a commonplace observation that Pinter is widely acclaimed by both the lay and the literary-critical public as a notable writer of realistic-sounding dialogue, then, in a book concerned with some of the relationships between play dialogue and naturally occurring conversation, some Pinter text was an obvious if not essential choice for close study and discussion. And on this parameter at least, it contrasts nicely with the Ionesco text and the public reactions to the ostensible artificiality of its dialogue. *The Dumb Waiter* has obvious procedural advantages in being relatively short, and relatively simple, at least in terms of its participants, there being only two characters on stage. It also seemed to be intuitively interesting and potentially rich with regard to conversational analysis, in that, whilst there is very little in the way of plot or action, there is certainly a great deal of talk. Admittedly the dumb waiter descends, bringing bizarre messages from an unseen third party. Similarly, matches arrive, instructions are given, and there is some unfinished action at the close of the play. Nevertheless, most of the stage time is taken up with 'mere' talk — a fact which enraged its original audience, and which has interesting implications for the distinction between small-talk in everyday life and 'small-talk' on stage. In terms of the microcosmic interaction, Ben and Gus are, to borrow Roy Turner's useful phrase, 'getting through time with talk' (Turner, 1972). In the macrocosm, the audience is given, to all intents and purposes, mostly 'talk' as their material, and in this way the interaction itself, and the interactants themselves, are what the play can be said to be 'about'. Quigley in his study of Pinter (Quigley, 1976), stresses the focus on what he calls 'the dominant inter-relational function' as opposed to any simpler referential function to be found in all Pinter's works:

The point to be grasped about a Pinter play is that language is not so much a means of referring to structure in personal relationships, as a means of creating it. Characters are constantly engaged in exploring or reinforcing or changing the relationship that obtains between them and the current situation. . . .Pinter has created a new dynamic of dialogue in which the coercive power of social conversation becomes the focus of character confrontation. The conflict that is essential to all drama is generated by interrelational coercive dialogue of characters who are at crucial points of adjustment between themselves and the environment to which they are currently exposed.

Certainly, during the forty-five-minute span of *The Dumb Waiter*, the audience's attention is focused on the characters of Ben and Gus as they are presented via the talk. In discussing the effects created in the language of the text, I want to begin by considering what seems to me to be a central and key feature of the play; the unequal statuses of the two participants, where, despite the odd battle for dominance, or occasional trouble from outside events, Ben is undoubtedly the dominating and superior interactant, and Gus is equally undoubtedly the dominated and inferior one. I will begin by discussing how we know this, working on the assumption that the creation of this impression lies in the work (in the ethnomethodological sense) that the fictional interactants do in the construction of their talk. I would want to suggest that Gus's seeming inferior, and his somewhat childlike interactive nature, obtain for him a degree of audience sympathy which enhances the pathos of his situation as potential 'victim' at the close of the play. Similarly, Ben's evident superiority, and his callous, controlling and dominant interactive behaviour make him easily acceptable as a villain in the piece. Thus Pinter, in choosing for the most part trivial or even humorous subject-matter for the conversationalists' topics, definitely establishes a type of relationship that evokes appropriate audience reactions when the play takes its menacing turn at the end.

After discussing how it is that we hear Ben as the dominant partner and Gus as the inferior one, in terms of adult–child interaction, I shall go on to focus on aspects of Gus's own behaviour that are specifically childlike in themselves.

Against this general textual norm, where Ben is the confident director of operations and persons, there are a few sections where this impression does not hold: after the matches arrive under the door, during the two arguments with Gus about lighting the kettle, during Ben's reading of the newspaper, during the activities demanded by the dumb waiter's messages, and when Gus starts to panic near the close of the play. The impression we get here is of a frailer side to Ben's character, and an awareness of his own subservient part in the mysterious 'organisation'. Whilst we do not condone his actions towards Gus at the end of the play, they appear understandably outside his control. I shall conclude this chapter by discussing aspects of the dialogue which create this particular set of impressions.

Let us consider Ben and Gus in conversation, with particular reference to adult–child interaction. The means by which Ben asserts his conversational dominance are numerous and pervasive. One highly relevant observation can be found in Abrahams (1972), where, writing of the differences between black American English house-talk culture, as compared with the street-talk between male peers, he describes an extreme version of the traditional British notion of the 'seen but not heard' convention that holds for children when interacting with adults. In his data this is a genuinely observed convention, rather than a more or less well-realized English myth. A succinct quote from Ward (1971) makes the relevant points rather clearly: 'Adults do not regard children as people to talk to. Conversations initiated by children are short-lived. . . .Rarely are questions asked for or answered, or is information volunteered.' In the course of the play, Ben makes it obvious by just these means that he does not regard Gus as a person to talk to, unless it suits his own purposes. It is useful and revealing to take each of Ward's observations singly, and to see how each is applicable to the interaction between Ben and Gus in both extreme and modified forms. There are other, related features which will be appended where appropriate. But to begin with we shall look at the following in detail: initiations, questions, requests for speaker's rights, requests for permission, the volunteering of information.

Whilst Gus continually does try to initiate conversations, in the sense that he tries to establish things to talk about, he is frequently just ignored by Ben, for example:

GUS   He's laid on some very nice crockery this time, I'll say that.
      It's sort of striped. There's a white stripe.
      (*BEN reads*)
      It's very nice, I'll say that.
      (*BEN turns the page*)

> You know, sort of round the cup. Round the rim. All the
> rest of it's black you see. Then the saucer's black, except for
> right in the middle, where the cup goes, where it's white.
> (*BEN reads*)

Similar examples can be found throughout the text: where Gus talks
about the forthcoming job; where he talks about the uncomfortable
bed; where he talks about the forthcoming victim; where he talks about
the putative café; where he talks about the job again, and their own
status within the organization; where he talks at length about their own
situation as contrasted with the possible people in the restaurant; where
he lets off steam about the owner of the house. Notice, in comparison,
whilst the topics introduced by Ben are few — the newspaper stories;
his interests; the job instructions; Gus's movements about the room —
they are never simply ignored by Gus.

A less extreme form of this conversational tactic emerges when Ben
does respond to and acknowledge Gus's chosen topics, but in doing so
makes it clear that he thinks they are foolish, unfounded, uninteresting,
unclear or otherwise suspect as contributions to an orderly conversation.
For example:

GUS I thought these sheets didn't look too bright. I thought they
     ponged a bit. I was too tired to notice when I got in this
     morning. Eh, that's taking a bit of a liberty isn't it? I don't
     want to share my bed-sheets. I told you things were going
     down the drain. I mean, we've always had clean sheets laid
     on up till now. I've noticed it.
BEN How do you know those sheets weren't clean?

And similarly, the same effects are created by the same means at the
following places: where Ben replies to the contribution about the
crockery by questioning Gus's need for a plate; where Gus's observation about tea is used as a cue for a directive about making the tea;
where Ben makes minimal replies, but refuses to express any interest
in the photograph of the first eleven; where he challenges Gus's expressed wish for a window, by asking him what he would want a
window for; where he responds to Gus's complaint about not having
time to look at the scenery, by pointing out that he has holidays for
that sort of thing; where he counters Gus's complaint that the holidays last only a fortnight, by pointing out that they do not work a full
week; where, when Gus has pointed out that they would get rheumatism

if they stayed long in that particular house, he stresses that they are not in fact staying for long; where he refuses to share Gus's enthusiasm about the following day being Saturday, until Gus explains the reason for this excitement; where he refuses to take up the suggestion that they could watch Aston Villa play, by saying that the team are not playing in Birmingham that week; where he backs up this objection, though not the truth value of the objection, by saying that they do not have the time to stay and watch football; where he contradicts Gus's retelling of the events of a previous football match; where he objects to the suggestion that they might watch Tottenham Hotspur, by saying that they too will be playing away; where he repeats that Aston Villa will be playing away; where Gus cites his mother as an authority on the figure of speech under debate, and Ben suggests that it is so long since Gus saw his mother that the authority is invalid; where he refuses to show any interest in the fact that the gas has gone out; where he reacts to Gus's complaint that they might not get a visit from the (to us) mysterious Wilson, and will thus get no money for the gas; by pointing out that he will just have to go without any tea; where he reinforces this two utterances later; where he challenges Gus's assumption about the man who owns the place they are in; where he challenges Gus's complaint about Wilson's infrequent visits, by saying that Wilson is a busy man with no obligation to visit; where he breaks into Gus's meanderings about the possibility that no one ever clears up after they have finished their apparently gruesome work, by pointing out that they are only a small part of a larger organization; where he follows Gus's complaint about the lack of food by telling him that eating is bad for him; and so on. Notice, on the other hand, that Ben's topics and statements are taken up with considerable interest, and usually no negative evaluation of the speaker (though see discussion below for a modification of this).

Another strategy that Ben employs centres on those places in the talk where Gus asks questions. Again, in some instances, Ben just completely refuses to answer, or even acknowledge in any way that a question has been put. For example:

GUS   You got any cigarettes? I think I've run out.

or:

GUS   You got any cigarettes? I've run out.

And see also utterances where Gus asks the following: when Wilson is going to get in touch with them; whether he should strike the match on his shoe; where Ben found his crisps; what happens to the putative restaurant when they are not there; what happens when they go; why Wilson does not get in touch; whether they are reliable in Wilson's eyes; what they are going to drink; what sort of food they have in the restaurant upstairs and how the people there manage; why he and Ben need to repeat the instruction routine; whether Ben is aware of not having made a mistake before; why they were sent matches when the sender knew there was no gas (twice); whether Ben remembers that Gus told him who owned the place they were in (twice). Notice that Gus never actually refuses Ben an answer in this way, thereby complying with Sacks's highly normative rule (Sacks, 1972) which he phrases thus: 'A person who has been asked a question, properly speaks and properly replies to it.'

An even more common occurrence, however, is that Gus may have to ask his questions more than once to get an answer, and in getting this answer, he also gets a negative evaluation from Ben, pointing out that his questions, like his topic-offerings, are in some sense foolish, illegitimate or simply a nuisance. For example:

GUS What time is he getting in touch?
     (*BEN reads*)
     What time is he getting in touch?
BEN What's the matter with you? It could be any time. Any time.

This happens consistently and routinely through the text: where Ben tells Gus he has assumed the wrong gender for the story referent; where Ben tells Gus not to hurry him when he gives the details of the second newspaper story; where he tells Gus to make his own referent (the lavatory tank) clearer; where Ben refuses to see any point to the question about the lavatory tank; where he denies the legitimacy of the question about the possibility of his getting fed up; where he suggests that Gus should have been asleep earlier, and therefore not in a position to have asked the question he has just asked about stopping the car; where he suggests that he has more information than Gus, and that the challenge Gus has just issued about being 'too early' thus has no substance; where he prefaces the answer with the information and complaint that he has already answered this particular question about what town they are in; where he refers to the conventions of the culture, which, by implication, any competent member of the culture should know ('It's a figure of speech' and 'It isn't done'); where he refuses to see the point of Gus's questions about the café and the stove (three times); and where he refuses to understand what Gus is trying to say about who has moved in upstairs and tells him to shut up, and similarly refuses to understand what Gus means by 'games' in, 'Well what's he playing these games for? That's what I want to know. What's he doing it for?' Notice that Gus, whilst he often asks for clarification, does not usually explicitly criticize Ben's talk in this way. The effect of Ben's tactics here is to force Gus to repeat and pursue his topics and questions, in a way that makes him sound annoyingly persistent and repetitively childlike (see below).

Similarly, Ben frequently responds to Gus's questions with vague answers, reminiscent of parents' replies to questions that are too difficult to be answered simply, and which can be put off with a generalized vague reply. For example, 'Well that all depends —' or 'That's not the point'. This is used particularly blatantly where Gus nags to be allowed to go and watch a football match the following day. He argues that since they are in Birmingham they could go and watch Aston Villa. Ben replies with the objection that Aston Villa are playing away. Gus then suggests they go to see Tottenham Hotspur, to which, again, the excuse that Ben gives is that they, too, are playing away. Gus twists this to his own advantage by saying that they might then be playing at Aston Villa:

GUS   If they're playing away they might be playing here. They
      might be playing the Villa.
BEN   (*tonelessly*) But the Villa are playing away.
GUS   Ben.
BEN   Away. They're all playing away.

Again, the impression we get is of the annoying child, being given evasive answers by a patient but non-complying adult.

Ben has yet another reaction to Gus's questions that is worth commenting on here, where he tries to stop Gus contributing altogether. He either tries to do this verbally, as in the following:

GUS   I asked you a question.
BEN   Enough!
GUS   I asked you before. Who moved in? I asked you. You said
      that the people who had it before moved out. Well who
      moved in?
BEN   (*hunched up*) Shut up.
GUS   I told you didn't I?
BEN   Shut up!

or, as this particular sequence progresses, he tries to stop Gus's contributions by physical means:

GUS   (*feverishly*) I told you before who owned this place didn't I?
I told you.
(*Ben hits him viciously on the shoulder*)
I told you who ran this place didn't I?
(*Ben hits him viciously on the shoulder*)

A common occurrence in the text, which is not covered in Ward's list of features above, is that Gus frequently requests permission to introduce certain, as yet unknown, topics. He thus classes himself as subordinate in a way in which Ben never does (see Sacks, 1972, on requests for speaker rights peculiar to small children). Ben does, though, use expressive particles to indicate that he wishes to hold the floor for an extended turn at story-telling (see Sacks, 1968), for which activity he needs some sort of acknowledgment from Gus before going ahead. Notice how Ben reacts to Gus's requests for speaking rights in two ways; one more extreme than the other. For example, he totally ignores the request, and behaves as if it had not occurred:

GUS   I want to ask you something.
BEN   What are you doing out there?

And see also: 'Oh, I wanted to ask you something', which is deflected by the story about the child killing a cat; 'Eh Ben', which eventually turns into the question about what town they are in; and 'I was going to ask you something', which is deflected by Ben's 'What are you sitting on my bed for?'

Alternatively, Ben may respond, but makes it quite explicit that he is annoyed by the request, as at:

GUS   Eh, I've been meaning to ask you.
BEN   What the hell is it now?

See also where Ben takes some time in chastising Gus, in the section where Gus is wondering about the forthcoming job, 'Oh, for Christ's sake', says Ben, and, 'Stop wondering. You've got a job to do. Why don't you just do it and shut up?'

These requests are connected with verbal activity, but notice also that it is only Gus who ever makes requests for permission connected with non-verbal behaviour, and similarly it is only Ben who implies that he is in the position of giving and withholding such permission. Thus we have the sequences to do with the food that Gus has been keeping in his bag — specifically to do with the Eccles cake and the crisps, where it is quite clear that Gus has been acting without Ben's prior permission in obtaining this food, and similarly where it is quite clear that Ben withholds permission for Gus to keep the food:

GUS   Do you mean I can keep the Eccles cake then?
BEN   Keep it?
GUS   Well they don't know we've got it do they?
BEN   That's not the point.
GUS   Can't I keep it?
BEN   No you can't.

When it comes to what Ward calls 'volunteering information' it is obvious to the reader/hearer that Ben has access to information that Gus wants and requests, yet Ben refuses him equal access to it. Some of the means for doing this have been covered above, in considering how often Ben avoids or counters requests and refuses to grant speaker's rights to Gus. The way these means cluster can be illustrated well by the following passage:

GUS   I wonder who it'll be tonight.
      (*Silence*)
      Eh, I've been wanting to ask you something.
BEN   (*putting his legs on the bed*) Oh, for Christ's sake.
GUS   No I was going to ask you something.
      (*He rises and sits on BEN's bed*)
BEN   What are you sitting on my bed for?
      (*Gus sits*)
      What's the matter with you. You're always asking me
      questions. What's the matter with you?
GUS   Nothing.
BEN   You never used to ask so many damn questions. What's
      come over you?
GUS   No, I was just wondering.
BEN   Stop wondering. You've got a job to do. Why don't you
      just do it and shut up.
GUS   That's what I was wondering about.
BEN   What?
GUS   The job.
BEN   What job?

GUS   (*tentatively*) I thought you might know something.
      (*BEN looks at him*)
      I thought perhaps you — I mean — have you got any idea who
      it's going to be tonight?
BEN   Who what's going to be?
      (*They look at each other*)
GUS   (*at length*) Who it's going to be.
      (*Silence*)
BEN   Are you feeling alright?
GUS   Sure.
BEN   Go and make the tea.
GUS   Yes, sure.

Similar sequences occur where Gus wants to know why Ben stopped the car earlier, but never gets anything more than a vague answer, which may be true, but we suspect is not; also where Ben refuses to respond to comments about the lack of contact, where he refuses to answer questions about the matches and the gas, where he refuses to answer about the people upstairs, where he refuses to comment on the reasons behind the tests. Notice that Gus seems to talk at length to fill all possible silences. As Sacks (1970) puts it:

> Routinely of course, people happen to talk for more than a sentence in an utterance, where it's not just that they didn't plan to, it's often that they didn't want to; i.e. they produce what they figure is a perfectly good sentence-utterance, and, nobody having started talking, they then find themselves 'continuing' so as in part to deal with the fact that a silence had emerged where under the more general rule of the turn-taking techniques we're dealing with, silence is a terrible thing. The turn-taking rules say that somebody should be talking all the time, not more than one person, but somebody. So a currently completing speaker, finding no-one's started may make it his business to keep off silence by going on.

We assume that Gus is not concealing any information at all, but searching around for possible ways of keeping off that silence.

On several fronts, then, Ben demonstrates to Gus and to us that he does not regard Gus as a person to talk to. He does this by exploiting the basic rules that apply for authoritarian adult–child interaction as given by Ward. Although Gus does not seem to take the hints offered to him so consistently, Ben, by taking the dominant role, forces the interaction to take the style that he chooses.

I also want to make out a case here for hearing Ben and Gus inter-acting in roles not dissimilar from the asymmetrical roles of teacher and pupil — though without many of the features that characterize class-rooms and the one-to-many discourse. To begin with, there are a few instances in the text where Ben refers overtly to this type of relation-ship, and himself as teacher, Gus as taught. For example:

BEN Who's the senior partner here, me or you?
GUS You.
BEN I'm only looking after your interests Gus. You've got to
     learn mate.

And similarly, there is an explicit training session to be found (and see also the instruction-giving sequence):

BEN Well come on.
GUS What do you do?
BEN See that? That's a whistle.
GUS What this?
BEN Yes, take it out. Pull it out.
     (*GUS does so*)
     That's it.
GUS What do we do now?
BEN Blow into it.
GUS Blow?
BEN It whistles up there if you blow. Then they know you want to
     speak. Blow.

However, more interesting than these overt references to a teacher–pupil relationship is the conversationalists' speech behaviour throughout the text, where there are many subtle and structural features that account for why we hear the text in this particular way. Again, with some notable exceptions (to be discussed below) there are a number of repeated patterns in Ben's talk which suggest that we are listening to a teacher talking to a pupil, and similar repeated patterns in Gus's talk that suggest that we are listening to the pupil. Notice that this pattern, like the adult–child patterns already discussed, is the norm of the text, against which sequences which move away from this pattern are seen as the oddities, the exceptions, the 'conflict that is essential to all drama' (Quigley above).

Some general features of teacher–pupil talk and relevant aspects of classroom situations are worth stating here. It is a defining feature of formal classroom talk that the pupils tolerate various types of monitoring of their own behaviour (including, of course, their talk) by the teacher, in ways to which conversationalists with equal speaking rights apparently object very strongly (see, for example, Garfinkel's created trouble, 1967). Various writers on the classroom have commented on this, but Stubbs (1974b) usefully formulates it as a descriptive rule in the style of Labov (1970):

> If A makes repeated and unmitigated statements about B's speech, or asks repeated and unmitigated questions about B's understanding of A, B will accept these statements or questions as legitimate and appropriate, only if B believes that A has the right to make such statements or ask such questions; and this right is inherent in only a limited number of role relationships of which the paradigm example is teacher–pupil, where A fills the role of teacher.

Sinclair and Coulthard (1975) and Mead (1976) also bring out the following features of teacher–pupil talk, that depend again on the unequal speaking rights embodied in the two complementary roles:

1 Teachers may monitor and control their pupils' verbal and non-verbal behaviour: by the issuing of directives which, in an orderly world, are properly carried out; by the giving or withholding of praise or the use of explicit criticism; by monitoring the timing of activities which are their responsibility; by reference to their authority or the current taken-for-granted social conventions.
2 Teachers may also explicitly monitor their pupils' verbal behaviour: by explicit metastatements about the form of pupil contributions; and the legitimacy of pupils' contributions to the talk.

I want to consider each of these points with reference to the text, in the following order: directives; praise and censure; monitoring time; authority and social convention judgments; metastatements about form, appropriateness and legitimacy.

Ben monitors Gus's non-verbal and verbal behaviour in all of the ways just suggested. Firstly, the text provides a substantial list of explicit, unmitigated directives (that is, imperative in mood), and also a substantial list of mitigated directives (that is, not imperative in mood, but items that in discourse terms (see chapter 6) clearly expect a 'react' as an appropriate response item from the other party). The explicit directives are as follows (asterisked examples denote directives referring to verbal behaviour specifically):

Listen to this!
Well, go on, make it.
Well, make the tea then, will you?
Wait a minute.*
Tell me one of your interests.*
Make the tea will you?
Get out of it.*
Don't make me laugh will you?*
Don't be silly.*
Pick it up.
Pick it up!
Open it.
Open it!
Show it to me.
Well, go on.
Open the door and see if you can catch anyone outside.
Go on!
Well, don't lose them.
Don't waste them!
Go on, go and light it.
Put on the bloody kettle, for Christ's sake.
Stop wondering.
Go and make the tea.
Scrub round it, will you?*
Get on with it, that's all.
Have a bit of common.
Read it.*
Let me see that.
Don't do that!*
Fetch me one of those plates.
Get the plate.
Put everything on the plate.
Get dressed will you?
Buck your ideas up will you.
Lend us your pencil.
Well, come on.
. . .take it out. Pull it out.
Blow into it.
Blow.
Speak into it!

Give me that!
Be quiet a minute.*
Let me give you your instructions.*
Let me give you your instructions.*
Shut the door behind him.
Enough!*
Shut up.*
Shut up!*
Stop it!

The mitigated directives are as follows:

What about the tea?
Well, you'd better eat them quick.
What about that tea?
When are you going to stop jabbering?*
Well, what are you waiting for?
What are you sitting on my bed for?
You've got a job to do. Why don't you just do it and shut up?
You'll have to wait.
You'd better get ready anyway.
We'd better send something up.
You'd better get ready.
Quick before it goes up.
You shouldn't shout like that.*
Have you checked your gun?
Why don't you ever polish it?
Look here. We'd better tell them.
That's enough! I'm warning you!*

In interesting contrast to this, Gus's directives number only four:

You got any cigarettes? [implicit]
You got any cigarettes? [implicit]
Ben, look here. [explicit]
Look. [explicit]

And, as usual, Ben ignores all but the last one, and even here it takes Gus two tries to actually attract his attention.

When it comes to items of praise or censure, there are again more and less explicit forms of control offered in the text. Ben offers Gus one explicit piece of positive evaluation when Gus guesses that the boy in the newspaper story was really to blame for killing the cat, and the following explicit negative evaluations:

> You kill me.
> You know what your trouble is?
> When are you going to stop jabbering?
> Don't be silly.
> The kettle, you fool.
> What's the matter with you?
> What's the matter with you?
> What's come over you?
> Are you feeling alright?
> What's the matter with you?
> You'll get a swipe round your earhole if you don't watch your step.
> A bloody liberty!
> You mutt.
> You birk!
> You're playing a dirty game my lad!
> I'll remember this.
> It's all your stupid fault, playing about!
> You're getting lazy, you know that?
> Buck your ideas up will you?
> You maniac!

On the rare occasions when Gus tries the same, for example, 'How many times have you read that newspaper?' and 'You've never missed that out before', considerable conflict arises. This will be considered in more detail below, but is worth mentioning here, in that even when Gus chooses to take the same speaking rights as Ben (which is not often), Ben very quickly makes it known that he does not accept this as a reasonable discourse situation.

There is also implicit censure indicated in the stage directions (see, for example, the very beginning of the play). Similarly, censure has been implied in the way that Ben deals with many of Gus's topic offerings, questions and requests for speaking rights, as described already. And the notion that Ben is a person with the right to comment on and control Gus's behaviour is persistently conveyed in what are evidently accusations — 'That's not the point', 'Where did these crisps come from', 'Eating makes you lazy, mate' — and checks on small details of Gus's behaviour — 'What are you doing out there?' and 'Where are you going?'

There are a number of occasions when Ben monitors Gus's behaviour with respect to time available, thus forcefully creating the impression that the organization of their time with respect to their work commitments is strictly his responsibility. Gus makes no such references.

> Time's getting on.
> We'll be on the job in a minute.
> Anyway there's no time. We've got to get straight back.
> Well what are you waiting for?
> You'll have to wait.
> You'll have a cup of tea afterwards.
> You'd better get ready anyway.
> Quick.
> You'd better get ready.
> Quick before it goes up.
> Get dressed will you. It'll be any minute now.
> Time's getting on.

The fact that Ben has to repeat so many of these reminders about time is interesting in itself, but will be taken up in more detail below.

Ben's overt references to his own authority are not many (in the argument about lighting the gas, about being the senior partner), but in that Gus makes none at all with reference to himself, and also complies explicitly with Ben's own definition of himself as the higher-status participant, they are a useful contribution to our overall impressions. Similarly, Ben's references to conventional judgments on behaviour, used as correction devices on aspects of Gus's behaviour of which he disapproves, are not many, but again reinforce the relationships in the talk:

> It's a figure of speech!
> It's common usage!
> That's not the point.
> It isn't done.
> Eating makes you lazy.

Gus only has one try at this sort of talk — 'They say put on the kettle'

— and this is in a section of talk where there is considerable conflict between the two men. This will be discussed further below, but notice that Ben wins the round.

Ben makes many implicit criticisms of Gus's verbal behaviour by the various means suggested above. Explicit examples are as follows:

Nobody says light the gas.
Don't do that. [in response to Gus's shouting]
You shouldn't shout like that.

And see also all the asterisked examples of directives. When Gus tries the same activity, arguing for 'light the gas' rather than 'light the kettle', there is conflict. One very neat example in terms of teacher–pupil talk occurs in the context where Ben is giving a long list of instructions about future events to Gus, which is seemingly a ritual activity they have carried out a number of times before, as shown in the following pair of utterances:

BEN   Be quiet a minute. Let me give you your instructions.
GUS   What for? We always do it the same way don't we?

as well as the routine way in which formulaic sections of talk are offered and repeated by Ben and Gus alternately. Later, we get the following criticism of the event from Gus:

GUS   You've missed something out.
BEN   I know. What?
GUS   I haven't taken my gun out according to you.

We have a suspicion that Ben has made a genuine error, but, if he has, he uses the teacher's technique of turning it to his own advantage, suggesting that it was designed specifically as a test question using a tactic based on the pervasive tacit assumption of the teacher's superior knowledge, and his right to ask questions to which he already knows the answer (see Stubbs, 1976b).

In discussing the superior status of Ben, we have in passing, and in contrast, already pointed to several characteristic features of Gus's talk which render him the inferior participant. I want here, though, to follow through the idea that not only is he inferior in the ways that we have already seen, but he has a specific childlike manner as well, and that one impression that one might take from the text is that Gus behaves in a recognizably and perhaps even annoyingly childlike way.

I want to begin by pursuing earlier observations about Gus's attempts to initiate conversational topics and the apparent difficulties he has when trying to find the means to do so. As we have already considered, in a sense some of the talk is provided for by the events that occur: the incoming matches; the messages on the dumb waiter. However, apart from Ben's re-telling of the newspaper stories and his various instructions about the tea or the job, all other conversational topics are, somewhat ineptly, introduced by Gus. Interestingly, most of them stem from objects around him in the room (apart from questions about earlier or later events). We have the impression that he is having considerable difficulty in getting any talk off the ground at all. Keenan and Klein (1974), in their work on the interactive speech of Keenan's twin sons (2:9 at the start of the research), are of considerable relevance here:

> In the case of young children, although the speaker may pre-
> suppose that the hearer *can* attend to the object in question,
> he may not always presuppose that the hearer *is* attending to
> the object. A critical task for the child is, in fact, to assure
> that the audience is attending to the topic at hand. This task is
> not always an easy one. The ethnomethodological literature for
> example, devotes considerable attention to the problem of topic-
> handling, topic-shift and so on among adult speakers (Sacks 1970).
> Children however, appear to experience even more difficulties in
> introducing topics than do adults. Their task is rendered more
> manageable when that 'topic' is an actual object in the environ-
> ment, that both speaker and hearer can perceive simultaneously.
> A new thing to look at is a new thing to talk about.

'A new thing to look at is a new thing to talk about' is certainly a tactic that Gus uses, and is a prominent feature of the part of the text which is specifically devoted to getting through time, that is, before the dumb waiter imposes demands on the participants' attention, talk and behaviour. In just this way Gus starts conversational topics about the crockery, the lavatory, the bed, the picture of the cricketers, the room they are in, the crockery and the room again, the lavatory again, the bed sheets, the envelope, the house, Ben's newspaper. In a sense Ben uses it to make conversation as well, when he refers to stories from his newspaper as 'something to talk about'. However, it is a much more marked feature of Gus's talk throughout.

Keenan also has an interesting comment on children's conversational repetitions that seems pertinent to the following mistake that Gus makes in repeating Ben's instructions to him:

BEN   He won't see you.
GUS   He won't see me.
BEN   But he'll see me.
GUS   He'll see you.
BEN   He won't know you're there.
GUS   He won't know you're there.
BEN   He won't know *you're* there.
GUS   He won't know I'm there.

This is a fairly simple mistake, given the routine in which the two are involved – itself reminiscent of comic-to-stooge routines in the music-hall, where just such a 'mistake' would be expected. Keenan, in discussing the way in which her own twins construct formally well-patterned discourse, says the following:

> It is a task of competent social actors to show that they are attending to one another's utterances and to be able to demonstrate that one has understood them correctly. Children can fulfil this obligation even though they do not always process utterances at all linguistic levels. A relevant response can be constructed by means of a fairly minimal low-level processing. . . .Formal modification serves as a basic resource for the performance of many speech act pairs, and a general strategy of the child may be: focus on the formal structure of a previous utterance and modify it (using the same lexical items) in your subsequent utterance.

In a sense this is all that Gus has to do throughout this instruction-giving sequence; to use Sacks's (1968) terminology, he merely has to 'show' understanding, rather than 'prove' it. This very simple mistake suggests that he is indeed following a childlike strategy for producing second-pair parts in the sequence. Notice, though, that shortly after this, in 'You've missed something out', Gus takes the upper hand for a while, thus demonstrating that he is at this later point listening properly.

Throughout the play, a feature that makes Gus sound childlike is the persistent questioning he indulges in. In a sense, of course, it is also Ben's refusal to answer these questions that makes Gus sound annoyingly persistent. It is interesting, though, that although a more adult participant might realize that Ben is deliberately avoiding involvement, Gus refuses to give way. Ben wins ultimately, thus reinforcing the sense

we have of Gus as nagging, or being a nuisance. One particularly pertinent example occurs with the first visit of the dumb waiter. Gus says
that the note they have just received is 'a bit funny', Ben replies by
saying that it used to be a café upstairs, and the next ten utterances are
taken up with Gus questioning the validity of this suggestion with
particularly sensible questions. Ben's rather weak conclusion, 'Well,
that all depends —', is helped to pass by the return of the dumb waiter
with yet more instructions. For a while the talk centres around these
notes and requests, but nearly fifty utterances later Gus persistently
returns to the café topic, with yet more objections to the reasonable-
ness of Ben's earlier suggestion. Again, he raises sensible objections, and
Ben avoids a direct answer, eventually refusing to answer at all, and is
saved from further problems by the return of the dumb waiter. This is
one very prominent and extended example of this type of talk that Gus
does throughout the text.

It was noted above that Ben has to keep repeating instructions and
suggestions to Gus. Thus, for example, reminders to make the tea come
at frequent intervals near the beginning of the play (eight times), and
reminders about the need to get ready come throughout the play
(seven times). This also contributes to the impression of Gus as a re-
calcitrant child — refusing to do household jobs, in need of continual
reminders and prompts, and ostensibly inefficient and lazy (see the
specific reference in 'Slack, mate, slack').

I want here to conclude by discussing those small sections of the
play where Ben, contrary to the norm of the text, appears as somewhat
less dominant and less in control than usual: the arguments with Gus,
and the activities forced upon them by the arrival of intrusive matches
or the dumb waiter's messages.

The arguments with Gus form three sections of the play. Firstly,
there is a trivial quarrel over the phrase 'light the kettle'; secondly,
there is a similar quarrel over Ben's reading of the newspaper; and
thirdly, there is what seems to be a much more serious argument over
the meaning of the dumb waiter's messages. In all of these, Ben wins
the arguments, but during each we get a sense of potential power in
Gus, potential frailty in Ben.

In the argument over the phrase 'light the kettle', Gus provokes the
row by commenting on the form of Ben's utterance:

BEN   Go and light it.
GUS   Light what?

BEN   The kettle.
GUS   You mean the gas.
BEN   Who does?

In doing this, he is of course usurping parental or teacher's speaking rights, in monitoring the form of the co-participant's utterance, an activity which, for the most part in the text, is Ben's prerogative. Interestingly, when Ben refuses to accept this, Gus resorts to methods of defence which Ben uses also, that is, reference to common cultural conventions: 'They say put on the kettle'. Ben of course cleverly turns this to his own advantage by demanding a specific instance of the generalized 'they', which Gus cannot legitimately give.

In the quarrel over the newspaper, Gus again takes on superior rights by commenting on the co-participant's non-verbal behaviour, in such a way that, despite a possible neutral interpretation, in the context Ben takes it up as a criticism (for a detailed discussion of the rules for this sort of interpretation see Sinclair and Coulthard, 1975, p. 32):

GUS   How many times have you read that paper?
        (*BEN slams down the paper and rises*)
BEN   (*angrily*) What do you mean?
GUS   I was just wondering how many times you'd —
BEN   What are you doing, criticising me?
GUS   No, I was just —
BEN   You'll get a swipe round your earhole if you don't watch
        your step.

Interestingly again, Gus refuses to give way at first, despite the times when Ben cuts off his protestations, and despite the explicit threats. He attempts to take a superior's conversational tactics:

GUS   Now look here Ben —

Again though, Ben twists this to his own advantage, by taking a literal interpretation of what was evidently meant to be a preface to some sort of claim to status and rights:

BEN   I'm not looking anywhere! (*he addresses the room*)
        How many times have I! A bloody liberty!
GUS   I didn't mean that.
BEN   You just get on with it mate. Get on with it that's all.

where finally, he resorts successfully to his strategy of empty, generalized, status-claiming utterance-use.

The final, more menacing argument, where Gus panics over the recent events, as well as presumably the impending job, is more interesting, in that Gus in his evident hysteria does in fact seem capable of dominating Ben, if only to the extent that Ben can find no verbal means of retaliating and reasserting himself. Some of the data were quoted above, to show Ben's extreme physical reaction to Gus's persistent questions here. Ben begins by using evasion techniques — often generalized counter-questions, appropriate as tokens in any conversation regardless of the specific lexical details or prior product utterances, for example, 'what are you talking about?', 'What's one thing to do with another?'. He then moves on to replying to Gus's questions by telling him forcefully to be quiet, and when this fails, resorts to answering him by hitting him. We certainly get the impression that Gus's questions are touching on important material here, and that Ben either cannot or will not answer. It is only the arrival of the dumb waiter, with yet another terse message, that resolves the situation.

Ben's behaviour in response to the arrival of the matches and the dumb waiter's messages are perhaps more revealing with regard to his own tentative position within the organization.

When the matches first arrive, he immediately takes on an authoritative role, directing Gus's actions, and not himself doing anything potentially dangerous. On his orders it is Gus who has to pick up the envelope, it is Gus who has to examine the envelope and its contents, and it is Gus who has to look outside the room for potential malefactors. In the section of the talk that follows this, it is Gus who suggests an optimistic interpretation of the event as a whole, and Ben, for once, takes on a trusting, supportive role:

GUS   Well they'll come in handy.
BEN   Yes.
GUS   Won't they?
BEN   Yes, you're always running out aren't you?
GUS   All the time.
BEN   Well they'll come in handy then.
GUS   Yes.
BEN   Won't they.
GUS   Yes, I could do with them. I could do with them too.

The talk centres upon this proposition of Gus's that the matches will 'come in handy'. The two men check and recheck the validity of this suggestion, but it is Gus who takes the reassuring role, confirming the need he has for them. Notice that, this having been established, Ben reverts to his superior position with an implicit criticism of Gus's usual behaviour in relation to matches in general:

BEN   Yes, you're always cadging matches. How many have you
        got there?
GUS   About a dozen.
BEN   Well, don't lose them.

And he reinforces this take-over by moving into a set of straight and explicit directives.

One of the most interesting features of the passage that occurs after the arrival of the dumb waiter's messages is Ben's eagerness to respond in some way to this mysterious and ostensibly crazy set of communications. In that he accepts the odd requests as legitimate summonses to be answered in some way (compare Schegloff, 1968) — however inappropriately — he demonstrates the insecurity of his own position *vis-à-vis* the people in the 'organization' who send him instructions. His panic shows itself in the meticulous way in which he sends up everything edible they possess — despite the mismatch with the articles that have been requested, and in his speech, in the way in which he urges Gus to assist him. When the dumb waiter returns with requests for Chinese food, he temporarily treats Gus as an equal if not superior — asking him for information that neither of them have; and he does so again, when the request for tea obviously cannot be met either.

For the most part then, the text sets up very clear participant relationships, with Ben as the superior, managerial member, and Gus forced into a subservient and inferior role. It is not always the case that Gus accepts this role, but Ben, having chosen the more forceful interactive part, imposes this interpretation on the discourse, and in so doing creates an impression of Gus as persistently annoying, and, in fact, even more childlike than if he had neatly complied with the unequal statuses to begin with.

91

Chapter 4

From dialogue to discourse and back again

I want here to consider briefly some of the possibilities, achievements and shortcomings inherent in the type of work presented so far in the studies of the individual plays in chapters 2 and 3. The aim there was simply to discuss, in rather general terms, the effects created by two contrasting modern drama texts, in terms of recent work in spoken discourse (or conversational analysis), in the hope of showing how useful this work in naturally-occurring conversation can be for the stylistician. Whilst it seems clear that discourse is certainly the appropriate level from which to approach an understanding of the effects in the dialogue (as opposed to, say, phonology or syntax), and similarly that it is indeed an illuminating and practical base from which to discuss simulated speech, several problems, some of them familiar to linguistic-stylisticians, have begun to emerge. Some are more serious and theoretically important than others.

Firstly, and very simply, there is the problem of length. Even using relatively short texts as items for study and discussion, and even being relatively selective about the number of features in the text on which to comment, the amount of descriptive prose thus generated is certainly formidable. Had the entire book been devoted in any straightforward or narrow way to one of these texts, then perhaps some more thorough and detailed analysis might have been both profitable and possible. However, given the broader aims of the work (contingent upon the current state of the arts of both stylistics and discourse analysis), which includes the complementary section using simulated dialogue as a means of developing discourse analysis itself (chapters 6 and 7), the work in this first section must remain as only a demonstration of the potential use that the stylistician might make of the ever-growing body of writing on conversational analysis, when discussing drama texts. It is a step forward for stylistics, and not, I hope, without interest, but there must be further work on the coherent theory of discourse analysis before anything more thorough and significant can be done. I shall discuss this further below. In the mean time, though, this is not to say that other such studies of drama texts need not be done. There is room for a great deal of interesting discussion of texts even at this problematic and tentative state of the art. (See chapter 8 for suggestions for further work.)

Another perennial stylistics problem is closely associated with the question of length, but has more serious theoretical issues contingent upon it; namely the inevitable limitations of any selective study of a text, if this work is undertaken under the auspices of linguistics rather than the traditionally more casual approach of literary criticism. One reason given for selectivity is, of course, precisely to avoid any over-long description, and certainly this is an important factor. However, there are more serious problems here that should be considered carefully by anyone involved in making stylistic analyses of texts. Overall it is essential for the analyst to consider carefully what demands might reasonably be made of any work that attempts to explain a text, at whatever level of explanation such a piece of work is situated. Similarly, it is essential to be aware of the peculiar problems of a discursive study, for, whilst insightful observations can be both illuminating and useful in a general literary-critical descriptive way, they are assuredly unhelpful in that they may well give the illusion of proper analysis when, clearly, if they are outside any rigorous, systematized, complete descriptive and theoretical framework, then they are nothing of the kind and cannot be justified as such. The possible illusion does a significant disservice to the very real powers of a full and adequate linguistic analysis, or any work that is moving towards such an analysis. To repeat a point made earlier, this is precisely why the accounts in chapters 2 and 3 are labelled 'studies' and not 'analyses'. A major difficulty with such discursive studies is that it is not usually clear (and probably it is not possible to be clear) about why some features of the texts in question are selected at the expense of others. Clearly, they are features which have struck the analyst as intuitively interesting, and features which link, in some inexplicable way, with observations encountered in other reading, or experience. (In this case, observations from a wide range of curiously related articles and books on naturally occurring conversation.) In this way, such studies have no clear-cut and replicable strategies of discovery to offer the reader or student, being very heavily dependent upon things like memory, intuition, fortuitous reading and so on. This is particularly relevant to work at the level of discourse, given the current state of linguistic enquiry and knowledge, and the fact that the analyst will be drawing on work that is often pre-theoretical, or situated in different, or even unstated, theoretical frameworks. Perhaps a brief comparison with more familiar linguistic-stylistic analyses at the phonological or syntactic level would make this point clearer.

If, say, an analyst of style wishes to describe the syntax of a lyrical poem, and the effects created in the text by its syntactic make-up, he or she can take one of several coherent and well-established syntactic theories and, against this background, work in a well-ordered, consistent and comprehensive manner, accounting for effects at all points in that theory. The fact that the syntacticians are elsewhere debating the niceties, the elegance, the parameters of their theories is, of course, of interest, but need not trouble the stylistician unduly at this stage. If an appropriate and reasonably adequate description of the syntax of the language is chosen, he or she will find a substantial and comprehensive list of categories and relationships through which to work in order to cover all possible aspects of the syntactic patterns and effects in the text under study. The fact that stylisticians often do not actually do this type of comprehensive analysis, but head instead for features that are foregrounded and are therefore of immediate interest, again need not trouble us here (but see Carter, 1979, for an excellent comprehensive study). Similarly, the fact that stylisticians may ignore poetics, at their cost, need not be an issue just here (see Fowler, 1979, for a strong argument against narrow stylistics). The point that does concern us is that the state of the art of syntactical analysis of ordinary language (and I use that term very casually) in no way prevents the linguistic-stylistician from making a thorough, detailed, and professional attempt at a rigorous stylistic description. A set of related principles and tools are readily available. Sensitive and sensible application of those principles and tools may be articulated, taught, learned and repeatedly achieved.

When it comes to discourse, however, we have no such resource. Although, in the last decade, articles, books and theses have begun to accumulate rapidly, there is no one general, fully articulated theoretical perspective from which to build a stylistics methodology, in order to allow us to discuss different 'styles' of talk. Style can only be understood and described comparatively and meaningfully against a coherent theoretical and descriptive background which provides an abstract set of categories and structures, some of which will be realized in

[handwritten margin note: but, that's just syntactic analyses; not stylistics]

[handwritten margin note: eh?]

94

different patterns and proportions in any particular text.

Whilst systematic analyses do, and must, leave out some interesting aspects of any text, this is precisely their strength; they focus on certain items quite specifically, at the expense of other items equally specifically and clearly. Notice though, that whilst some features at some levels must be ignored in this way, systematic analyses do also insist that everything that is there in the text must be described at some particular and designated level. Thus awkward problems cannot just be ignored. Even if the use of an analytical category may sometimes involve an arbitrary or temporary decision of some sort, then at the very least, problem areas in the base descriptive system are clearly highlighted. So, as is desirable in all disciplines, the practical application of theoretical frameworks may feed back into the development and refinement of that theory, such that practical application may be undertaken much more efficiently and effectively. More problems may occur. More refinements may be needed. Thus some sort of progression of knowledge is effected.

All this is not to say that I see no value at all in the discursive, observational approach to a text, merely that I think it is extremely important to be fully aware that it remains theoretically unsatisfactory from the linguistic-stylistician's point of view. Ultimately, such work must be seen to be, though linguistically interesting, not a central part of linguistics at all. Drawing on linguistics as a means of relating scattered impressions is useful if talking casually about a text, and if it is the text itself that is your final interest, but it is by no means linguistically sound practice, being far too dependent on luck rather than informed judgment.

Where then should this type of work fruitfully proceed? I want now to describe briefly the material the reader will encounter in the second main section of this book, 'Discourse', and make clear its motivation, which is of two kinds. The first is relevant to the concerns of any sociolinguist and discourse analyst. The second is of interest to the stylistician in particular.

In 'Discourse', I take the most fully articulated, explicit and systematic descriptive framework for spoken discourse that is available (Sinclair and Coulthard, 1975). This is work which is based on data collected in formal talk situations, which developed a functional and systematic way of describing the componence, structure and relationships in and between the utterances in these speech events. I describe this work fully in chapter 6, and concentrate there on its strengths, so will not

95

go into further detail here except to point briefly to some of its short-comings.

Its overall weakness as a descriptive apparatus is that it cannot adequately account for talk outside a formal situation. The data collected was from formal chalk-and-talk classrooms, doctor–patient interviews, media discussions, committee meetings and so on. Whilst the ultimate aim for discourse analysis must be to describe any type of spoken interaction, the data collected did, I believe, preclude certain types of insights in that all sorts of conversational options simply do not occur there. To gloss these options extremely casually, there are no instances of features like people arguing, ignoring each other, being stubborn, being unhelpful, perverse or in any way odd. Thus the data that were formative in building the descriptive model were all of a collaborative-consensus kind. Certain options that are actually rather basic to most talk were simply not realized in the formal data, and thus were given no place in the apparatus.

The first motivation for the work presented in chapter 7 is of specific interest to the discourse analyst. Drama dialogue which sounds like naturally-occurring conversation (and I am aware of the possible naivety of that description, but will let it pass for the time being), if used and analysed as if it were a transcript of real conversation, is an extremely powerful heuristic device for the discourse analyst trapped into a way of seeing by other styles of data. Analysing such material forces radical shifts in the perception of the structure of talk, that is not possible when studying data collected under some mandate, particularly if this happens to be collaborative-consensus material, since there no radical shift proved necessary. The interesting problem is to make these shifts as far as possible within the original framework of the basic model. Principles and categories are maintained wherever possible, but nevertheless necessary adjustments must be found to be compatible, such that the talk in the playscripts (and indeed in any script) may be comprehensively and replicably analysed.

The motivation for stylistics should be obvious. If every script can be charted comprehensively against this altered model, then the talk in those scripts can be discussed efficiently and clearly in comparative terms. Using syntax stylistics for comparison and clarification again, in such work we might initially be able to compare one poem with another, in that the one might be made entirely with sentences in declarative mood, the other with sentences entirely in the imperative. So, with dialogue texts analysable in an analogously precise way, stretches of talk might be compared as being, say, 100 per cent Elicitation versus 50 per cent Elicitation and 50 per cent Informing. I offer these descriptions merely as shorthand examples. By no means do I wish to suggest that the discussion of style is merely a question of counting isolated features. Nevertheless, any discussion of the language of any text or stretch of language must be based on a consistent analysis of its constituent parts and overall structure. We can only do this once we have a systematic vocabulary for isolating, recognizing and describing these constituent parts. We must be sure we are comparing like features with like features, if we are not to produce nonsense. Labov (1970) puts it succinctly:

> no useful purpose would be served by counting the number of questions that someone asks in an interview. The relation of argument and discourse to language is much more abstract than this, and such superficial indices can be quite deceptive. When we can say *what* is being done with a sentence, then we will be able to observe how often speakers do it.

In this more precise way, though, the stylistician might very professionally demonstrate, say, the difference in style between X's earlier and later dialogue, or perhaps account for the similarity intuitively perceived between dialogue in play Y and play Z. The usual possibilities are then open. Interestingly, the stylistician might then be able efficiently to say why, for example, the dialogue in play P sounds like courtroom talk, even though it takes place (on stage) in a drawing-room.

And this, of course, brings us full circle. We are again considering the relevance of such analysis for the straight discourse analyst. It has been a feature of discourse analysis so far that analysts have gone out to collect data based on social-situational variables. Thus it has been decided that individuals or project teams will collect 'therapy talk', 'science lectures', 'trade-union discussions', 'seminar discussions', 'mother-child talk' or even 'comparisons of middle-class mothers and children with working-class mothers and children'. This has been a misguided and unhelpful approach. Whilst, clearly, there is a certain sense in this, in that it is a linguistic commonplace to recognize that different social situations call for and produce different types of talk, this common-sense observation is of no lasting or interesting linguistic significance. Linguistically, it is much more relevant to collect samples of talk, un-tagged by these situational labels, and to compare them precisely as styles of talk, against a model suitably powerful and abstract

97

to allow all talk to be measured and compared against its presentation of possible underlying structures. In this way, stretches of talk may be compared with stretches of talk for their sociolinguistically salient features. Styles that emerge as descriptively similar (for example, mother–child talk and formal classroom talk) or dissimilar (for example, doctor–patient interviews and 3-year-old children talking together) will do so because they have certain linguistic features in common or not.

In part 2, then, the reader will be introduced to this more accurate and sound way of describing both discourse and dialogue. Though the emphasis will be on the features of that descriptive model, rather than on lengthy analyses of style in dialogue, it will, I hope, be available as a model for anyone with either linguistic or literary interests to use in just that way.

Part Two: Discourse

Chapter 5

The alienated analyst: an argument for rich data for the discourse analyst

I want to present and discuss the idea that playscripts in general, and modern playscripts in particular, are an extremely rich resource for the conversational analyst, who is ultimately interested in accounting for and describing the structures and sociolinguistic constraints that are the rules for naturally occurring conversations. A key concept I want to use in this argument is that of the Alienation Device, or Alienation Effect, as defined and used by Bertolt Brecht (1937):

> THE PHILOSOPHER: If empathy makes something ordinary of a special event, alienation makes something special of an ordinary one. The most hackneyed, everyday incidents are stripped of their monotony when represented as quite special.

In a sense all conversation requires at least two primary Alienation Devices imposed on it by the analyst to make it in any way accessible to either analysis or theory: tape recording and transcription. Hardened analysts tend to forget the strength of these Alienation Devices, but the surprised reactions of those presented with these materials for the first time, say, first-year undergraduates, are a salutory reminder of the effects thus achieved. Particularly frequent reactions include (1) the inability to understand a recording without a transcript, and (2), given a transcript without its complementary recording, a refusal to believe that 'talk looks like that'. In an early paper about naturally occurring talk, David Abercrombie (1959), in his suggestions for those unfamiliar with thinking about conversational structure, makes these very apposite comments:

> Try, when you are present at an informal discussion among a number of people (if possible an intellectual discussion when people are thinking as they talk), withdrawing yourself from participation

for a while, and picturing to yourself, in your mind's eye, what the flow of words which is taking place, would look like if it was written down exactly as spoken. One sees conversation in a new light by doing this; it brings out features one had never noticed before.

Alienation concepts will be referred to below as (amongst other things), 'estrangement devices' (Garfinkel, 1967), and 'foregrounding' (Prague Structuralists, *passim*). I shall argue that the concept of 'making strange' the otherwise too-familiar is employed by researchers and creative writers in the several disciplines that serve as a reasonable background for a conversational analyst. In each of these disciplines, observers and theorists argue convincingly that Alienation Devices enable analytical thought to penetrate the otherwise intangible aspects of the everyday world. Since I take it that the conversational analyst's most severe problem is that of having communicative competence in the very object he wishes to analyse, I also take it that he shares the need for an Alienation methodology in order to analyse effectively his member's knowledge.

So, I want to draw together here what seem to me to be extremely interesting interrelated concepts, methods and theoretical procedures in complementary disciplines, mainly of course from the point of view of their reference to the conversational analyst, but also to point out a significant epistemological trend which, whilst not actually new in terms of either technicalities or practice, has nonetheless found novel currency among twentieth-century analysts, theorists and creative writers in the humanities.

Firstly, it is clear that creative literature itself can be seen and used as an Alienation Device on social life, as in the use of imaginative literature as data in the recent work on the 'Sociology of the Everyday'. It is a well-known feature of the work of Erving Goffman, for example – always interesting in his considerations of methodology – that as exemplification for higher-level theoretical concepts he draws on a wide range of literary references, taking the point of view that the professional sociologist can learn a great deal from the lay observers of social structures and behaviour and of underlying beliefs, taboos, prejudices and so on. In *Stigma* (Goffman, 1963), he makes this quite explicit: 'In this essay, I want to review some work on stigma, especially some popular work, to see what it can yield for sociology.' This work, like all his others, is peppered with eclectically drawn references like (p. 15), 'The management of class stigma is of course a central theme in the English novel', which assert the implicitly recognized universality of his categories and their properties, as exemplified in the culture's Culture. Many smaller pieces of detailed analysis are similarly to be found as demonstrations of author-sociologists, and here, the references are appropriately small and well-detailed themselves. For example, in the same work (p.41) there is the following point in the main text: 'Before taking the standpoint of those with a particular stigma, the normal person who is becoming wise may first have to pass through a heart-changing personal experience of which there are many literary records.'

In passing, it is interesting to note the use of the term 'records', to be taken up further below in connection with the work of Webb *et al.* (1966), and Glaser and Strauss (1967), who compare literary documents with traditional archives. However, to return to my main point, the footnote to Goffman's observation above reads as follows:

N Mailer, 'The Homosexual Villain' in *Advertisements for Myself*, New York, Signet books, 1960, pp.200–205, provides a model confession detailing the basic cycle of bigotry, enlightening experience, and finally recantation of prejudice through public admission. See also Angus Wilson's introduction to Carling, op. cit. [Carling, 1962] for a confessional record of Wilson's re-definition of cripples.

The particularly interesting work of Webb *et al.* (1966) has two points of relevance here. They present ideas which concentrate on suggesting novel and stimulating methods with which the sociologist can collect meaningful and contrastive information, in ways which differ from the traditional quantitatively based and inter-reactive procedures, with all their accompanying and inherent distortions. Firstly, like Goffman, they also implicitly use the assumption that a literary author may be a perceptive lay-sociologist. They, too, refer to literary examples to substantiate their observations, and demonstrate that notions they are putting forward are common conventions of the social world. Thus, for example, there are references to and extended quotations from Dickens (p.112), F. Scott Fitzgerald (p.151) and Stephen Leacock (p.115).

Secondly, they review sociological work that has used literature as data for sociological observation and correlation. Thus (p.78), they describe the work of Ray (1965), who examines the values of Hitler's Germany as compared with those of other countries by making content analyses of contemporary plays (detailed in McGranahan and Wayne, 1948). This, taken in conjunction with other studies of the mass media and popular culture of the period, proves a valuable source of information. Middleton (1960) is also cited (p. 58), for work that studies fertility levels and values in American society by comparing fertility levels as expressed in American magazine fiction with actuarial fertility levels. Researching three separate periods (1916, 1936, 1956) he estimates fertility levels by noting the size and composition of fictional families in American magazines, and observes that the shifts recorded therein closely parallel shifts in recorded United States fertility levels. This seems to justify the idea that literature may well embody members' knowledge of their social life in rather fine detail, and, where there is a precedent of reliable fact–fiction correlation, to provide a tentative hypothesis on the reliability of imaginative literature as data for sociological observation and comment. It is important to note, however, that this would only be appropriate in areas where concepts such as irony, parody or satire do not intrude upon the reliable representation of the subject matter.

Sociolinguists also use literature for data in this way. Brown and Gilman (in Sebeok, 1960), in their work on the pronouns of power and solidarity, make the distinction between the search for diachronic data, where imaginative literature is essential, and for synchronic data, where it is useful as a comparative rather than a primary resource:

> Among secondary sources, the general language histories have been of little use, because their central concern is always phonetic rather than semantic change. However, there are a small number of monographs and doctoral dissertations describing the detailed pronoun semantics for one or another language — sometimes throughout its history . . . sometimes for only a century or so . . . and sometimes for the works of a particular author. . . . As primary evidence for the usage of the past we have drawn on plays, on legal proceedings and on letters. We have also learned about contemporary usage from literature, but, more importantly, from long conversations with native speakers of French, Italian, German and Spanish.

A much more positive and emphatic view is taken by Glaser and Strauss (1967). Again, there is advice here for the sociologist concerning both the collection and analysis of data, with insightful and remarkably stimulating passages on theory building, the richness of comparative data and the generation of grounded theory from data-based study, where 'grounded theory is derived from data, and then illustrated by characteristic examples of the data' (p.5). They make a general recommendation of the library and its books as a hoard of rich materials and insights for the imaginative sociologist (p.163):

> Every book, every magazine article, represents at least one person who is equivalent to the anthropologist's informant, or the socio-logist's interviewee. In these publications, people converse, announce positions, argue with a range of eloquence, and describe events or scenes in ways entirely comparable to what is seen and heard during fieldwork. The researcher needs only to discover the voices in the library to release them for his analytic use.

Their work is highly relevant to the overall theme of this paper, in that, although they use no actual equivalent of 'Alienation', the concept runs beneath the book as a whole. Thus they argue that grounded theory is most efficiently and interestingly generated from a general method of comparative analysis, and that the analyst in rebellion against simple verification rhetoric and research must look for 'what concepts and hypotheses are relevant for the area one wishes to research', as opposed to 'theory generated by logical deduction from *a priori* assumptions'. Of this comparative data they write (p.34):

> allowing substantive concepts and hypotheses to emerge first, on their own, enables the analyst to ascertain which, if any, existing formal theory may help him generate his substantive theories. He can be more faithful to his data, rather than forcing it to fit a theory.

With this in mind, and as a general methodological procedure, they recommend that (p.49), 'The researcher chooses any groups that will help generate to the fullest extent, as many properties of the categories as possible.' As a specific point of detail they underline the value of comparing 'the seemingly non-comparable' (p.54): 'Comparing as many differences and similarities in the data as possible. . .forces the analyst to generate categories, their properties and other interrelations as he tries to understand his data.'

In their own particular field of research, Glaser and Strauss comment specifically on the usefulness of studying highly alien and strange data as a comparison with, and for enlightenment on, the more familiar aspects of their own culture. Thus, with reference to the reactions of families to a dying patient, an observation of Malayan practices and customs at a late stage of their own research programme revealed pertinent characteristics of the more familiar situation in the USA, and they found themselves (p. 57) 'noticing abroad what we had missed in America'.

Following on from this, notice that modern Sociology of the Everyday develops, quite explicitly, the notion of exploiting Alienation Devices as a useful means to understanding an over-familiar world. Garfinkel (1967) using Herbert Spiegelberg's phrase, refers to this as 'aids to a sluggish imagination', and details his concept of estrangement as a sociologist's tool, in a section called 'Making commonplace scenes visible'. His description of the sociologist's dilemma is significantly reminiscent of both the modern dramatist's dilemma (see below) and the general problems facing the conversational analyst. A well-known quotation is relevant here:

> In accounting for the stable features of everyday activities, sociologists commonly select familiar settings such as familial households, or work places, and ask for the variables that contribute to their stable features. Just as commonly, one set of considerations are unexamined: the socially standardized 'seen but unnoticed', expected, background features of everyday scenes.

Notice, incidentally, the use of words like 'settings', 'scenes', 'background': playwrights' terms, highly reminiscent here of Goffman's extended dramaturgical metaphor (1959). With a special focus on the difficulties facing the analysis of the persistently ungraspable aspects of everyday life, Garfinkel continues:

> The member of the society uses background expectancies of interpretation. With their use, actual appearances are for him recognizable and intelligible as the appearances-of-familiar-events. Demonstrably he is responsive to this background, while at the same time he is at a loss to tell us specifically of what the expectancies consist. When we ask him about them he has little or nothing to say.

He then points to the difference between this situation and that of an anthropologist studying an alien culture, with suggestions for a possible methodology that a sociologist of his own society might adopt:

> For these background expectancies to come into view, one must either be a stranger to the life-as-usual character of everyday scenes,

or become estranged from them. . . .Procedurally it is my preference to start with familiar scenes, and ask what can be done to make trouble. The operations one would have to perform in order to multiply the senseless features of perceived environments; to produce and sustain bewilderment, consternation and confusion, to produce the socially structured effects of anxiety, shame, guilt and indignation, and to produce disorganized interaction, should tell us something about how the structures of everyday activities are routinely produced and maintained.

If we recognize his 'disorganized interaction' as being realized in certain types of modern plays, say in Ionesco (1950), Pinter (1957, 1960, 1967), Orton (1967), Simpson (1957) and Stoppard (1968, 1969), to name but a few examples, then Garfinkel's comments are doubly appropriate to the overall topic of this chapter, concerning the use which the conversational analyst might make of modern drama dialogue. These playwrights similarly distort the otherwise familiar domestic scenes and settings of bourgeois theatre. They provide material where 'trouble' has already been made. In this vein also, Garfinkel writes of his own studies, where otherwise familiar environments are disturbed by a participant sociologist taking an intentionally perverse and distorted interactive part in the proceedings. He says, 'I have found that they produce reflections through which the strangeness of an obstinately familiar world can be detected'. Conversation is a notable feature of this obstinately familiar world, and many of Garfinkel's insights are focused on interactive dialogue. Since the plays listed above use estranged dialogues of different sorts as their medium towards variably larger messages, the playscripts allow specifically similar insightful reflections for the analyst of everyday conversations.

Like sociologists, linguists also write in a general way about the same analytical problem. Thus Chomsky, in *Language and Mind* (1968), says the following:

One difficulty in the psychological sciences lies in the familiarity of the phenomena with which they deal. A certain intellectual effort is required to see how such phenomena can pose serious problems or call for intricate explanatory theories. One is inclined to take them for granted as necessary, or somehow 'natural'. . . . Phenomena can be so familiar that we do not really see them at all, a matter that has been much discussed by literary theorists and philosophers. For example, Viktor Sklovskij in the early 1920s developed the idea that the function of poetic art is that of 'making strange' the object depicted, 'People living at the seashore grow so accustomed to the murmur of the waves that they never hear the sea. By the same token, we scarcely ever hear the words we utter. . . .We look at each other, but we do not see each other any more. Our perception of the world has withered away; what has remained is mere recognition.'

We will return to ideas of 'making strange' by literary theorists below (an idea that had actually been articulated for some years before this representative quotation from Sklovskij), but the linguist's solution to the problem Chomsky states here is noticeably analogous to the solution found by the sociologist. That is, they both often begin their work with situations that are noticeably and intuitively marked out as odd or un-usual. In this respect, work in both language pathology and language acquisition is interesting for its useful contribution to the study of less markedly unusual language use and users. This quotation from John Laver (1970) is a good representative for this school of thought:

> The strategy of inferring properties of control systems from their output can be applied not only to the efficient operation of these systems, but also to their output when malfunctions occur. The evidence from characteristic malfunctions is, if anything, more penetrating than that obtained when the system is operating efficiently. We can distinguish five different conditions of speech to which this strategy can be applied: error-free continuous speech; speech containing errors such as slips of the tongue, and their corrections; speech containing discontinuities such as hesitation signals; speech during the language acquisition period in young children; and 'speech in dissolution', in the gross malfunctions of the speech production process in speech pathology.
>
> It seems very probable that studies of language acquisition and speech pathology will eventually make an important contribution to the development of an adequate, neurolinguistic model of the normal, healthy, adult brain.

Similarly, of course, linguists in other branches of the discipline examine materials which are marked intuitively as odd or unusual as catalysts for the developments of new ideas in exploratory fields: stylisticians repeatedly seize upon e.e. cummings, Gerard Manley Hopkins, Hemingway and James Joyce; students of syntax look for the unacceptable or marginally acceptable sentences; commutation tests or strict formalism are useful because, among other things, they can provide absurd results; and the very generalized notion of the counter-example is in itself a pure instance of Alienation methodology.

Among linguists, discourse analysts in particular have specifically and explicitly begun their work by taking unusual and intuitively less complex interaction situations, as distinct from casual or desultory conversations: the classroom (Sinclair and Coulthard, 1975; Stubbs, 1974b, 1976a and b); doctor–patient interviews (Coulthard and Ashby, 1976); committee-talk (Stubbs, 1973); media discussions (Pearce, 1973); telephone calls (Schegloff, 1968, and Schegloff and Sacks, 1973); and 'talk as data' therapy-talk (Turner, 1972). As Sinclair and Coulthard put it, they decided it would be productive to begin with 'a more simple type of spoken discourse, one which has much more overt structure, where one participant has acknowledged responsibility for the direction of the discourse, for deciding who shall speak when, and for introducing and ending topics.' Grimes too (1975), in his rather different, and particularly impressive, work on narrative discourse, makes a very clear recommendation that the analyst should begin working towards considering his complex problems by studying the simpler examples of data available, so that, once these simple structures are perceived and understood, the analyst can later move to more difficult data (p. 35):

> Texts with flashbacks or that begin in the middle of things should be left to one side at the start.
>   To begin analysis with simple narrative does not, of course, imply that we stop with the study of simple narratives. Like any exploration of the complex, discourse study should begin in shallow waters and only later progress into the depths. What is learned in the study of simple narratives becomes the starting point that allows progress into other areas.

The Prague Structuralists give the most explicit statement on methodology, as well as the most coherent and sustained account of language forms made strange, or 'foregrounding'. Havránek (1932) explains the term as follows: 'By foregrounding. . .we mean the use of the devices of the language in such a way that this use attracts attention and is perceived as uncommon'; whilst Garvin (1964) gives an account of the use of the concept in general structuralist analysis – with reference not only to linguistic phenomena but to the culture in general:

'Automatisation refers to the stimulus normally expected in a social situation; foregrounding. . .on the other hand, refers to a stimulus not culturally expected in a social situation, and hence capable of provoking special attention.'

A statement by Mukařovský about foregrounding in language is particularly interesting here, because of its very marked similarity to comments made by Garfinkel above: 'Foregrounding brings to the surface and before the eye of the observer even such linguistic phenomena as remain quite covert in communicative speech, although they are important factors in language.'

It should be noted that the practical work in descriptive linguistics in Prague is mostly directed towards the lower end of core linguistics, and general statements are made mainly with reference to poetic language as a specific focus. However, their more abstract observations and definitions are equally applicable to patterns in conversation structure. So, whilst Garvin goes on to define foregrounded language as 'the esthetically intentional distortion of the linguistic components', provided that we accept that discourse study falls within the province of linguistics, then the notion of foregrounding is certainly applicable to such multi-level theoretical notions as, say, 'turn-taking', 'greeting', 'topicality', 'question–answer sequencing', 'initiation–response–feedback', 'presuppositions', 'side-sequencing' and so on. And anyone at all familiar with post-absurd drama will be aware that it is just such items that are frequently intentionally distorted by such dramatists for aesthetic purposes. Although there is no methodical study of conversation *per se* in Prague Linguistics, notice that, in line with the idea that Structuralism as an epistemological point of view should be relevant to cultural research in general, there are useful sporadic comments which demonstrate the linguists' awareness of the appropriateness of their general conceptual apparatus to such phenomena as conversations or discourse. Thus Havránek writes, 'The automatisation of the language of science, or even just workaday technical speech, used in conversational speech, becomes foregrounded.'

In this connection, one thinks immediately of plays such as Ionesco's *The Bald Prima Donna*, where some of the conversation is supposedly based on the drill structures found in a foreign learner's text book. Similarly there is a little Pinter sketch, 'Trouble at the works' (1961c), with its emphasis on ambiguous nominal group structure, referring to the technical apparatus of the factory. Also there is the case of the Inspector in Jo Orton's *Loot* (1967), pretending to be an official from the water board, but 'giving himself away' by slipping into the stereo-typical stage-talk of a stage-policeman. Havránek has an appropriate suggestion here too: 'A transfer of automatisations of a certain field into an entirely uncommon environment is at the root of many verbal jokes, which are instances of foregrounding.'

Mukařovský (1932) makes it quite plain that the value of studying foregrounded language is in clarifying rules of non-foregrounded lan-guage. He takes it that all literature is foregrounded in some way, poetry above all (compare Levin, 1963). But he emphasizes, 'The theorist of the standard language. . .wants to know above all to what extent a work of poetry can be used as data for ascertaining the norm of the standard.'

In drama texts, many different levels of language can be exploited and foregrounded. Some texts undoubtedly offer strange 'conversations'. Where this is intuitively so, it seems that from the linguist's point of view there are powerful precedents to suggest that those texts would prove a source of insights into naturally occurring conversation *per se*.

Having considered literature as a useful resource, and Alienation as a useful methodological device, in rather general terms, I want also to consider both modern literature and the dramatic genre in this context. The overall point being that plays are a means of presenting the social world in a specifically alienated, and therefore graspable, way. Simi-larly, modern literature can be seen to be in a self-consciously designed Alienation tradition, whose central aim is to shock and disturb 'those members of the audience who leave their brains with their hats and coats in the cloakroom' (Brecht, 1937). Thus, modern drama, em-bodying both sets of characteristics, should again be particularly useful for the analyst of social interaction.

Plays are of course a particularly interesting and valuable literary genre for this purpose, in that, unless peculiarly anarchic, they have to be concerned with human interaction, and have to be realized by human dialogue. If we are considering drama working in a post-Brechtian ethos, an anti-emphatic theatre tradition, then the statement by the Prague Structuralist Veltruský (1940), 'the theatre can show us new ways of perceiving the world', can be seen as a positive, calculated intention built into the text, rather than the description of a probable and incalculable effect of the text. The fact that plays, unlike other literary forms, are framed in a specific limit of physical space and actual time, and the fact that the audience is constrained to see and interpret what is presented in that space and time as integrated into a structurally coherent unit, with a coherent communicative intent, leads to a focus on the medium *per se*; in other words, on the dialogue and the interaction.

However opaque the reference, however minimal the concessions from the playwright to the audience's conventional expectations, however blatant his exploitation of theatre as a communication situation, the audience will none the less interpret what is set before it as representationalist art — merely because the vehicles for the author's work and words are human beings interacting. Veltruský again has a relevant statement here:

> In the theatre. . .the action is an end in itself and it lacks an external practical purpose which might determine its properties.
> The action is here geared towards being understood by the audience as a coherent meaningful series.

I take it that there are two basic assumptions that we need here, with reference to the analysis of play-texts: that conversation is a part of this 'action'; and that an audience will strongly resist accepting anarchy and total non-meaningfulness in a text. Thus, for example, if the medium were to be gobbledegook, then the higher order message would at least be something like 'all communication is phatic'.

Veltruský also raises some points which are relevant to the communicative function of the theatre, and which, though written in 1940 and therefore of questionable applicability to recent drama, are none the less highly accurate in considering bourgeois audience expectations. Firstly, he suggests, 'The theatre uses only those signs which are needed for the given dramatic situation', and later continues, 'The spectator of course understands even those non-purposive components of the actor's performance as signs'. Given the date and place of Veltruský's article, he was, I suspect, referring only to a limited type of theatre — the traditional realist paradigm against which Futurismo, Dada, Oulipo, the Absurdists and all Formalist avant-gardes have been reacting and acting since the turn of the century, though more markedly in the last forty years, and more successfully in the last twenty years (see Burton, 1973; Lodge, 1977; Gardner, 1977). Thus, his statements are, in the sense of theatrical potential, an oversimplification of the case. To pinpoint specific examples for his statements, I take it that the first refers to something like the 'well-written' text — well-written in the sense that the plot holds together, and the author manages to give us necessary background information about characters and their histories in a relatively uncluttered and natural way. I understand the second to mean that 'performance errors', say, stuttering, hesitations, false starts, etc., are interpreted wherever possible by the audience to mean something like 'that character is nervous' rather than 'that actor is nervous'. It is interesting, incidentally, that the term 'performance error' suggests that linguists have their own type of dramaturgical metaphor too.

Whilst these statements may not apply to recent drama, they none the less demonstrate the audience expectations against which such theatre may be reacting, and therefore, of course, suggest the very features that avant-garde drama exploits. There is a dilemma for any audience trained by experience in traditional theatre, traditional film, traditional fiction or poetry or representationalist art. A sophisticated recipient, whatever his aesthetic preferences, may still pick up a book or go to a play, not knowing as he does so whether he is to willingly suspend his disbelief or not. Veltruský's 'signs' may be seen as analogous to other more conventional linguistic signs. Modern literature exploits the conventions of both, so modern drama does, in a very marked and complex sense, give us new ways of perceiving the world. The very act of putting common human-oriented events on a stage is a primitive Alienation Device, used to enable the spectators to consider their own world. Where modern drama deals with everyday situations and interactions, with a pronounced focus on interactive dialogue, its marked conversational patterns enable the spectators to see this particular aspect of their world afresh.

Returning to Brecht, which was where this chapter started, there can be seen to be a strong link between his concept of Alienation and that expressed by writers in other disciplines. For each, it is seen as a general procedure to enable observations and critical or descriptive thought, in a movement towards data-based theory. In each, whilst of course there is a certain focus on the writer's own discipline, there is also a set of generally reciprocal references and statements, pointing out that the method itself is applicable in all sorts of analytical frameworks and contexts. Brecht himself makes this point (1950):

> The A-effect as a Procedure in Everyday Life. The achievement of the A-effect constitutes something utterly ordinary, recurrent, it is just a widely practised way of drawing one's own or someone else's attention to a thing, and it can be seen in education as also in business conferences of one sort or another. The A-effect consists in turning the object of which one is to be made aware, to which one's attention is to be drawn, from something ordinary, familiar,

immediately accessible into something peculiar, striking and unexpected. What is obvious is in a certain sense made incomprehen-
sible, but this is only in order that it may then be made all the
easier to comprehend. Before familiarity can turn into awareness,
the familiar must be stripped of its inconspicuousness.

This, in different ideological frameworks, can be taken as an underlying concept for modern art and literature in general. Thus, modern
fiction experiments with form to make the reader aware of hitherto
ignored formal criteria. Thus, too, modern plastic art experiments with
form to make the audience aware that form is as much a possible
subject matter as 'mere' medium. Similarly minimalist poetry experiments to make strange, and therefore prominent, the fundamental
components of linguistic and poetic form. The fact that theatre has a
very specific link with naturalistic social interaction means that Alienation can be used to a specific purpose and effect, that is of interest to
the conversational analyst. For as well as exploiting aspects of theatrical
taken-for-granteds (see Turner, 1970, and Goffman, 1974), it can make
strange, and therefore clear, the commonplace of everyday interaction.
Again Brecht has a relevant comment: 'The new alienations are only designed to free the socially-conditioned phenomena from that stamp of
familiarity which protects them against our grasp today.' Conversation
being the fundamental wherewithal of both naturally occurring interaction and stage interaction, there is a special case for the conversational analyst directing his attention to this kind of theatre.

I have, so far, been offering a wide range of generally related views
on Alienation devices and techniques, as used in various disciplines
with notably different aims and focuses. My own particular use (see
chapter 7), will involve treating a playscript 'as if it were' a transcript
of naturally occurring talk, in order to extend the descriptive range of
a recent rigorous analytical system for discourse (Sinclair and Coulthard, 1975), which was built on a limited collection of data (see
chapter 6) so that the system as it stands can only deal adequately with
an equally limited type of interactive situation. By using the playscript,
the analyst is forced into perceiving ways in which the descriptive
apparatus has to be changed in order to account for the dialogue. It will
be part of the work of the last chapter of the book to consider aspects
and analytical implications of the relationship between real and 'framed
for viewing' activity (Goffman, 1975), real talk and talk on stage,
transcripts of naturally occurring conversation and playscripts. However,

a few observations about the last of these distinctions would seem to be particularly pertinent here.

Drama scripts are markedly tidied-up versions of talk, adhering closely to the two rules that Sacks declares are the most basic conversational rules available (Sacks, 1970), that is, that 'one party speaks at a time' and 'speaker change recurs'. Many of the problems inherent in recordings and transcripts of naturally occurring talk are therefore not present. There are no problems of unclear utterances, overlaps or false starts, which are not intended as oddities by the dramatist. Similarly, many of the paralinguistic problems are removed, in that we are in possession of as much of the paralinguistic information that the dramatist considered necessary for our understanding, and no more. Thus, we do not have clear and explicit indications about intonation, kinesics, proxemics, non-verbal props and so on, but we have enough to get by. I want to suggest that, given the particular goal of furthering descriptive work in the analysis of conversation, and the present state of the art (see chapter 6), it is in fact to our advantage to take situations with some of the problems removed. (See the quotation from Grimes above, and also the quotation from Sinclair and Coulthard.) It may be the case that, just as dramatists adhere closely to those two basic rules, they may also maintain the more fundamental mechanisms of conversation in general. Discovering what is happening in their edited naturalistic-sounding or absurd talk may well offer guidelines towards the ultimate task of working out the rules that operate in real casual conversations. It would not be wise, of course, to make this claim about the maintenance of fundamental rules too strongly, but if it is the case that this edited material does help us extend the basic requirements of discourse-analysis apparatus, such that other researchers can more easily construct whatever else is needed to analyse their own naturalistic data, then drama data will have proved an extremely useful and important catalyst.

It is also the case that drama data do not depend on any *a priori* notions of institutionalized situations, either in terms of functional goals for the talk, participant categorization or relative statuses. Of course the data do demonstrate such variables in use, but they become apparent via the talk, and not because the analyst has collected doctor–patient interviews or mother-child interactions and so on. It is also in the nature of drama (several notable avant-garde writers excepted) to produce interesting interactions. Thus peculiar events arise, and the analytical apparatus has to be enriched in order to cope with them.

Most importantly here, in regard to the possible extension of the framework given in Sinclair and Coulthard (1975) (see chapters 6 and 7), drama dialogue presents conflict. This conflict is a complex matter, and will be further discussed below, but this feature alone makes drama data radically different from almost all other data collected and analysed in this framework before. Crudely, the interactants — fictitious as they are — argue, try to assert themselves, insult each other, ignore each other, refuse to do what they are asked to do, don't bother to be polite, create unnecessary obstacles and so on. In short, they exhibit all sorts of conversational behaviour that will not fit into the collaborative-consensus model that the Sinclair and Coulthard system represents. Here as elsewhere, drama data force the analyst to re-examine his taken-for-granted assumptions, and provokes powerful and fascinating insights into everyday conversational structures.

Chapter 6

The linguistic analysis of spoken discourse

In this chapter, I concentrate primarily on explaining the descriptive apparatus for spoken discourse developed at Birmingham University, English Language Research, by Sinclair, Coulthard, Ashby and Forsyth on a project funded by the Social Science Research Council (1970–2), 'The English used by teachers and pupils', and written up in Sinclair *et al.* (1972) and Sinclair and Coulthard (1975). This work is a substantial contribution to discourse analysis, quite differently oriented and constructed from the work by sociolinguists referred to throughout chapters 2 and 3, and will be discussed in detail here.

This work in discourse analysis, in English Language Research, has been in progress for over a decade. Early ideas are presented informally in Sinclair (1966b), Quigley (1969) and Short (1970). More rigorous work was undertaken by project teams under the auspices of two SSRC-funded research projects: the classroom work mentioned above, and 'The structure of verbal interaction in selected situations' (1972–4). This has been and will be supplemented by the research work of various individuals: Pearce (1973), Williams (1974), Brazil (1975, 1977, 1978), Stubbs (1973, 1974a), Willes (1975), Mead (1976, forthcoming) and Montgomery (1976, 1977). Similarly, researchers at other institutions have also been trying to apply and adapt the original descriptive apparatus, in complementary studies: Krumm (1977), Leitner (1976), McTear (1976), McKnight (1976) and Stocker-Edel (1976). Experience has shown that, for those outside the institution, or not in immediate contact with members of the Birmingham research unit, much of this interesting and important material is not at all easily accessible, perhaps because it is unpublished, or published obscurely, or, in the case of the main publication (Sinclair and Coulthard, 1975) written explicitly for at least two audiences (see the opening of their chapter 3, and the range of journals in which the book has been reviewed). It is therefore difficult for those with specific research interests to use the work in any constructive and practical way. It is part of my object in this chapter to explain, locate and comment on aspects of this work. I hope to draw together what I see as significant features of the descriptive system, and to foreground problem areas. I need to do this specifically to enable the reader to understand my own contribution to work in discourse analysis (detailed in chapter 7), which is an adaptation of this approach. If, in so doing, it makes it easier for those outside Birmingham to appreciate and perhaps use the characteristic features of this particular approach to the linguistic analysis of talk, then so much the better.

There are perhaps three main schools of conversational analysis that are interesting and significant as trends in humanities research in Britain and the USA. There are the sociological analyses of the ethnomethodologists and ethnographers (see, for example, Sacks, 1970, 1972; Schegloff, 1968; Turner, 1974; Gumperz and Hymes, 1972), the philosophically oriented work on speech acts and conversational implicature (see, for example, Austin, 1961, 1965; Searle, 1969; Grice 1957, 1967; Kempson, 1977), and the linguistically focused work from Birmingham English Language Research. There are also, of course, many stray individuals whose particular concerns overlap in varied ways with the preoccupations of all these, and, indeed, it would be perverse to see even these three models as distinct and hermetic — they too have overlapping aims, principles, references and results. Nevertheless, I think most conversational analysts would agree that they represent three distinctive paradigms. Whilst all three are insightful, stimulating and rich in ideas, the differences in focus are extremely important. The strong features of the Birmingham work, from the linguist's point of view, are well elaborated by Sinclair and Coulthard (1975). They are fully explicit about their allegiance to an established theoretical-linguistic framework (the early Hallidayan model), using terminology, apparatus and graphic representation that is contingent upon Halliday (1961), and proposing discourse as a linguistic level higher than grammar, but which none the less displays a hierarchical rank scale analogous to those in the more studied levels of grammar, phonology and graphology. They also make it clear that, in their search for organization in discourse, they have borne in mind the sorts of organization available for consideration at other levels of language, both in drawing parallels and in observing new features of patterning. They also reproduce a set of four criteria to be used in the construction of descriptive schemes (see Sinclair, 1973), which puts them squarely within the general principles of linguistics, and distances them from the exciting, but less rigorous, notions and approach to data which characterize, say, the ethnomethodologists' work. They are in line here with an early pronouncement by Firth (1935): 'We must avoid loose sociological linguistics without analytical rigour'. The four crucial criteria to be borne in mind are as follows:

1 The descriptive system must be finite
2 Symbols used in the descriptive apparatus must be explicitly and precisely relatable to the data, so that coding is both clear and replicable
3 The apparatus must account for *all* the data
4 In order to make a structural statement of any standing whatsoever, there must be at least one impossible combination of symbols. (These points are elaborated and exemplified in Sinclair and Coulthard, p. 17.)

It is this sort of approach to the work – collecting a corpus of naturally occurring talk, and developing a descriptive apparatus that follows these sorts of criteria, that distinguishes the work of English Language Research from the other (undoubtedly rich and often brilliant) work produced by the scholars in the above-mentioned associated fields.

It would probably also be useful to locate where the Birmingham work stands in relation to both sociolinguistics and functionalism; to both of which it lays claim to belong. The first of these is quite easy, in that we can make the usual distinction (see Fishman, 1965) between macro-sociolinguistics (language planning, correlational studies of substantial samples, work on class and sex differentials, large-scale cultural and political phenomena) and micro-sociolinguistics (the study of the minutiae of verbal interaction in a small data-based corpus). Undoubtedly the macro and the micro have much to offer each other (see Burton and Stubbs, 1976, on this point), but certainly in an area as new and relatively uncharted as conversational analysis, a small collection of data, and a thorough, detailed and specific account of those data, is the only sensible way to proceed. There is an interesting comparison to be made here with several of the emergent fields within linguistics, children's acquisition of language, or pathological linguistics, for example, both of which require powerfully rich and detailed analyses of the case-study type if they ever hope to progress to work of greater generality, in either the practical or theoretical sense.

The precise relation of the English Language Research work to functionalism is less easy to bring out. There is certainly a stated link with the anthropological-linguistic tradition of Malinowski–Firth–Halliday, where all instances of language are seen as variations on the theme of 'I am communicating with you', and where 'things get done' through talk. But the Birmingham discourse work is placed, quite decidedly, within a very microcosmic notion of functionality, so that, for example, the analyst needs to consider questions like, 'what does this utterance do, in terms of the actual discourse it contributes to? Does it request a verbal response? Does it mark a boundary in the flow of talk? Does it mark the fact that something interesting is coming later?' This, it seems to me, is a significantly different focus from other functionalist-based work, which considers functional relationships between the utterance and the much wider situation, which includes, of course, the rest of the discourse and participants to that discourse, but which usually looks outside the very minute relationships implied in Birmingham discourse analysis (see for comparison Jakobson, 1960; Soskin and John, 1963; Burke, 1945; Halliday, 1969, Hymes, 1972b). Again, the larger-focused work and the smaller-focused work should have much to offer each other. For the time being, however, it is important to understand exactly what is being referred to in the Birmingham work when functions are mentioned. Perhaps a small example would help to make the point. The classroom description lists, amongst its 'Acts', an item labelled 'Aside', where the teacher might mutter to himself something like, 'Now where did I put the chalk?', or, 'Brr, it's freezing in here'. In the description of the definitions and realizations of the twenty-two Acts in Sinclair and Coulthard, all the other Acts are described, amongst other things, in terms of their function, but Aside is given no such description — implying that it has no function at all. Now clearly, in some functionalist models it would have a very definite function — 'phatic' perhaps, or 'phatic/expressive' if one were considering Jakobson's model (Jakobson, 1960). Within the working of the actual conversation, however, it serves no prospective or retrospective function. That is, it neither sets up an expectation for a following utterance, nor fulfils one from a previous utterance. It is in this sense, then, that it has no function. It does not, in fact, contribute to the ongoing talk itself in any constructive way. Unless one has a very clear understanding of what is meant by 'function' in the Birmingham descriptive framework, much confusion can, and does, arise. Perhaps I have laboured the point rather, but the concept has substantial consequences for the rank scale, and particularly for any adaptations that researchers might want to make of it, and it is precisely because students and researchers have been confused by the issue (see, for example, McKnight, 1976, p.25) that I have spent time and space here in an attempt to clarify the situation.

Both sociolinguistics and functionalism are foregrounded in the discussion of 'situation' and 'tactics' (Sinclair and Coulthard, pp. 28–34). These two labels indicate the ways in which individual utterances can be coded for what they do in the real world and in the discourse. Turner (1970) very sensibly points out a particular problem for linguists working on real talk, which is that there is no simple, mechanical way in which the analyst can tell, simply from the words on his transcript, what speech act is being used and responded to. Sinclair and Coulthard offer a classic example, 'Is that your coat on the floor?', which is, of course, ostensibly an interrogative (in terms of syntax) or a question (in terms of sentence action). But in certain situations, for example, a father to a son in a cross tone of voice, when the son knows he is not supposed to leave his coat on the floor, this utterance constitutes a command, meaning something like, 'Pick it up and put it away!'. Sinclair and Coulthard state their position as follows:

> To handle this lack of fit between grammar and discourse we
> suggest two intermediate areas where distinctive choices can be
> postulated: situation and tactics. . . . *Situation* here includes all
> relevant factors in the environment, social conventions and the
> shared experience of the participants. . .*tactics* handles the syntag-
> matic patterns of discourse: the way in which items precede, follow
> and are related to each other. It is place in the structure of dis-
> course which finally determines which act a particular item is
> realizing, though classification can only be made of items already
> tagged with features from grammar and situation.

Clearly, 'situation' is, and must be, a vague notion, where utterances may well be open to various styles of interpretation from different individuals. This in itself is a fascinating area of study (see Garfinkel, 1967; Cicourel, 1973). It is none the less a reasonable, common-sense and workable state of affairs. Again, perhaps an example would help to make clear the last part of the above quotation. Consider the difference between these two teacher utterances:

1 'What about this one?' (*Pause*)

2 'What about this one? (*No pause*) This I think is a super one. Isobel, can you think what it means?'

Considering just the first four words: in the first (hypothetical) utterance they function as what is labelled as an Elicitation — a question eliciting a verbal response. In the second (genuine) utterance, the same four words are 'pushed down' to the position of Starter — a question, statement or command, whose function is to draw attention to, or provide information about, an area, in order to make more likely a correct Response to the Initiation as a whole. In this case, the set of three (orthographic) sentences form an Opening Move, the head of which is the Elicitation, 'can you think what it means?' In terms of tactics, the first four words fill a possible pre-head position in the Move, whose total possible structure is reproduced in Table 6.1.

Table 6.1 *RANK IV: Move (Opening)*

Elements of Structure	Structures	
signal(s)	(s) (pre-h)h(post-h) (sel)	s:marker
		pre-h: starter
pre-head (pre-h)	(sel) (pre-h)h	h:choice of elicitation/
		directive/informative/
head (h)		check
		post-h: choice of
post-head (post-h)		prompt/clue
		sel: ((cue) bid) nomi-
select (sel)		nation

Again, to avoid misunderstanding, I think it is probably advisable to say a little about the status of the descriptive system as published, particularly in relation to further work in discourse study. Sinclair and Coulthard indicate throughout that they hope that their work will be used, extended and modified in further conversational analysis research:

There will be a few. . .who will want to use the system in their own research work and for whom this chapter will have to act as a coding manual [p.19] .

We would stress the preliminary nature of this work, we are confident that sufficient progress has been made for more ambitious studies to be successfully undertaken [p.112] .

We are hopeful that our efforts to provide a systematic account of samples of spoken language from a small number of classrooms will be of use to others with similar interests and stimulate further empirical studies both in educational and other contexts [p.112].

Implicit in these remarks, and more explicit elsewhere, is an acknowledgment of the limitations of their study (p.112): 'The most we can claim is to have begun to evolve one possible approach to the analysis of spoken texts, while working with a relatively small data sample taken from one situation type.' It is the 'one situation type' that is crucial to my point here. Elsewhere the authors again point out this problem with their analysis:

> The system. . .is now able to cope with most teacher/pupil interaction inside the classroom. What it cannot handle, and of course was not designed to handle, is pupil/pupil interaction in project work, discussion groups or the playground [p.113].

A particular problem I have encountered with recent researchers has been on this point, and in connection with the descriptive status of the discourse model as outlined in the book by Sinclair and Coulthard. The corpus itself was homogeneous, and a normative description inevitably emerged, which, as the authors themselves stress (p.121), 'must be abandoned as soon as substantial sociolinguistic variables are allowed to vary'. They are equally explicitly aware of the dangers of forcing new data into categories constructed for other data, but inevitably, of course, any later researcher wanting to test the strengths and weaknesses of the paradigm must begin by trying to force his data into those categories, in order to see how near or how far the new material is, in terms of its organization, and to see whether minor or even major amendments are feasible. The contingent danger is, of course, the difficulty in seeing what sort of new or modified structure might be required to handle the non-homogeneous data. Again, researchers have often mistaken the status of the classroom discourse model, and have reacted with surprise on finding that it fails to meet their needs precisely. It must be borne in mind that classroom discourse was originally singled out for study (see p.6) because it was intuitively felt to be 'easier to handle', 'more highly structured than casual conversation' and, therefore, in some sense 'odd'. Since this is the case, it is similarly important for conversational analysts not to regard classroom discourse as central and other situations as variations upon it. Again, as Sinclair and Coulthard point out (p.123), a linguist who has intuitively selected a type of discourse as in some way unusual, then has the job of proving that there is some overlap between this type and others.

As already stated above, the practical descriptive apparatus for handling classroom data is built as a rank-scale model, with the usual hierarchical implications. The basic structure is shown in Figure 6.1,

Lesson
∨
Transaction
∨
Exchange
∨
Move
∨
Act

Figure 6.1.

where Lessons are made up of Transactions, Transactions are made up of Exchanges, Exchanges are made up of Moves, and Moves are made up of Acts. The analogy with the grammar-rank scale (Halliday, 1961) is helpful here, particularly at the lower end of the scale, with a comparison between word-morpheme and Move-Act, since it is important to remember that although the Act is the smallest unit, it is the Move which is the minimal free interactive unit, and, although a Move may be realized by a single Act, Acts are essentially bound units, some of which cannot be used singly.

I find the very informal presentation of the way this rank scale developed (Sinclair and Coulthard, p.21) very helpful as a preliminary to understanding the rank scale in detail and depth, and will summarize this description briefly here.

1 The researchers began by considering two units only: the utterance (one speaker's contribution), and the exchange (two speakers' joint contribution to the talk (question and answer, for example).
2 They then noticed that a vast number of teacher utterances had a boundary in mid-utterance (compare Turner, 1970). A very typical teacher utterance might have this form for instance:
   'Paris, that's right.
   And Mary, what's the capital of Sweden?'

They therefore decided to recognize a unit smaller than an utterance, which they labelled 'Move'. In the hypothetical example just
given, the teacher uses two Moves — one which tells one pupil that
he has just given her the right answer to a previous question, and one
which asks another, specifically nominated pupil a similar question,
requesting a different, but analogous, answer. It might be useful, at
this stage, if I extend this hypothetical, but recognizably typical
discourse, to produce two complete Exchanges (two teacher
Eliciting Exchanges), and lay them out in Table 6.2, using the
graphic system given in Sinclair and Coulthard's book.

Table 6.2.

Opening move	Act	Answering move	Act	Follow-up move	Act
John	n	Paris	rep	Paris	acc
What's the capital	el			that's right	ev
of France?					
And Mary	n	Stockholm	rep	Stockholm	acc
What's the capital	el			Good girl	ev
of Sweden?					

3 The researchers then decided that the typical Exchange structure
for classroom discourse can be described as having three parts,
Initiation, Response and Feedback (IRF).
4 The next thing they noticed was a small set of words and phrases
that recurred in teacher-talk, like 'Right', 'Well', 'OK', 'Now', produced with a sharply falling intonation and followed by a pause.
These could be seen to be marking boundaries in the flow of the
talk, indicating the end of one stage and the beginning of the next.
This they labelled Frame.
5 This framing item was often followed in the data by a metastatement about the discourse. This they labelled Focus. Notice
that Frame and Focus are both Moves, together with Opening,
Answering and Follow-up Moves. But whereas Opening, Answering,
and Follow-up Moves combine to form what are called Teaching
Exchanges, Frame and Focus combine to form what are called
Boundary Exchanges.
6 Frame and Focus provided the first positive evidence for a rank
above Exchange. This was labelled Transaction. As yet there is no
evidence for a structural description of Transaction. It is suggested

that this may be a feature of different teachers' styles. So that,
for example, a particular teacher may mark the boundary of the
Transaction, follow this with an Informing Exchange, follow that
with, say, five Eliciting Exchanges and follow that with a
Directing Exchange, and when the action that he has commanded
the class to do has been completed, the teacher may explicitly
mark the end of the Transaction with another Boundary Exchange,
whose Metastatement in the Focusing Move refers backwards to the
job just completed.

7 They then realized that Moves had an internal structure of their
own, and devised criteria for recognizing twenty-two different
Acts, some of which have already appeared in the example above:
Nomination (n); Elicitation (el); Reply (rep); Accept (acc); and
Evaluate (ev).

In the following pages I will set out the rank scale completely, more
or less as it appears in Sinclair and Coulthard, but with a few minor
modifications which, hopefully, make it easier to read, and correcting
some misprints in the first edition of the book. I will also append
comments, when appropriate, on some of the inherent problems con-
tained in the scheme. In part, this anticipates some of the points I
shall make in chapter 7, but it also reflects areas where the authors
themselves are anticipating alterations to the model.

Table 6.3 *RANK I: Lesson*

Elements of Structure	Structures	Classes
	an unordered series of transactions	

Notes:
Clearly this is a very vague structural statement, and points up the difficulty
inherent in any rank-scale model apropos of its highest unit. Notice, though, the
implications for 'rule-bound creativity', for, whilst the lower ranks are very explicitly and tightly restricted, at the higher ranks there is clearly room for varia-
tion in 'discourse-style' and therefore 'teaching method' within an orderly and
consensus discourse. (See Bernstein, 1971, on the notion of frames and freedom.)
   For different speech situations, different common-sense terms are, of course,
easily substituted: 'committee-meeting'; 'interview'; 'service-encounter'. For more
abstract discussion, Hymes's notion of speech event is an appropriate item to be
borrowed (Hymes, 1972b), wherever the interaction is co-terminous with that
event.

Table 6.4 *RANK II: Transaction*

Elements of Structure	Structures	Classes of Exchange
Preliminary (P)	$PM(M^2...M^n)(T)$	P, T: Boundary (II.1)
Medial (M)		M: Teaching (II.2)
Terminal (T)		

Note:
The optional terminal element is worth some consideration. Whilst it is quite a common option used in classroom discourse, where the teacher is often concerned to point out the structure of his or her talk as clearly as possible to the audience, it is not so obviously in use in other, less formal situations. It may often be the case that the closing of a particular Transaction can only be recognized after the event. That is, the hearer knows that Transaction 1 has finished because Transaction 2 has explicitly started. Pearce (1977) and Tadros (forthcoming) have pointed out the same characteristic for the analysis of written discourse, and this may well be an important feature with regard to how participants understand all kinds of discourse. If it is the case that we assume we are still within one unit, mode, or framework until the producer of the discourse we are reading or hearing explicitly indicates that we have moved to another, then this notion could well be used to explain various sorts of malfunctioning discourse — whether deliberate (like jokes, or avant-garde writing) or accidental (foreigners' mistakes, socio-psychologically problematic situations).

Table 6.5 *RANK III: Exchange (Boundary)*

Elements of Structure	Structures	Classes of Move
Frame (Fr)	Fr (Fo)	Fr: Framing (III.1)
Focus (Fo)		Fo: Focusing (III.2)

Note:
The structure is represented thus in Sinclair and Coulthard (p. 26): (Fr) (Fo).
If it is intended to indicate that the Boundary Exchange can be made up of either a Frame or a Focus, or of both together, then linked brackets would make this clearer, (Fr ⫧ Fo), and would be more in line with current conventions. However, I understand that in the classroom data the Frame is obligatory and the Focus only optional (Sinclair, personal communication), so I have altered the structural statement as above.

Table 6.6 *RANK III: Exchange* (*Teaching*)

Elements of Structure	Structures	Classes of Move
Initiation (I)	I (R) (F)	I: Opening (III.3)
Response (R)		R: Answering (III.4)
Feedback (F)		F: Follow-up (III.5)

Notes:
The basic rank scale is presented at primary delicacy only. Eleven sub-categories of this Exchange type are also isolated and presented in Sinclair and Coulthard. Of these, six are Free Exchanges, and five are bound to preceding Free Exchanges:

Free

Teacher-Inform	I(R)
Teacher-Direct	IR(F)
Teacher-Elicit	IRF
Pupil-Elicit	IR
Pupil-Inform	IF
Teacher-Check	IR(F)

Bound

Teacher-ReInitiation	IRI^bRF
Teacher-ReInitiation	$IRF(I^b)\,RF$
Teacher-Listing	$IRF(I^b)RF(I^b)RF$ etc.
Teacher-Reinforce	IRI^bR
Teacher-Repeat	IRI^bRF

Notice that in the discursive writing in the book, the authors claim that IRF is the most usual structure. This is, of course, the primary pattern only, and whilst it certainly does cover a large number of Exchanges in the data, a more delicate description is possible and desirable.

TABLE 6.7 *RANK IV: Move* (*Opening*)

Elements of Structure	Structures	Classes of Act
signal (s)	(s) (pre-h) h (post-h) (sel)	s: marker (IV.1)
pre-head (pre-h)	(sel) (pre-h) h	pre-h: starter (IV.2)
head (h)		h: system operating at h; choice of
		elicitation
		directive
post-head (post-h)		informative
select (sel)		check (IV.3)
		post-h: system operating at post-h: choice of
		prompt
		clue (IV.4)
		sel: ((cue) bid) nomination (IV.5)

Note:

I have corrected the rather misleading printing of the second column which appears in Sinclair and Coulthard thus:

(s) (pre-h) h (post-h)
(sel)
(sel) (pre-h) h

Presumably the printer ran out of space, and the resulting presentation is somewhat confusing. My amendment is supposed to make clear that there are only two alternative structures for an opening move.

Table 6.8 *RANK IV: Move (Answering)*

Elements of Structure	Structures	Classes of Act
pre-head (pre-h)	(pre-h) h (post-h)	pre-h: acknowledge (IV.6)
head (h)		h: system operating at h; choice of
post-head (post-h)		reply
		react
		acknowledge (IV.6)
		post-h: comment (IV.8)

Notes:

There are several problems with the item Acknowledge which I will discuss below at Act rank. For the moment, notice that it is given here as occurring at two distinct places in the structure of this Move — pre-head or head. Taking account of the push-down mechanism would simplify any coding problems with this item. That is, it would be coded as head if there were no following head realized by Reply or React.

The book misprints Acknowledge (as head) as IV.7 in the third column. I have corrected this to IV.6.

Table 6.9 *Move (Follow-up)*

Elements of Structure	Structures	Classes of Act
pre-head (pre-h)	(pre-h) (h) (post-h)	pre-h: accept (IV.9)
head (h)		h: evaluate (IV.10)
post-head (post-h)		post-h: comment (IV.8)

Table 6.10 *RANK IV: Move (Framing)*

Elements of Structure	Structures	Classes of Act
head (h)	hq	h: marker (IV.1)
qualifier (q)		q: silent stress (IV.11)

Note:
The distinction between the head and qualifier is not immediately obvious since both of them are obligatory. The distinction resides in the fact that Markers can also occur in Opening Moves, but, if followed by the Silent Stress, the Move is recognized, and recognizable, as a Framing Move.

Table 6.11 *RANK IV: Move (Focusing)*

Elements of Structure	Structures	Classes of Act
signal (s)	(s) (pre-h) h (post-h)	s: marker (IV.1)
pre-head (pre-h)		pre-h: starter (IV.2)
head (h)		h: system operating at h; choice of
		metastatement
post-head (post-h)		conclusion
		post-h: comment (IV.8)

Note:
Notice the similarity between this and the Opening Move; both begin with possible Marker and possible Starter, whilst the difference occurs in the actual choice of head. However, whereas Opening Moves choose between Elicitation/Directive/Informative/Check, Focusing Moves choose between Metastatement and Conclusion. This has substantial implications for notions of the continuous classification of talk, in that hearers cannot tell, until the speaker produces the head of this utterance, whether they are supposed to be attending to a possible Opening Move or a possible Focusing Move.

Classes of Acts

Table 6.12

Reference no.	Label	Symbol	Realization and Definition
IV.1	marker	m	*Realized* by a closed class — Well/OK/Now/Good/Right/Alright. Falling intonation, and silent stress following when acting as the head of a Framing Move *Function* to mark boundaries in the discourse *Occurs* in Opening Moves as signal Framing Moves as head Focusing Moves as signal

Table 6.13

Reference no.	Label	Symbol	Realization and Definition
IV.2	starter	s	*Realized* by statement/question/command *Function* to provide information about, or direct attention to, an area, in order to make a correct response to the initiation more likely *Occurs* in Opening Moves as pre-head Focusing Moves as pre-head

Notes:
Although there are no such examples in the data, it would be quite feasible for this Act to be realized by a moodless item, for example, 'Easy one this'. Again, it is important to be quite clear about the relationship between the statements set out in the presentation of the system, and real discourse. The authors claim that they present only what occurs in the data. That these descriptive statements take on a categorical and definitive implication is unfortunate and misleading.

Notice the similarity between this item and Clues. They are indeed almost identical in terms of realization, but they are labelled according to where they occur in the structure of the talk (see, again, the discussion of Tactics, above). Thus, Starters occur in both Opening and Focusing Moves as pre-head, but Clues occur in Opening Moves as post-head. This again points up the importance accorded to continuous classification, and again has important implications when it comes to considering later researchers' suggestions for other Acts, and Moves for different discourse types, some of which are extremely uneconomical.

Table 6.14

Reference no.	Label	Symbol	Realization and Definition
IV.3.1	elicita-tion	el	*Realized* by a question *Function* to request a linguistic response *Occurs* in Opening Moves as head cf. IV.3.2/IV.3.3/IV.3.4

Note:
See below for remarks on an interesting overlap problem between Elicitation and Directives.

Table 6.15

Reference no.	Label	Symbol	Realization and Definition
IV.3.2	check	ch	*Realized* by a closed set of polar questions to do with being 'finished'/'ready', having 'problems'/'difficulties', being able to 'see'/'hear'. Real questions, in the sense that the teacher does not already know the answer *Function* to enable the teacher to ascertain whether there are any problems preventing the progress of the lesson *Occurs* in Opening Moves as head cf. IV.3.1/IV.3.3/IV.3.4

Table 6.16

Reference no.	Label	Symbol	Realization and Definition
IV.3.3	directive	d	*Realized* by a command. Its function is to request a non-linguistic response

Notes:
The original text states that a Directive is realized by an imperative, thus confusing the distinctions made on p.29, which presents the relationships between discourse categories, situational categories and grammatical categories. Since imperative is clearly a grammatical category, I have changed this to a discourse equivalent above.

There is an interesting problem of overlap between Directive and Elicitation when the teacher produces an utterance like this:

'Tell me your name'

In one sense this is clearly an utterance that requests a verbal response (which is one reason for classifying it as an Elicitation), in another sense it is clearly a command (which is one reason for classifying it as a Directive). It is not an uncommon example. Either it is necessary to set up a new opening and answering pair (like Elicitation-Reply and Directive-React) to cope with this problem, or, more economically, it is possible to see this as a Directive whose corresponding React happens to involve a verbal noise. It is this classification that seems more in line with a common-sense understanding of the discourse situation, in that, clearly, a Directive implies an instruction to perform something, and that performance might well include a verbal performance. Thus 'Sing the National Anthem backwards' would have the same classification.

It is interesting that Bauman (1976) uses the term 'solicitation' to cover both Elicitations and Directives.

Table 6.17

Reference no.	Label	Symbol	Realization and Definition
IV.3.4	inform-ative	i	*Realized* by a statement. Differs from other uses of statement in that its sole *Function* is to provide information. The only necessary response is an acknowledgment of attention and understanding *Occurs* in Opening Moves as head cf. IV.3.1/IV.3.2/IV.3.3

Notes:
Notice the negative definition of this act.

In terms of classroom discourse this Act seems perfectly adequate, but in other situations, particularly ones which are not set up as 'time for the transfer of information' but where, nevertheless, referential content is undoubtedly passed between the participants, a finer notion of this item is definitely called for. See comments in chapter 7.

Table 6.18

Reference no.	Label	Symbol	Realization and Definition
IV.4.1	prompt	p	*Realized* by a closed class of items, e.g., 'Go on'/'Have a go'/'Come on'/ 'Quickly' *Function* to reinforce a Directive or Elicitation by suggesting that the response is no longer requested but demanded *Occurs* in Opening Moves as post-head cf. IV.4.2.

Table 6.19

Reference no.	Label	Symbol	Realization and Definition
IV.4.2	clue	cl	*Realized* by statement, command, question or moodless item *Function* to provide additional information which helps the pupil answer the Elicitation or comply with the Directive. Thus subordinate to head *Occurs* in Opening Moves as post-head cf. IV.4.1

Note:
See the remarks on Starters above.

Table 6.20

Reference no.	Label	Symbol	Realization and Definition
IV.5.1	cue	cu	*Realized* by closed class of items (only three exponents in the data), 'Hands up'/'Don't call out', etc. *Function* to evoke an appropriate bid *Occurs in* Opening Moves as select cf. IV.5.2/IV.5.3

Table 6.21

Reference no.	Label	Symbol	Realization and Definition
IV.5.2	bid	b	*Realized* by closed class of verbal and non-verbal items: 'Sir'/'Miss'/teacher's name/raised hand/finger clicks *Function* to signal a desire to contribute to the discourse *Occurs* in Opening Moves as select cf. IV.5.1/IV.5.3

Note:
Notice that this description allows two speakers to contribute to a single Move, which, if allowed to stand, has far-reaching consequences for the descriptive system. Sinclair and Coulthard are aware of the problem:

> our rank of move is concerned centrally with each discrete contribution to a discussion made by one speaker. We resist recognizing as a move a structure in which more than one speaker contributes since that is more typical of the next rank up, exchange [p.123].

> It would be possible to suggest that teaching exchanges actually have a structure of five moves, with both bid and nomination as separate moves. The argument for this would be that a new move should begin every time there is a new speaker. We rejected this alternative, because it would have created as many difficulties as it would have solved. When a teacher nominated without waiting for a bid, we would have had to regard this as two moves, one consisting of a single word, and at times even embedded inside the other move. Such a solution would also have devalued the concept of move. We prefer to say that a move boundary signals a change in the speaker who is composing/creating the discourse, and that therefore a move boundary is a potential change in the direction of the discourse, whereas a child making a bid must choose from a very limited set of choices. Thus we regard the function of an opening move, with elicitation or directive as head, as not only requesting a reply or a reaction but as also deciding who should respond. . . . An opening move ends after the responder has been selected [p.46].

The problem occurs in other data as well (Krumm, 1977; Stubbs, 1973), and has been partially considered in Sinclair (1977), with a notion of an Act called 'Engage', and a suggestion that this problem is more appropriately considered at Act rank. I will discuss this more fully below (chapter 7) and merely point it out as a problem here.

Table 6.22

Reference no.	Label	Symbol	Realization and Definition
IV.5.3	nomi-nation	n	*Realized* by closed class: names of all the pupils/'You' with contrastive stress/ 'Anybody'/'Yes' *Function* to call on, or give permission to, a pupil to contribute to the discourse *Occurs* in Opening Moves as select cf. IV.5.1/IV.5.2

Note:
This is a very clear example of the way in which the analyst cannot move from a closed set of formal items (the children's names) to a functional categorization. If, say, the class were an unruly one (and notice, in passing, that this descriptive apparatus does not provide the tools necessary for describing unruly classes, since the data came from well-ordered classrooms), then the use of a child's name, spoken with, say, tone 4 (Halliday, 1970), could well be used and heard as a warning to stop behaving in ways that violate spoken and unspoken rules of classroom behaviour. (See Sinclair and Coulthard, p. 30–2, for a full discussion of the overlapping interpretations of command/request, and the dependence on situational knowledge for interpretive rules. See also Willes, 1975, for part of a case study of a child who clearly does not share situational knowledge.) As in Scale and Category grammar, used as a descriptive tool for the study of text, interpretation depends upon a combination of the examination of meaning, componence and structure (see Sinclair, 1972, p. 37).

Table 6.23

Reference no.	Label	Symbol	Realization and Definition
IV.6	acknow-ledge	ack	*Realized* by 'Yes'/'OK'/'Wow' and certain non-verbal gestures and expressions *Function* simply to show that the Initiation has been understood, and, if the head was a Directive, that the pupil intends to React *Occurs* in Answering Move as pre-head Answering Move as head cf. IV.7.1/IV.7.2

Note:
As in Informing above, it seems unsatisfactory not to distinguish between different types of Acknowledge, like 'Yes' and 'Wow'. Again, this may not be particularly important in the classroom, where the range of choices open to the pupil are so very limited (although I can imagine sarcastic exploitation of 'Wow' by unruly pupils that could totally demolish the planned lesson, and would thus need to be shown in the description of that discourse), but outside the classroom this is a rich and therefore problematic area. This matter of the rights and possibilities of answering speakers will be taken up more fully in chapter 7.

Table 6.24

Reference no.	Label	Symbol	Realization and Definition
IV.7.1	reply	rep	*Realized* by statement, question, moodless item and non-verbal surrogates like nods *Function* to provide a linguistic response appropriate to the Elicitation *Occurs* in Answering Moves as head cf. IV.7.2/IV.6

Table 6.25

Reference no.	Label	Symbol	Realization and Definition
IV.7.2	react	rea	*Realized* by a non-linguistic action *Function* to provide the appropriate non-linguistic response defined by the preceding Directive *Occurs* in Answering Moves as head cf. IV.7.1/IV.6

Table 6.26

Reference no.	Label	Symbol	Realization and Definition
IV.8	comment	com	*Realized* by statement or tag question subordinate to the head *Function* to exemplify, expand, justify, provide additional information *Occurs* in Answering Moves as post-head Follow-up Moves as post-head Focusing Moves as post-head

Note:
The book again confuses grammatical and discourse categories. 'Tag question' here means 'a declarative with an interrogative tag'. I have altered 'Realized by statement and tag question' to 'Realized by statement or tag question' to try to make this clearer.

Table 6.27

Reference no.	Label	Symbol	Realization and Definition
IV.9	accept	acc	*Realized* by a closed class of items 'Yes'/'No'/'Good'/'Fine'/repetition of pupil's reply, all with neutral low fall intonation. *Function* to indicate that teacher has heard/seen and that the Reply or React was appropriate. *Occurs* in Follow-up Moves as pre-head

Table 6.28

Reference no.	Label	Symbol	Realization and Definition
IV.10	evalu-ate	e	*Realized* by statements or tag questions including words and phrases like 'Good'/'team point'/'interesting' *Function* to comment on quality of pupil Reply, React or Initiation *Occurs* in Follow-up Moves as head

Note:
See my amendment above to 'Comment', with regard to tag question. I have done the same here.

Table 6.29

Reference no.	Label	Symbol	Realization and Definition
IV.11	silent stress	Λ	*Realized* by a pause, following a marker *Function* to highlight the marker when it is serving as the head of a Boundary Exchange, indicating a Transaction Boundary. *Occurs* in Framing Moves as qualifier

Note:
It is not immediately obvious why this should be termed a 'qualifier' and not 'post-head', but see my comments on Boundary Exchanges above, where I point out that if, and only if, a Silent Stress follows a Marker (that is, qualifies it), that Marker is heard as starting an Opening Move, rather than a Framing Move. The Silent Stress is thus only considered important as a bound qualifier to Markers.

Table 6.30

Reference no.	Label	Symbol	Realization and Definition
IV.12.1	meta-state-ment	ms	*Realized* by a statement which refers to future time *Function* to help pupils to see the structure of the lesson and understand the purpose of the subsequent Exchange *Occurs* in Focusing Moves as head cf. IV.12.2

Note:
Whilst the data has no examples of Metastatements referring to present time, it is by no means an impossible construct. For example, a teacher might well say 'What we're doing now is creating energy'.

Table 6.31

Reference no.	Label	Symbol	Realization and Definition
IV.13	loop	l	*Realized* by closed class of items 'Pardon'/'What did you say'/'Eh'/ 'Did you say'/'Do you mean' *Function* to return the discourse to the stage it was at before the pupil spoke, and from where it can proceed normally *Occurs* Anywhere

Note:
I am reminded of a method Garfinkel employed 'to create trouble', which was to get his students to repeatedly produce Loops to other participants' Informs (see Garfinkel, 1967). By no means did the discourse proceed normally! This means that, again, this item is open to disruptive exploitation.

Table 6.32

Reference no.	Label	Symbol	Realization and Definition
IV.14	aside	z	*Realized* by statement, question, command, moodless item. Seems to be the teacher talking to himself 'It's freezing in here', 'Where's the chalk', for example *Function* not given *Occurs* Anywhere

138

Note:

See my remarks on this item at the beginning of this chapter. The fact that this item is not assigned a function means only that it does not contribute anything to the discourse and is not taken up in any way by other participants. I suspect that this item is far more a feature of formal talk situations than informal ones, where it could be a very embarrassing item. This item is also open to exploitation by perverse interactants.

I hope then, to have clarified what I see as the essential features in this type of rigorous linguistic approach to the analysis of spoken discourse. The later project work, and less central issues, are described in detail in Burton (1978), chapter 5. I came to this work from a background interest in conversational analysis that was much more strongly oriented to sociological and ethnomethodological concerns, and I was, at first, rather sceptical about it. However, it was when I wanted to describe actual data, and when I forced myself to come to grips with the details of this descriptive apparatus, that I realized the precision and descriptive power it allowed me. Of course, many fine points of detail about the nature of the spoken interaction are lost if the data are coded in this way without annotation, but, at the level at which the data are described, they can be described fully and accurately. So stretches of talk can be charted comparatively in a significant way. There are alterations to the apparatus which must be made if it is to accommodate data other than purely formal talk, and I describe a possible set of changes in the next chapter. Given a concept of underlying conversational structure sufficiently abstract to cope with any type of spoken discourse, which is what the work in chapter 7 is supposed to represent, then data charted against that framework, together with explanatory annotation, can truly be discussed in terms of style.

Chapter 7

Towards an analysis of casual conversation

In this chapter, I describe in detail the descriptive apparatus closely based on the model in Sinclair and Coulthard (1975), with alterations which enable, initially, an efficient coding of the plays studied and discussed in chapters 2 and 3; but also, hopefully, this adaptation made for the tidied-up talk in the playscripts will prove useful for analysts of naturally occurring talk as well. The work here is specifically intended as a contribution to the linguistic analysis of all spoken discourse. I begin with an informal, though thorough, discussion of the changes that seemed necessary if the general principles of Sinclair and Coulthard's model were to be applied fruitfully and rigorously to non-formal conversational data. I continue with a formal presentation of the general descriptive apparatus for analysing all conversation, and I conclude with some examples of coded data (taken from *The Dumb Waiter*) in an attempt to clarify this approach.

Firstly, then, there seem to be two sets of problems that recur when analysts of data, other than classroom data, try to apply the Sinclair–Coulthard coding scheme. The simple problems concern the topmost and bottommost ranks – Interaction, Transaction, Act – where the analyst needs only to see what recognition criteria are descriptively adequate, to account for these structures and items. Apart from questions of economy, precision, delicacy, this activity is not unduly difficult, and alterations are not necessarily radical.

The really interesting interactive ranks are those of Exchange and Move. And since the description of Exchange structure hinges on what Moves are used in what orders and relationships, and since Move is also the minimal interactive unit, it seems that most analytical problems centre on this rank first and foremost.

Outside the classroom there are several specific problems with the notion and description of Moves as set out in Sinclair and Coulthard.

140

Firstly, 'Feedback' or 'Follow-up' hardly ever occur. Only in minimal ritual encounters (see Goffman, 1971, chapter 3), or in extended formal talk, or among people acting out classroom situations, can this be seen as a recurrent feature that needs a special place in a structural description of conversations. I think it may be used in informal talk as a device for conveying sarcasm, but irony, jokes, sarcasm and so on require another paper to themselves (see the apposite Sacks comment quoted in Labov's footnote, Labov, 1970). I will not dwell on that suggestion here, except to say that, if it is the case that casual conversationalists can use Feedback items *per se* as a sarcasm device, regardless of the realizations of that item, then it must also be the case that Feedback does not occur as a norm in the structure of those casual conversations. This repeated lack of Feedback or Follow-up being the case, any coder using the layout of three major columns – Opening, Answering, Follow-up – that works so neatly for the classroom data, merely finds himself with an empty third column: surely an adequate reason for deleting that third column.

This leaves the analyst with Opening and Answering Moves. Inside the classroom all parties are agreed that time will be spent in the transfer of information from teacher to pupils, with a ritualized structure of Informatives, Elicitations and Directives, and so on, to be employed by the Teacher to that end, and a set of appropriate reciprocal Acts and Moves to be employed by the Pupils to assist in the attainment of the Teacher's end. The teacher is in control of structural choices right through the hierarchy, in that when the pupils, or selected pupils, are given a place to interact, the type of Act they can appropriately use is selected and predetermined by the preceding Teacher Act. The teacher is also in control of content right through the hierarchy, in that he or she selects the topic for the lesson, the topic for Transactions, the topic for Exchanges, the topic for appropriate Moves and Acts. Outside the classroom it is no news to anyone that the situation is nothing like as simple, particularly since interactants, far from having a job to do by means of the talk, may simply talk for the sake of talking.

Certainly, structural and topical control are rarely in the hands of one participant only; indeed the common-sense interpretation of a conversationalist finding himself in such a position would be that his co-conversationalist was 'difficult to talk with'. Whilst Openings which coincide with Transaction boundaries are easy to find, in that of course the recognition criteria also coincide, other following Moves are often difficult to categorize, in that they can seem simultaneously to answer

141

a preceding Move and open up the way for a new Move. An extreme analytical view would be to see multiple Openings, where anything that was not a simple appropriate response to a preceding Act, say a Reply to an Elicitation, or an Acknowledge to an ongoing Inform, would be seen as another Opening. This would not, however, be of much structural or descriptive interest, since there are clearly relationships between successive utterances in casual conversations, even though they do not fit the classroom format. The biggest difference between classroom data and everyday talk is of course the wide range of verbal activities available to anyone answering an Opening. The polite consensus-collaborative model just has no room for the number of possibilities, where, for example, the 'answerer' can refuse to answer, can demand a reason for the question being asked or can provide an answer that simultaneously answers a preceding Move, but opens up the next exchange. This last possibility appears in many people's data, and analysts feel (wrongly) that they need to 'double code'. It certainly appears in my data, such that to remain within two simple columns representing Opening (including Framing and Focusing) and Answering would only be possible by forcing the data into categories that they do not really fit, and by ignoring other interesting structural complexities that should be represented.

My solution to these problems has been to reconceptualize conversational Moves in a fairly common-sense way, in that it seemed to me to be true that, given an Opening Move by speaker A, B has the choice either of politely agreeing, complying and supporting the discourse presuppositions in that Move, and behaving in a tidy, appropriate way in his choice of subsequent Moves and Acts, or of not agreeing, not supporting, not complying with those presuppositions, and possibly counter-proposing, ignoring or telling A that his Opening was misguided, badly designed and so on. This range of possibilities open to B (and of course subsequently to A, then to B and even to C, D and E) seemed to divide into two types of conversational behaviour, which, for mnemonic convenience only, I labelled 'Supporting' and 'Challenging' Moves. I am trying here to keep within the 'game' analogy suggested loosely by the notion 'Move'. Whilst it would be misguided to press this analogy too far, it is nevertheless helpful to see Moves as items which define the positions of the participants' utterances in relation to each other in the course of, say, a round of talk, leaving a different set of information to be conveyed by the choice of constituent Acts for these Moves.

The problem then was to find explicit criteria for recognizing these Moves (as well as other more familiar types of Move), an endeavour that became increasingly problematic as the data became more familiar, and I found that I had begun to conceptualize, say, A as 'aggressive', B as 'subservient', using these characterizations unconsciously as a way of determining what was being done in the talk instead of the other way round. I eventually realized that the problem could be resolved quite neatly by importing three concepts: (1) a notion of *Discourse Framework,* based on patterns of reciprocal Acts and cohesion; (2) Keenan and Schieffelin's (1976) idea of *Discourse Topic Steps,* necessary for establishment of a discourse topic; and (3) an extension of Labov's (1970) preconditions for the interpretation of any utterance as a request for action. I think the clearest way to explain the rank scale I am using is from the bottommost rank upwards, so I will do that, and explain these three concepts more fully under my description of Moves.

Considering Acts first, wherever it was possible I tried to restrict my coding at Act rank to the twenty-two Acts listed in Sinclair and Coult-hard (pp.40–4). Obviously, though, where this would have meant forcing the data into inappropriate categories, I revised and reconsidered that list. For the most part the twenty-two Acts were adequate, but I made some alterations and some additions. Some of the classroom Acts do not happen to occur in my data, for example, 'clue'. I think it would be unwise, at this stage, to delete them, as possibly they will occur in other data. I have not, however, given them a place in the apparatus here, though it is not difficult to imagine where they might fit, using intuitive examples. A list of newly-found or modified Acts follows: Marker; Summons; Accept; Accuse-Excuse; Inform-Comment; Preface.

There are other realizations for Markers. In the classroom, this item is realized by a closed class including 'Well', 'Right', 'OK', 'Good', 'Alright'. Its function is to mark boundaries in the discourse, and it occurs either as the pre-head signal in an Opening Move, or as the head of a Framing Move, in which case it is used with a falling intonation and followed by a silent stress. Maintaining this functional criterion, and given that I also recognize both Framing and Opening Moves in my data (the latter somewhat amended – see below), I also find this set of Markers, but need to extend the realization list to include items which, following Schegloff in Keenan (1977), I call 'expressive particles'; for example:

```
BEN  Kaw!              Marker + Silent Stress
     What about this?
     Listen to this!
```

Notice that in cases like this one, I take the exclamation mark to represent something like the equivalent of a silent stress.

I also found items I call 'Summonses'. An attention-getting item recurs in my data, when one participant uses the name of another in order to establish contact before introducing a discourse topic. Again, this marks boundaries in the discourse, and can occur either as the head of a Framing Move or as the Signal in an Opening Move. I have again borrowed the term itself from Schegloff (1968) in that this verbal item seems structurally and functionally analogous to non-verbal summonses like telephone or door bells. Both the verbal and non-verbal items occur in my data, and I refer to them both as Summonses:

```
GUS  Ben.              Summons
BEN  What?
GUS  Look here.        Directive
```

A similar item recurs, being Metastatements requesting speaking rights. Like Summonses, these requests for speaker's rights (compare Sacks, 1972) occur as pre-topic items, being variations on the classic 'You know what' formula of small children with restricted speaker's rights, or questions, or statements containing 'tell', or 'ask', for example:

```
BEN  You know what your trouble is.
```

or

```
GUS  I've been meaning to ask you something.
```

They occur as the heads of Focusing Moves, like Metastatements or Conclusions. It seems appropriate to list them as a sub-category of Metastatement, in that they do contain explicit reference to doing talking, and since, outside the classroom, there seems only a very fine line between these items and items that are more clearly Metastatements as described by Sinclair and Coulthard, in that they indicate what the next piece of talk is going to be about, for example:

```
BEN  Let me give you your instructions.
```

The important structural distinction between the use of Metastatements inside the classroom and outside it is that in the latter situation other participants may choose not to allow the speaker using the Metastatement

144

to go ahead with his designated talk. Thus, since both ordinary, classic Metastatements and these requests for speaker's rights require the approval of the other speaker, and occur in the same structural place, it would seem economic to see them both as Metastatements.

Outside the classroom, then, Summonses, Metastatements and requests for speaker's rights do not always go unchallenged, and, as a consequence of this possibility, in fact usually require some sort of 'go ahead' signal from a co-participant. This may be realized by a non-hostile silence, appropriate attention-giving gestures or formulaic responses, such as, A 'Do you know what?', B 'What?', or A 'Can I tell you a story?', B 'Yes' and so on. I label these 'Accept', bearing in mind part of the functional definition of that Act in Sinclair and Coulthard, 'to indicate that the Teacher has heard or seen and that the preceding Act was appropriate'. Of course in the classroom, Accept is a Follow-up Act, whereas in my coding it is the head of a Supporting Move.

Greetings do not of course occur in the classroom, although they frequently do so outside it. In that they are inevitably markers of boundaries in the talk, I see them as similar to Summonses for an opening greeting, and Accepts for a reply greeting. The first-pair part is coded as Summons, the second-pair part as Accept; thus they can be coded as the head of a Framing Move, followed by the head of a Supporting Move.

A particular feature that again does not seem to be relevant in the classroom, but recurs often in my data, occurs when speaker A uses a statement, question or command that is heard as requiring either an apology or an excuse/explanation, or else a justification (compare Austin, 1965). This statement, question or command varies in intensity from mild criticism to serious attack. Wherever the responses to this type of Act can be coded as an apology or excuse, I label the first-pair part 'Accuse', the second-pair part 'Excuse'. The rather nice ambiguity between the meaning of the noun 'excuse' and the verb 'excuse' covers the related but different types of response rather well.

Where there are long passages of Informatives offered in the text, it seems inadequate to give one label of 'Informative' to the whole passage, or even to label the first clause 'Inform' and all subsequent units 'Comment' — using the definition of Comment in Sinclair and Coulthard as 'to exemplify, expand, justify, provide additional information'. I have here followed some of the ideas suggested in Montgomery (1976) in his analysis of the discourse structure of information-transfer lectures. His very neat and interesting work is described in detail in Burton

(1978). In coding my data, I have found the following categories useful: Additive, Adversative and Causal items; Repeat, Restate and Qualifying items. It seems to me that the first three are sub-categories of Informative, as the head of an Opening Move, and the last three are sub-categories of Comment. Later Informing Acts can easily be classified under these six headings. Montgomery adapts the first three from Winter's more complex suggestions (Winter, 1977) on causal relationships. Additive items are typically but not necessarily introduced by 'and'. Adversative items are typically but not necessarily introduced by 'but'. Causal items are typically but not necessarily introduced by 'so'. They represent, of course, the three primary relationships to which, according to natural logic, all propositions can be reduced.

All these types of Informative can then be 'expanded' by the use of the other three Comment items. Repeats are Acts which, more or less, repeat the exact words, or some of the words, of an earlier Informative. Restate items rephrase an earlier Informative, while Qualifying items modify the general applicability of a preceding Informative. All Comment items may also be used, of course, to expand preceding Comment items. Coding with these seven labels is no longer coding at primary delicacy, but in that the data do not conform to the rather simple informing patterns required by the information transfer of the classroom, it seems uninteresting to do less. In my formal representation of the rank scale, I have restricted items to the two primaries, Inform and Comment, but these should be understood as superordinates. See also the notes below on coding conventions.

Following work on committee data (Stubbs, 1973), I have labelled Acts which introduce Re-Opening Moves as Prefaces. Stubbs recognizes three types of Prefaces — Misplacement Prefaces, Interruption Prefaces and Personal-Point-of-View Prefaces — which for my purposes I find it adequate to collapse into one general Act.

Misplacement Prefaces point out that the utterance following them will in some way be out of sequence. The term is borrowed from Schegloff and Sacks (1973), where they consider the notion of Misplacement Markers. They are typically, in committee data, rather elaborate:

Just one other comment Mike — you asked me just now what. . .

or

John — y'know this other information. . .

Stubbs gives the full possible form of a Misplacement Preface as follows:

1	2	3	4	5	6
term of address	mitigation	account	place-ment marker	self-referential metaterm	meta-reference to other speakers' talk

and produces a hypothetical example of how the full form of a Misplacement Preface might be realized:

1	2	3
John —	erm I think perhaps	it would be useful

4	5	6
before we go any further	if I sum up	some of the things Harry was saying

Interruption Prefaces are described as a particular type of Misplacement Preface, exhibiting surface markers which typically preface items designed to break into a flow of talk, for example:

> look — look let me let me let me let me make it patently clear . . .

The markers include: repetition of the first syllable or two; addressing someone by name; standard adversative words and formulae — 'but', 'no but'; items such as 'can I', 'could I', 'I must', 'let me', plus a self-referential statement. His suggestion for the full form of an Interruption Preface looks like this:

1	2	3
term of address	can I	self-referential metastatement
	could I	
	I must	
	let me	

Personal-Point-of-View Prefaces overlap to a certain extent with Interruption Prefaces in terms of their exponents. If, however, there is a clear indication that the speaker is expressing his own point of view, then the item is categorized specifically as a Personal-Point-of-View Preface, for example:

> personally I think we really . . .
> my real opinion is . . .
> I certainly don't . . .

Only one example in her labelled text!

This list, though useful for committee data, is in fact rather overbuilt for my own data — particularly since it is very much tidied-up talk. Thus I have collapsed the three types of Preface into one category of Preface.

I want to add a word or two here about my conventions in coding Acts on the analysis sheets (see below). I have loosely followed a suggestion in Halliday and Hasan (1975), where they analyse texts for cohesion, in that I have given each Act, usually a single clause (given the inclusion of Montgomery's categories), a number, indicating its sequential position within the Transaction. In this way the coded sheets can show relationships between Acts, these relationships being rather more complex than the often simple sentences exhibited in classroom data. Again this is arguably not coding at primary delicacy, but it seemed interesting to add this rather simple feature in the coding for the sake of extra information that it gives.

In the data I recognize seven types of Move: Framing, Focusing, Opening, Supporting, Challenging, Bound-Opening, Re-Opening. A discursive description follows.

Frames and Focuses are explicit markers of Transaction boundaries, and involve Acts that are essentially attention-getting, pre-topic items. Thus Frames are made up of a head which is either a Marker or a Summons, and silent stress as qualifier. Focuses comprise an optional signal (Marker or Summons), followed by an optional pre-head (Starter), a compulsory head (Metastatement or Conclusion) and an optional post-head (Comment — including Montgomery's additions to this).

Opening Moves may also be Transaction-initial, in which case the recognition criteria are the same as those for Transaction boundaries where Frames and Focuses are not employed; that is, they are Informatives, Elicitations or Directives which have no anaphoric reference to the immediately preceding utterance. This preceding utterance can then be seen to be the concluding utterance of a Transaction. Occasional problems occur in the data, for example, where a new Transaction can be recognized in this way, but where the very next utterance, from another speaker, adds what can be understood in a common-sense way to be another utterance in the Transaction just closed by the preceding Transaction-initial utterance. Where this does occur, I annotate the analysis sheet, but in general I have chosen to see such cases as overlapping ends and beginnings, rather than as a succession of new Transactions. Opening Moves then are essentially topic-carrying items which are recognizably 'new' in terms of the immediately preceding talk.

Where they are not Transaction-initial, they follow directly after Frame and/or Focus, where these have been used to attract the attention of the co-participant(s), to announce that a new topic will be coming.

Supporting Moves occur after all the other types of Move: Frames, Focuses, Openings, Challenges, Bound-Openings and Re-Openings. The data contain chains of Supporting Moves, but essentially the notion of a Supporting Move involves items that concur with the initiatory Moves they are Supporting. This means that in these chains, each Supporting Move can be related back to one of the other six types of Move. This being the case, whilst a Supporting Move may in fact follow another Supporting Move, functionally it serves to support a preceding Initiatory Move. Recognition of Supporting Moves depends upon a concept of Discourse Framework, which I will outline briefly here.

Discourse Framework concerns the presuppositions set up in the Initiating Move of an Exchange (that is, in any Move other than a Supporting Move), and the interactional expectations dependent on that Move. I want to argue that, for casual conversation, Exchanges can be seen to last as long as this Framework holds. The Discourse Framework set up by an Initiating Move has two aspects, which, loosely following Halliday (1971), I shall label (1) ideational and textual, (2) interpersonal.

The first of these, the ideational and textual, is defined lexico-semantically, and can be retrieved from the lexical items used in the topic-component of any initiating Move. The potential Discourse Framework dependent on that Move then includes all items that can be categorized as cohesive with that Move, using the notions covered in Halliday and Hasan (1975): substitution, ellipsis, conjunction and lexical cohesion.

The second aspect, the interpersonal, concerns interdependent or reciprocal Acts, where certain initiating Acts set up the expectations for certain responding Acts. Here the Discourse Framework can be retrieved differently from the Acts used pre-topically (in the optional initial Moves of a Transaction — Frames and Focuses) and from Acts used in topic-carrying Moves (in the compulsory Opening Move of a Transaction, and subsequent Re-Openings, Bound-Openings and Challenges).

Pre-topic Acts include the following:

Markers
Summonses
Metastatements

Topic-carrying Acts include the following:

Informatives
Elicitations
Directives
Accusations

If the appropriate and expected second-pair parts are added to these initiatory Acts the outline for the interpersonal aspect of the Discourse Framework is as follows:

Marker . . . . Acknowledge (including giving attention/
    non-hostile silence)
Summons . . . . Accept
Metastatement. . . . . . Accept
Informative . . . . . Acknowledge
Elicitation . . . . Reply
Directive . . . . React
Accuse . . . . Excuse

Given this concept of Discourse Framework, a Supporting Move is any Move that maintains the framework set up by a preceding Initiatory Move. If speaker A sets up the framework, then once speaker B has supported it, he may support it too. The idea in general is that in casual conversation speakers can Support a previous piece of *text* rather than a previous speaker.

As Supporting Moves function to facilitate the topic presented in a previous utterance, or to facilitate the contribution of a topic implied in a previous utterance, Challenging Moves function to hold up the progress of that topic or topic-introduction in some way. Challenging Moves can occur after any other Move, with the exception, in two-party talk, of following a Supporting Move. There are different types of Challenging Move, whose recognition depends on three different concepts – the idea of Discourse Framework outlined just above, the idea of discourse-topic steps, presented in Keenan and Schieffelin (1976), and an expansion of the necessary preconditions for interpreting any utterance as a request for action, as suggested by Labov (1970). I shall take each of these separately.

Firstly, Challenging Moves and Discourse Framework. A simple kind of Challenging Move is made by withholding an expected or appropriate reciprocal Act, where the expectation for this Act was set up in a preceding Initiatory Move. Thus, absence of, say, a Reply after an

Elicitation, or an Accept after a request-for-speaker's-rights Meta-statement, is seen as a Challenge (compare Sacks, 1972; Turner, 1970; and Schegloff, 1968; on the notion of justifiable absences).

Similarly, a Challenging Move can be made by supplying an unexpected and inappropriate Act where the expectation of another has been set up: for example, by producing a Marker where a React has been indicated as appropriate. At its most extreme, of course, this type of Challenge filters upwards through the system and brings about the opening of a new Transaction. Notice that although I have chosen the mnemonic 'Challenge', I certainly do not intend it necessarily to indicate hostility. A Challenging Move may divert the ongoing talk in quite an amicable way.

Secondly, Challenging Moves and discourse-topic steps. Keenan and Schieffelin's very interesting paper on topic as a discourse notion suggests that the following four steps are required, in order for the speaker to make his topic known to his hearer:

1 The speaker must secure the attention of the hearer
2 The speaker must articulate clearly
3 The speaker must provide sufficient information for the listener to identify objects, persons, ideas included in the discourse topic
4 The speaker must provide sufficient information for the listener to reconstruct the semantic relations obtaining between the referents in the discourse topic

To reformulate this in terms of Challenging Moves, the listener in this above-described situation may do one of four types of Challenge; again, either hostilely, or because of poor recipient design in the first place:

1 He may refuse to give his attention
2 He may ask for a repetition of the utterance
3 He may ask for clarification of information about the identification of objects, persons, ideas in the discourse topic
4 He may ask for more information concerning the semantic relations that obtain between the referents in the discourse topic

Thirdly, Challenging Moves and Labov's rules of interpretation. Labov, amongst his other extremely useful rules of interpretation linking 'what is said' with 'what is done', offers a general rule for interpreting any utterance as a request for action — a Directive.

"valid"?

If A requests B to perform an action X at a time T, A's utterance will be heard as a valid command only if the following preconditions hold: B believes that A believes that (it is an AB-event that)

1 X should be done for a purpose Y
2 B has the ability to do X
3 B has the obligation to do X
4 A has the right to tell B to do X

His own data is interesting in that it shows a speaker directly challenging several of these preconditions.

To these four I want to add more preconditions for hearing any utterance as either a valid Informative or a valid Elicitation:

"valid"?

If A informs B of an item of information P, A's utterance will be heard as a valid Informative only if the following preconditions hold: B believes that A believes that (it is an AB-event that)

5 A is in a position to inform B of P
6 P is a reasonable piece of information
7 B does not already know P
8 B is interested in P
9 B is not offended/insulted by P

odd use of "valid"

If A asks B for a linguistic response from B concerning a question M, it will be heard as a valid Elicitation only if the following preconditions hold: A believes that B believes that (it is an AB-event that)

10 B hears M as a sensible question
11 A does not know M
12 It is the case that B might know M
13 It is the case that A can be told M
14 It is the case that B has no objection to telling M to A.

Again, each of these preconditions has its corresponding Challenging Move, as Labov himself makes clear in his own data. In my coding of the data, I index each Challenge, where it is not a simple breach of the Discourse Framework, with reference either to Keenan and Schieffelin (KS 1, 2, 3, 4) or to Labov (L 1–14), in order to indicate what sort of Challenge I understand the data to represent.

Bound-Opening Moves occur after a preceding Opening, Bound-Opening or Re-Opening Move has been Supported. They specifically enlarge the Discourse Framework by extending the ideational-textual aspect of the original Opening Move, employing the various types of

Informative and Comment Acts presented in the discussion of Montgomery (1976) above.

Re-Opening Moves occur after a preceding Opening, Bound-Opening or Re-Opening has been Challenged. They reinstate the topic that the Challenge either diverted or delayed. They are made up of optional Prefaces, as pre-heads, with compulsory Informs/Comments as heads.

[handwritten margin note: etc.? or Elicits or Directives or Acts...]

As we move up the rank scale, I recognize two types of Exchanges: Explicit Boundary Exchanges and Conversational Exchanges. Explicit Boundary Exchanges are optional Exchanges at the openings of Transactions. They are made up of a Frame or a Focus, or a Frame and a Focus together, and must be Supported by another speaker. This Support may be negatively realized (as it is in the classroom) and it is then a matter of interpretation for both the analyst and the co-participants to determine whether Support has in fact been given. Conversational Exchanges begin with an initiation which may be either an Opening, a Re-Opening or a Challenging Move. They may be followed by one or several Supporting Moves, and may then be followed by a Bound-Opening, which may itself be Supported one or several times, after which Bound-Openings may recur together with recursive Supports.

Since Transactions either begin with Frame, Focus or an Opening Move, the recognition criteria for Transaction boundaries are the same as those for the beginnings of these Moves. It might be useful, however, to repeat them here. (1) Frames: the presence of a Marker or a Summons, together with Silent Stress. (2) Focuses: the presence of a Metastatement (which may be a request for speaker's rights) or a Conclusion. The optional use of a Marker or Summons preceding this, and the optional use of a Starter immediately before the Metastatement or Conclusion. (3) The presence of an Informative, Elicitation, Directive or Accusation with no anaphoric referent in the preceding utterance. This may be preceded by a Marker or Summons, and/or a Starter, and may of course be followed by a Comment or Prompt.

Transactions themselves are made up of an optional Explicit Boundary Exchange, a compulsory Conversational Exchange with an *Opening* Move as Initiator, an unordered sequence of Conversational Exchanges with Bound-Openings, Re-Openings and Challenges as their Initiators.

A formal description of the rank scale follows. I here adopt the layout used in Sinclair and Coulthard.

Discourse

RANK I: Interaction

Elements of Structure	Structures	Classes of Transaction
	An unordered string of Transactions	

RANK II: Transaction

Elements of Structure	Structures	Classes of Exchange
Preliminary (P)	$(P)O(C(R)^n)^n$	P: Explicit Boundary
Opening (O)		O: Conversational with Opening as Initiator
Challenging (C)		C: Conversational with Challenge as Initiator
Re-Opening (R)		R: Conversational with Re-Opening as Initiator

RANK III: Exchange (Explicit Boundary)

Elements of Structure	Structures	Classes of Move
Frame (Fr)	$(Fr \text{ } Fo) S$	Fr: Framing
Focus (Fo)		Fo: Focusing·
Supporting (S)		S: Supporting

RANK III: Exchange (Conversational) —(*Opening, Challenging, Re-Opening*) eh?

Elements of Structure	Structures	Classes of Move
Initiation (I)	$I(R(I^r(R)^n)^n)^n$	I: Opening or Challenging or Re-Opening
Responses (R)		R: Supporting
Re-Initiation (I^r)		I^r: Bound-Opening

RANK IV: Move (Framing)

Elements of Structure	Structures	Classes of Act
head (h)	hq	h: Marker or Summons
qualifier (q)		q: Silent Stress

154

RANK IV: Move (*Focusing*)

Elements of Structure	Structures	Classes of Act
signal (s) pre-head (pre-h) head (h) post-head (post-h)	(s) (pre-h) h (post-h)	s: Marker or Summons pre-h: Starter h: Metastatement or Conclusion post-h: Comment

RANK IV: Move (*Opening*)

Elements of Structure	Structures	Classes of Act

signal (s)
pre-head (pre-h)
head (h)
 	
post-head (post-h)
	(s) (pre-h) h (post-h)	s: Marker or Summons
		pre-h: Starter
		h: Information or
		  Elicitation or
		  Directive or
		  Accusation
		post-h: Comment
		  or Prompt or Clue

RANK IV: Move (*Supporting*)

Elements of Structure	Structures	Classes of Act

pre-head (pre-h)
head (h)
post-head (post-h)
	(pre-h) h (post-h)	pre-h: Accept
		h: Acknowledge or
		  Reply or React
		  or Excuse
		post-h: Comment

RANK IV: Move (*Challenging*)

Elements of Structure	Structures	Classes of Act

pre-head (pre-h)
head (h)
post-head (post-h)
	(pre-h) h (post-h)	pre-h: Starter or Preface
		h: Informative or
		  Elicitation or
		  Directive or
		  Accusation
		post-h: Comment
		  or Prompt

Discourse

RANK IV: Move (*Bound-Opening*)

Elements of Structure	Structures	Classes of Act

pre-head (pre-h)
head (h)
post-head (post-h)
	(pre-h) h (post-h)	pre-h: Starter or Preface
		h: Informative or
		    Elicitation or
		    Directive or
		    Accusation
		post-h: Comment or
		    Prompt

RANK IV: Move (*Re-Opening*)

Elements of Structure	Structures	Classes of Act

pre-head (pre-h)
head (h)
post-head (post-h)
	(pre-h) h (post-h)	pre-h: Starter or Preface
		h: Informative or
		    Elicitation or
		    Directive or
		    Accusation
		post-h: Comment or
		    Prompt

Summary of the Acts

Label	Symbol	Realization and Definition
Marker	m	Realized by a closed class of items — 'Well', 'OK', 'Now', 'Good', 'Alright' and expressive particles, e.g. 'Kaw', 'Blimey'. Its function is to mark boundaries in the discourse and to indicate that the speaker has a topic to introduce
Summons	sum	Realized by a closed class of verbal and non-verbal items — the use of the name of another participant, or mechanical devices like door bells, telephone bells, etc. Its function is to mark a boundary in the discourse, and to indicate that the producer of the item has a topic to introduce once he has gained the attention of the hearer

Label	Symbol	Realization and Definition
Silent Stress	Λ	Realized by a pause, indicated in the text by either an exclamation mark or a stage direction following a Marker. It functions to highlight the Marker or Summons when they act as the head of a Boundary Exchange
Starter	s	Realized by a statement, question, command or moodless item. Its function is to provide information about, direct attention or thought towards an area, in order to make a correct response to the coming Initiation more likely
Metastatement	ms	Realized by a statement, question or command which refers to a future event in the ongoing talk, or a request for speaker's rights. Its function is to make clear the structure of the immediately following discourse, and to indicate the speaker's wish for an extended turn
Conclusion	con	Realized by an anaphoric statement, which can be seen as the complement to Metastatement, in that its function is to make clear the structure of the immediately preceding discourse
Informative	i	Realized by a statement whose sole function is to provide information. The appropriate response is the giving of attention and indication of understanding
Elicitation	el	Realized by a question. Its function is to request a linguistic response. Occasionally it may be realized by a command requesting a linguistic response
Directive	d	Realized by a command, and functions to request a non-linguistic response
Accusation	accn	Realized by a statement, question, command or moodless item. Its function is to request an apology or a surrogate excuse

bosh!

157

Label	Symbol	Realization and Definition
Comment	com	Realized by a statement, question, command or moodless item, and functions to expand, justify, provide additional information to a preceding Informative or Comment
Accept	acct	Realized by a closed class of items — 'Yes', 'OK', 'Uhuh', 'I will', 'No' (Where the preceding utterance was negative). Its function is to indicate that the speaker has heard and understood the previous utterance and is compliant
Reply	rep	Realized by a statement, question, moodless items and non-verbal surrogates such as nods. Its function is to provide a linguistic response appropriate to a preceding elicitation
React	rea	Realized by a non-linguistic action. Its function is to provide an appropriate non-linguistic response to a preceding directive
Acknowledge	ack	Realized by 'Yes', 'OK', 'Uhuh' and expressive particles. Its function is to show that an Informative has been understood, and its significance appreciated
Excuse	ex	Realized by a formulaic apology, or a statement or moodless item which substitutes for an apology and is thus heard as an excuse. Its function is to provide an appropriate response to a preceding accusation
Preface	pr	Realized by combinations of placement markers, self-referential meta-terms and meta-reference to preceding talk. Its function is to show that a diverted topic is being re-introduced

Label	Symbol	Realization and Definition
Prompt	p	Realized by a closed class of items — 'Go on', 'What are you waiting for', 'Hurry up'. Its function is to reinforce a preceding Directive or Elicitation
Evaluate	ev	Realized by a statement, question, command or moodless item. Its function is to comment on the appropriateness of a preceding utterance

The following coded pages take the first ten Transactions of Pinter's *The Dumb Waiter*. Whilst it was not possible to find a reasonably sized selection that would demonstrate all the coding categories, I think that this piece contains a representative sample of problems, and will, I hope, serve to clarify my approach to the data in general.

It will be obvious that I am coding only one interpretation of the text, and, as we do not have precise information about the intonation patterns here, many utterances are necessarily ambiguous. Where stage directions are relevant they are included to substantiate this interpretation, but otherwise, I have had to make decisions about what is happening in the text in the same way that actors or directors would have to do. For example, in Transaction 1, I have coded utterances 13–21 as Supporting items, 'hearing' them as expressing interest or fascination in the news story rather than simple disbelief, simply because a recent production I attended presented the actors playing the lines that way. It would, of course, be possible to take the alternative view, in which case some of Guy's utterances would be coded as Challenges, and the subsequent analysis contour would look very different. I do not want to dwell on this issue here, though it is interesting to observe how some writers give explicit clues for their interpreters, and some give no hints at all. This means of course that there are differing amounts of freedom of interpretation available in different texts, and the descriptive apparatus is one way of showing exactly what happens to the network of choices available, once a single item is realized in different ways. For the present, I ask only that you see my coding as a reasonable and possible interpretation of the words in the text — not by any means as the only analysis.

	Challenging Move	Act	Opening Move	Frame	Act	Supporting Move	Act
Trans. 1 Boundary			1 B Kaw	Frame	m		
Opening			2 What about this?		s		
			3 Listen to this!		s		
			4 A man of 87 wanted to cross the road		inf		
			5 But there was a lot of traffic see		adv4		
			6 He couldn't see how he was going to squeeze through		add5		
			7 So he crawled under a lorry		cau		
Challenge	8 G He what? (KS 2)	el					
Re-Opening			9 He crawled under a lorry		rep7		
			10 A stationary lorry		qual9	11 G No?	ack 10
Bound-Opening			12 B The lorry started and ran over him		add7		
						13 G Go on!	ack 12
						14 B That's what it says here	com 12
						15 G Get away!	ack 12

See top p146 ~150 143

	Challenging Move	Act	Opening Move	Act	Supporting Move	Act
					16 B It's enough to make you want to puke isn't it?	ack 12
					17 G Who advised him to do a thing like that?	ack 12
					18 A man of 87 crawling under a lorry	rept 4, 7
					19 G It's unbelievable	ack
					20 B It's down here in black and white	com
					21 G Incredible	ack
Trans.2			Focus			
Boundary			1 G I want to ask you something	ms		
Challenge	B (no response) (KS 1)					
Trans.3						
Opening			1 B What are you doing out there?	el	2 G Well I was just –	rep 1
Bound-Opening			3 B What about the tea?	el	4 G I'm just going to make it	rep 3

161

	Challenging Move	Act	Opening Move	Act	Supporting Move	Act
Bound-Opening			5 B Well go on, make it	dir	6 G Yes, I will	rea
Trans.4 Opening			1 G He's laid on some very nice crockery this time	inf		
			2 I'll say that	com 1		
			3 It's sort of striped	qual 1		
			4 There's a white stripe	qual 3		
Challenge	(Ben reads) (KS 1)					
Re-Opening			5 G It's very nice	rest 11		
			6 I'll say that	rept 2		
Challenge	(Ben reads) (KS 1)					
Re-Opening			7 G You know sort of round the cup	qual 4		
			8 Round the rim	qual 7		
			9 All the rest of it's black you see	qual 3		
			10 Then the saucer's black	rest 9		
			11 Except for right in the middle	qual 10		
			12 where the cup goes	rest 11		
			13 where it's white	rest 11		
				12		

	Challenging Move	Act	Opening Move	Act	Supporting Move	Act
Challenge	(Ben reads) (KS 1)					
Re-Opening			14 G Then the plates are the same you see	add		
			15 only they've got a black stripe	qual 14		
			16 — the plates —	rept 14		
			17 right across the middle	qual 15		
			18 Yes, I'm quite taken with the crockery	rest 1		
Challenge	19 B What do you want plates for? (L 6)	el				
	20 You're not going to eat	com				
Challenge	21 G I've brought a few biscuits (L 10)	rep				
Challenge	22 B Well you'd better eat them quickly (L 9)	dir				
Re-Opening			23 G I always bring a few biscuits	inf		
			24 Or a pie	qual 23		
			25 You know I can't drink tea without anything to eat	com		

	Challenging Move	Act	Opening Move	Act	Supporting Move	Act
Challenge	26 B Well make the tea then will you (L 8)	dir				
	27 Time's getting on	com				
Trans.5						
Opening			1 G You got any cigarettes?	el		
			2 I think I've run out	com		*why not inf?*
Challenge	(no response) (KS 1)					
Trans.6						
Opening			1 G I hope it won't be a long job this one	inf		*why not com?*
Challenge	(no response) (KS 1)					
Trans.7						
Boundary			1 G Oh Focus	m		
			2 I wanted to ask you something	ms		
Challenge	(no response) (KS 1)					
Trans.8						
Boundary			1 B Kaw! Frame	m		
					2 G What's that?	acct

	Challenging Move	Act	Opening Move	Act	Supporting Move	Act
Opening			3 B A child of 8 killed a cat	inf	4 G Get away	ack
					5 B It's a fact	com 3
					6 What about that eh?	ack 3
					7 A child of 8 killing a cat	rept 3
Bound-Opening Challenge	9 B It was a girl (L 10)	inf	8 G How did he do it?	el		
Re-Opening			10 G How did she do it?	el	11 B She –	rep
Challenge	12 B It doesn't say (L 12)	inf				
Challenge	13 G Why not? (L 6)	el				
Challenge	14 B Wait a minute (L 14)	dir				
Re-Opening			15 B It just says Her brother, aged 11 viewed the incident from the woodshed	pref		
				rep 10		
Challenge	16 G Go on! (L 6)	ack				
	17 That's bloody ridiculous	ack				
Re-Opening Challenge	19 B Who? (KS 3)	el	18 G I bet he did it	inf		

Challenging Move	Act	Opening Move	Act	Supporting Move	Act
Re-Opening					
		20 G The brother	rep19		
				21 B I think you're right	ev
				22 What about that eh?	ack
				23 A kid of 11 killing a cat and blaming it on his little sister of 8	rest 3
					18
				24 It's enough to —	com
Trans.9					
Opening					
		1 G What time is he getting in touch?	el		
Challenge					
(Ben reads) (KS 1)					
Re-Opening					
		2 G What time is he getting in touch?	rest 1		
Challenge					
3 B What's the matter with you? (L 10)	el				
4 It could be any time	rep 2				
5 Any time	rest 4				
Trans.10					
Boundary					
		Focus			
		1 G Well I was going to ask you something	ms		
				2 B What?	acct

	Challenging Move	Act	Opening Move	Act	Supporting Move	Act
Opening			3 G Have you noticed the time that tank takes to fill?	el		
Challenge	4 B What tank (KS 4)	el				
Re-Opening			5 G In the lavatory	rep 4	6 B No.	rep 3
					7 Does it?	el
					8 G Terrible	rep 7
Challenge	9 B Well what about it? (L 10)	el				
Re-Opening			10 G What do you think's the matter with it?	el	11 B Nothing	rep 10
Challenge	12 G Nothing? (L 6)	el				
Challenge	13 B It's got a deficient ballcock, that's all (L 10)	rep 12				
Challenge	14 G A deficient what? (KS 3)				15 B Ballcock	rep 14
					16 No? Really?	ack 15
					17 B That's what I should say	rest 14
					18 G Go on!	ack 17
					19 That didn't occur to me	qual 18

Chapter 8

Suggestions for further research

In this final chapter, I hope to draw together a range of suggestions for further work in the related fields of dialogue and discourse studies. These suggestions vary from the highly specific (that is, work that would have been presented in this book, had there been world enough and time and space) to much wider topics concerning research in the general area of literary-linguistic practice and theory. As a preliminary to these suggestions, I shall offer here a summary of what I see as the main characteristics of the work so far presented.

The book is an attempt to relate some recent work in discourse analysis to a neglected area of linguistic-stylistics: the effects created in modern drama texts. The original aim was simply to further work and ideas in these two areas simultaneously; firstly, using discourse-analysis findings to explain effects in simulated talk, and secondly, using this simulated talk as a heuristic device to suggest modifications and innovations in the analysis of spoken discourse. Particularly, I was hoping to extend the scope of application of a rigorous linguistic analysis of conversation. Given the state of both stylistics and discourse analysis, it has been necessary to proceed in rather general terms, and in a sense there are several potential other books lurking behind each chapter. However, to have expanded any one detailed area at the expense of a broader perspective would certainly have been unwarranted here. The very fact that there is no simple body of secondary literature on dialogue and discourse to review is a clear indication of how much preliminary work is still to be done. Interested readers may perhaps like to compare the following, however: Coulthard (1977), chapter 9; Widdowson (1979); Willes (1976); Short (forthcoming).

I have, then, deliberately maintained a very general approach, trying to set out quite basic parameters, demonstrating both possibilities and limitations of the enterprise. Hopefully, the suggestions encapsulated

168

explicitly or implicitly here will enable further research and other researchers to develop what is potentially a very rich field of linguistic and literary interdisciplinary study.

I would like to make explicit some areas of research that seem to arise immediately out of earlier chapters. I shall offer brief suggestions relating to dialogue, brief suggestions relating to discourse and then an extended consideration of ways of understanding overheard interaction in the theatre and in general.

With reference to the study of *The Bald Prima Donna* in chapter 2, it would be both feasible and profitable for a bilingual English–French speaker to study this text in its original French, together with the translation, in terms of discourse analysis specifically. I deliberately avoided any amateur discussion of the French text myself, although a tentative hypothesis concerning politeness phenomena was offered at one stage. Clearly, for this type of work to be properly undertaken, the discourse analyst would need to have user's competence in both languages. Extending this bilingual approach to stylistics, discourse analysis and translation, a particularly interesting writer to focus on in this way would be Samuel Beckett, who writes his texts in his second language, and only then translates or approves a translation into what is his first language. There has, of course, been interesting work on these texts (see, for example, Jones, 1972), but not yet at the linguistic level of discourse. These sorts of studies would have direct relevance both to considerations about the status of translated text, and to the value of discourse analysis as part of the art of translation. They would also be of direct benefit to work in discourse analysis, as the practical analyses of these texts would undoubtedly highlight a host of translation problems at discourse level, which would foreground new insights for analysts of discourse in whichever languages were concerned.

It would also be interesting to extend the approach used in chapters 2 and 3 to studying represented speech in other genres; both literary (prose-fiction, poetry) and non-literary (foreign language textbooks, transcripts of legal proceedings and so on). Here, and particularly obviously in the first case, other formalist features of the structure in the texts would have to be appropriately located as well. A blend of stylistics with poetics is both feasible and desirable, however.

Just as dialogue (when naturalistic sounding) can demonstrate what authors, as lay-sociologists, know and have observed about naturally occurring conversations, so too do many contextualizing narrative comments in, say, prose-fiction. A study of any individual author, or

169

set of authors, which focused on these types of comments, in comparison with observations made by sociolinguists, would be very revealing, both in terms of the writer(s) and the text(s), and also in terms of the academic status of work in conversational analysis.

Suggestions for further work in discourse analysis concern the model presented in chapter 7. It was devised, over time and with some difficulty, with reference to *The Dumb Waiter* and *The Bald Prima Donna*. Whilst it seems to account adequately for these data, it needs to be checked, and perhaps modified, against other data. These could be drawn from drama, or, more importantly, given the overall aim of extending the analysis of discourse to cope with casual conversation, from naturally occurring conversation. The model also certainly requires input from intonation studies (see, especially, Brazil 1978; Coulthard, Brazil and Johns, forthcoming).

Should the model prove usable in this way, it would be interesting to try to classify different conversations from the evidence of the coded analysis sheets, as opposed to the current practice of classifying conversations on common-sense notions of 'situation'. Crudely, this might mean that a transcript which frequently utilized the left-hand column would be a more competitive conversation than one which utilized the right-hand column. And conclusions could be drawn about the interactants from the amount of Transaction boundaries they produced, or whether they favoured Bound-Openings, and so on.

As was indicated in chapter 7, the coded sheets represent only one interpretation of the text, and that is made here without the benefit of any audial clues. Two research possibilities are immediately suggested in relation to this. Firstly, different productions of the same text could be recorded and analysed. Without doubt, they would produce different interpretations, and thus different coding contours. The analysis charts might then be a reasonable means of graphically representing such variable interpretations, similar to records of choreography in different productions of ballets. Secondly, it would be interesting to study different playwrights in terms of just how much leeway they allow their interpreters. If, for example, they use very few stage directions (like 'angrily' or 'hesitantly'), and offer many utterances with little propositional content, then their texts should leave a great deal of room for interpretation. Similar work could be done on dialogue in novels, of course.

As an extension of these ideas, it would be interesting for new pieces to be written, where the writers have a set of interpretations in mind, in terms of the discourse functions of the represented speech. They could experiment with informants to see whether these intentions could be deduced from the text, and if so, by what means such interpretation might be facilitated.

Clearly, there is a very rich and wide field waiting to be explored by linguists interested in literary text. Whilst the relationship between discourse analysis and stylistics can only be at a tentative stage at present, it is hoped that the work here may provide a basis for further studies in this area. I shall now, though, turn to the rather large and important subject of theatre interaction and 'overheard conversation'.

I want to clarify some aspects of theatre interaction, in order to locate and facilitate various types of further discussion and analysis, and to avoid any over-simplistic assumptions or implications being drawn from the discussion presented in chapters 2 and 3 and 7. Clearly no 'interaction situation' or 'context of situation' can ever be charted in full (see Winograd, 1972, for a possible modification of this), but there are a number of specific observations that can be made about interaction in the theatre that are relevant to the topic of this book. Goffman (1974, p. 127) states the central problem thus:

> In considering legitimate stage performance it is all too common
> to speak of interaction between performer and audience. That
> easy conclusion conceals the analysis that would be required to
> make sense of this interaction, conceals the fact that participants
> in a conversation can be said to interact too, conceals, indeed,
> the fact that the term 'interaction' equally applies to everything
> one might want to distinguish.

I am particularly interested here in distinguishing pertinent features of both interaction in the theatre *per se*, and also interaction on stage as compared with interaction in everyday life.

When I began to try to work out ideas on this topic, I turned my attention to three closely related types of literature which, I assumed, would prove a fruitful source of material and ideas. Loosely these can be categorized as follows:

> 1 Work by sociologists who write about the theatre and its similarity to everyday life (for example, Simnel, 1898; Gurvitch, 1956; Duvignand, 1965).

> 2 Work by sociologists who write about life and its similarity to drama (Goffman, 1959; Turner, 1970; Burns, 1974; Rockwell, 1974; Lyman and Scott, 1975).

3 Work by dramatists who demonstrate the fine line that divides
drama and life (for example, Pirandello, 1922; Stoppard, 1967).

These approaches seem to me to have a very direct bearing on general
notions in the sociology of drama, and more particular relevance to the
sociolinguistics of drama. Clearly, there is a complex area of related
work here that needs to be considered and compared before the sociolinguist can talk intelligently about lifelike stage-talk, or talk in the
theatre at all.

When I tried to reconcile the observations and statements in these
three areas, which were, certainly, very rich and stimulating, I immediately encountered severe difficulties. There is an interesting if tantalizing feature in the style of much of this work, in that the writers concerned very often use neatly structured epigrammatic statements that
simultaneously state and demonstrate the complexities of the descriptions and definitions they are trying to make. For example,
Duvignand (1965):

> The theatre in society: society in the theatre

or Gurvitch (1956):

> The theatre is a sublimation of certain social situations, whether
> it idealizes them, parodies them, or calls for them to be transcended.
> The theatre is simultaneously a sort of escape hatch from social
> conflicts and the embodiment of these conflicts. From this point
> of view it contains a paradoxical element or rather, a theatrical
> dialectic, which is supremely a dialectic of ambiguity. The theatre
> is society or the group looking at itself in various mirrors.

Erving Goffman's famous caveat in his extended dramaturgical metaphor (Goffman, 1959) sums up the complexity of this writing very
well: 'All the world is not, of course, a stage, but the ways in which it
is not are difficult to determine.' Writing such as this, and certainly the
intricate problems posed by the dramatists themselves, undoubtedly
reinforces the fascination of the topic, but, unfortunately for the
critic or analyst, only increases the mystery of the very phenomena he
is trying to understand. Tantalizing questions and stimulating problems
are continually and repeatedly offered, but satisfactory answers and
clear definitive descriptions are not in evidence.

My early attempts at putting together and comparing the arguments
and statements to be found in these three literatures floundered hope-
lessly as the actual, formal details of situations that they were supposed

to be presenting for the reader's comprehension slipped uneasily from anecdote to epigram. Juxtaposed examples in the texts seemed to demonstrate little in the way of any organization towards rigorous conclusions. And I was certainly far from being able to answer the fundamental question posed in the introduction to Hymes (1972a): 'Which of the many aspects of verbal behaviour do we observe, and what concepts do we utilize in classifying what we observe, to ensure comparability of data?'

The aim was indeed to be able to talk *comparatively* about a range of interaction situations, whose intricacies could be perceived haphazardly and intuitively, but whose parameters and relationships it was extremely difficult to specify precisely. What I then tried to do was to find a formal model to represent the basic features in all the interaction events that the three types of writers described and presented, so that the similarities and differences in the examples they were using could be mapped out both quickly and precisely.

I want to describe here, then, a model I have devised that helps me to understand and compare what is being said and done in different play-texts. I also want to describe a problem encountered when first formulating the model. Like Schegloff (1968) I found that my first assessment and formulation of the speech event I was trying to analyse failed to match the data. But a significant reformulation of the features of the speech event enabled me to account efficiently for even more material than I had originally envisaged. I think the model can help to make clear some rather delicate features of individual utterances that are difficult to grasp and describe in a rigorous, comparative way by any other means — the lengthy prose of the work already described, for example. I think it is also useful as a way of characterizing longer stretches of play-talk in a linguistically interesting way.

I want to begin by focusing on the idea of potential channels of verbal interaction that hold for the theatre. This seems to be a central problem for the sociolinguist who is interested in understanding and describing features of drama dialogue. I should make it clear from the beginning that the theatre for which I am going to provide a model is the standard fourth-wall realistic bourgeois theatre. With this as a standard or norm, it is also of course possible to show precisely which features the various avant-garde writers have chosen to exploit in order to shock their audiences' expectations. Similarly, it would be easy enough to demonstrate relationships that hold between this and earlier conventions in drama, both in western and oriental cultures; however, this is outside my interests at the present time. I realize that to sophisti-cated readers, this type of theatre is only one type among many. None the less, it does still hold a central position in the theatre industry, and this, together with the undoubted evidence of the powerful responses evoked by avant-garde writers at various times and in various places this century, convinces me that any central, basic model of theatre interaction must have this as its first paradigm.

All literary discourse involves complex channels of interaction (see Widdowson, 1973 or 1975), but I want to focus entirely on what can be said about channels of interaction within a theatre building, and during a performance. I am here leaving aside all ideas about the author, editor or producer, or any other background figure, and am concen-trating on what happens when an utterance is produced by a character on the stage, and is heard both by other characters and the audience simultaneously. For, clearly, whilst stage-talk shares certain characteris-tics with real-talk, there is one absolutely fundamental difference, in that stage-talk is routinely produced to be 'overheard' by a party not (usually) involved in that discourse in the microcosm.

In passing, let me point out that there is a related situation and problem here for the analyst of naturally occurring conversation, in that talk may often be produced for the benefit of people outside the interaction itself – bystanders, passers-by, onlookers and so on (see Goffman *passim*, but in particular 1971). Sinclair and Coulthard (1975, p.115) make this point too:

> Most verbal interaction is private in the sense that it is intended
> solely for the participants, but there are situations where the
> speaker is conscious of two audiences, the one that is verbally
> interacting with him, and the one that is listening in to the
> situation. It is arguable that as soon as one puts a tape-recorder
> into a situation it is no longer strictly private, but private situa-
> tions can still be distinguished from public ones according to
> intention, whether the interaction is directly aimed at a second
> audience. In media discussions, for example, one of the functions
> of a chairman is to clarify for the audience, references which may
> not be readily understandable by the audience. The effect of the
> audience on the interaction and the way in which participants take
> notice of the audience are obviously highly complex questions and
> at the moment we are not sure how to begin answering them.

'To begin answering' these questions is precisely what I hope to do below, although I think the notion that public and private situations can be distinguished from each other by intention is over-simple, as it begins with observations on the wrong sorts of external criteria. I am sure that any model that helps to clarify what is happening in talk-on-stage and in a theatre can also help to clarify what is happening in these frequently occurring everyday overheard conversations. What the analyst needs, in both cases, is a means of efficiently grasping and describing the basic aspects of all kinds of 'overheard' interactions.

An existing model that strikes me as particularly relevant to this problem is Jakobson's adaptation of Bühler's work on the primary functions of the utterance (see Jakobson, 1960; and Bühler, 1933). There are of course several other models of a similar sort (for example, Hymes, 1972b, 1974; Burke, 1945; Soskin and John, 1963; Halliday, 1969; Ervin-Tripp, 1964). In a sense any of these would have suited my purposes equally well, but since all of them have their associated problems and inadequacies, I have chosen Jakobson's because it is relatively simple and easy to handle, as well as being probably the most familiar to other readers. It would, though, be sensible if I gave a brief summary of the relevant part of his paper, to make his underlying assumptions clear. We should perhaps bear in mind that his overall purpose in the paper was to demonstrate the essential place of poetics within the linguistic-literary analysis, and theory, of literary text.

Within this framework, Jakobson sets up a schematic representation of the ways in which the linguist can differentiate channels of information exchange (in the widest sense — see Laver and Hutcheson, 1972, p.12) in any utterance, looking for the 'means used' and 'the effects aimed at'. Whilst mentioning Sapir's statement that 'ideation reigns supreme in any language', he goes on to set up a description of the other complementary functions that need to be taken into account in the production and comprehension of any utterance. He starts with what he calls the six basic aspects to be distinguished, and which are observable as the constitutive factors of any speech event:

The ADDRESSER sends a MESSAGE to the ADDRESSEE. To be operative the message requires a CONTEXT (referred to as 'referent' in another, somewhat ambiguous nomenclature) seizable by the addressee, and either verbal or capable of being verbalized, a CODE fully or at least partially common to the addresser and the addressee (or in other words to the encoder and the decoder of the message); and finally a CONTACT, a physical and psychological

175

connection between an addresser and an addressee enabling both
of them to stay in communication.

These are schematized in Figure 8.1.

CONTEXT

MESSAGE
ADDRESSER. . . . . ADDRESSEE
CONTACT

CODE

Figure 8.1.

Onto this he maps six basic functions which complement these
aspects of any speech event. Thus, he matches EMOTIVE or EX-
PRESSIVE function to the addresser, in much the same way as the
original Prague School thesis did — the focus being on the direct expression of the speaker's attitude to what he is speaking about. He cites
a story of a Stanislavskyan actor saying 'Good evening' in forty intonation patterns, thus indicating forty different interpretations of the
speaker's general attitude. The opposite orientation — with a focus on
the addressee — he calls the CONATIVE function. This is most clearly
expressed in imperatives, which have a direct and observable effect on
the addressee. The other staple for Bühler was the REFERENTIAL
function, with its focus on context. This is in some sense 'what the
message is about': the ideational or propositional content. To this
Jakobson adds the PHATIC function, with its emphasis on estab-
lishing and maintaining contact. A simple example would be any ritual
greeting that functions strictly as a greeting, and not in terms of its
propositional content. Thus, the appropriate ritual reply to 'How are
you' is a similar greeting, not a description of your gouty leg. He also
adds a function that focuses on code, and calls it METALINGUAL.
This is talk about talk, glossing or any reference to the code that is
being used. Thus, for example, much teacher-talk is quite specifically
metalingual; for example, 'That's not a proper sentence'. The set
towards the message itself he calls the POETIC FUNCTION, and thus
accounts for a focus on form or pattern for structural or aesthetic

reasons. Rhyme, alliteration, parallel clause structures are simple examples of this.

His cursory description has been even more cursorily described here – but sufficiently I hope to make the mapping of aspects and functions clear in Figure 8.2.

CONTEXT
(REFERENTIAL)

MESSAGE
(POETIC)

ADDRESSER . . . . ADDRESSEE
(EXPRESSIVE)   (CONATIVE)

CONTACT
(PHATIC)

CODE
(METALINGUAL)

Figure 8.2.

What is absolutely crucial for his purposes, and mine, is the assumption that in most normal speech situations all of these aspects and functions are routinely usable, observable and accountable. However, any particular utterance, speech act or text can and must be described according to which of these functions are highlighted, foregrounded or stressed. Also, of course, some odd speech events may be described according to an absent aspect or function. As Jakobson says himself:

> Even though a set towards the referent, an orientation towards the CONTENT. . . is the leading task of numerous messages, the accessory participation of the other functions in such messages must be taken into account by the observant linguist.

When it comes to play-talk, clearly we have, somehow, to map on another dimension to cope with the fact that, when a character is speaking to his fellow characters, he is also in some sense, and possibly indirectly, speaking to the audience as well. Thus the addresser has two

177

Discourse

different categories of addressee – one in the microcosm of the play, one in the macrocosm of the theatre. My original idea assumed that since the addresser/addressee relationship held on two channels, then it seemed plausible that all the other aspects and functions that Jakobson described should also fit around these two channels, and that this schematization might well enable me to distinguish rather fine points of descriptive detail with respect to audiences listening to play-talk. This original formalization was as shown in Figure 8.3, where the vertical axis represents the microcosm – the fictional world of the play – and the horizontal axis represents the macrocosm – the real world of the theatre.

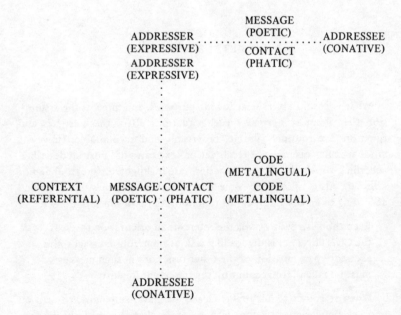

Figure 8.3.

178

I then went on to try to gather together examples from well known drama texts that would exemplify each category of the diagram, partly for the purpose of making the diagram clear for other people, partly to see if it served any useful purpose for me and partly to check its adequacy. The obvious way to begin was to find a set of simple examples to demonstrate the set towards each of the twelve functions separately, though the reader should remember that most utterances will utilize all possible functions, and that the examples I present here are only to demonstrate different emphases. These examples of emphasis are as follows:

1 Focus on the expressive function in the microcosm — orientation towards the addresser and the fictional world. An example of this would be Hamlet's speech in *Hamlet,* act 1, scene 2, which begins 'O, that this too too solid flesh would melt':

> O, that this too too solid flesh would melt,
> Thaw, and resolve itself into a dew;
> Or that the Everlasting had not fix'd
> His canon 'gainst self-slaughter! O God! O God!
> How weary, stale, flat, and unprofitable
> Seem to me all the uses of this world.

Whatever intonation patterns the actor chooses to use here, there can be no doubt that the text of this speech is focused on presenting the speaker's state of mind and attitude to whatever he uses as referential content.

2 Focus on the expressive function in the macrocosm — orientation towards the addresser and the real world. This seemed problematic. I initially thought of instances like Archie Rice in the music-hall scenes of *The Entertainer* (Osborne, 1957) talking straight into the auditorium, or Alan Bennett's Headmaster in *Forty Years On* (Bennett, 1969) talking to the audience as if they were the parents of his pupils, attending the end-of-term play. But what is really happening here is that although the micro and macro addressees seem to be conflated, we know without doubt that Archie and the Headmaster are not talking to us at all, but to a set of unseen fictional addressees who are somehow in the auditorium with us. Also, of course, we have superior knowledge and insights to these fictional addressees: herein lies the success of satire and humour in all such exploitations. The only true examples I could finally produce were utterances where, to use Goffman's (1974)

phrase, the actor in some sense 'breaks frame' — that is, he steps out of his actor-role and demonstrates his dual identity as both an individual 'real' person and the fictional character the real person has to play. So, for example, when Morecambe and Wise, in the middle of a serious conversation, let their facial muscles twitch and let us see that they are holding back laughter, and pass comments on the interaction to us, then we have a focus on the macro-expressive function. However, this raises a problem for the model, in that we are no longer thinking of the utterances as issuing from a character within the play, but from the actor overtly portraying that fiction. I will return to this problem below.

3   Focus on the conative function in the microcosm — orientation towards the addressee and the fictional world. Examples are easy to find: Birdboot telling Moon to 'Have a chocolate!' in Stoppard's *The Real Inspector Hound* (Stoppard, 1968); Hamlet giving instructions to the player-king (*Hamlet,* act 2, scene 2); Ben telling Gus to 'Make the tea, will you?' in Pinter's *The Dumb Waiter* (Pinter, 1957); Guildenstern telling Rosencrantz to 'glean what afflicts him' or 'address me' in Stoppard's *Rosencrantz and Guildenstern are Dead* (Stoppard, 1967).

4   Focus on the conative function in the macrocosm — orientation towards the addressee and the real world. This function is commonly used in modernist theatre, so that Brecht's plays, for example, are peppered with admonitions to the audience: to watch carefully; to think about what they're seeing; to take relevant action and so on. An example would be the conclusion to *The Good Woman of Setzuan* (Brecht, 1940, translated by Bentley):

> How could a better ending be arranged?
> Could one change people? Can the world be changed?
> Would new gods do the trick? Will atheism?
> Moral rearmament? Materialism?
> It is for you to find a way my friends,
> To help good men arrive at happy ends.
> *You* write the happy ending to the play!

As Raymond Williams has pointed out (1968), this sort of direct instruction to the audience is certainly not a new practice, and this sort of conative relationship can clearly be seen in classic theatre too. Thus, for example, at the end of *A Midsummer Night's Dream,* act 5, scene 2, Robin Goodfellow asks for applause: 'Give me your hands if we be friends'. I suppose the ultimate in really effective use of the conative-macro function is when the audience prevent the 'death" of Tinkerbell in J.M. Barrie's 'Peter Pan and Wendy' (Barrie, 1911) by applauding loudly – as they reliably do at every performance. I sometimes fantasize about the possibility of persuading an entire auditorium to refrain from applause in this play.

5 Focus on poetic function in the microcosm – orientation towards the form of the message in the fictional world. Much Shakespearean fool-talk is built on this function. Thus, for example, we have Feste in *Twelfth Night* twisting the words of Olivia, the Fool in *King Lear* twisting the words of Lear. There is a simple but perhaps more subtle use of this focus in *Hamlet*, act 3, scene 4, where Hamlet's reply to his mother's 'Hamlet, thou hast thy father much offended' exactly parallels her choice of structure, with only the vocatives and pronominals changed to make his point: 'Mother, you have my father much offended.' A modern example would be Rosencrantz and Guildenstern 'playing questions' (Stoppard, 1967).

6 Focus on the poetic function in the macrocosm – orientation towards the form of the message and the real world. Examples here are again numerous. Presumably the whole of Shakespeare would come into this category, in the sense that, apart from the examples like those under the previous heading, the language of the plays is poetic only for the audience, and certainly not for the interactants within the fiction. Whilst we do, and are supposed to, notice a nice turn of phrase here, a clever rhyme there, a subtle bit of structuring elsewhere, it would be most inappropriate if the characters of the play were to react in this way. The same holds for modern drama of course – presumably only we hear the Women of Canterbury in *Murder in the Cathedral* (Eliot, 1935), or the conversationalists in *The Cocktail Party* (Eliot, 1949) as talking poetry. In exactly the same way, although the focus is on different formal properties, the well-structuredness of, say, a Pinter 'conversation-like' dialogue is for the most part for our attention and not for the interactants on stage.

7 Focus on phatic function in the microcosm – orientation towards the contact aspect in the fictional world. Again, examples are easy to find. Any greeting will do – Gertrude to Hamlet, Prospero to Caliban, Birdboot to Moon and Moon to Birdboot. Ionesco exploits the humorous potential in this by a stretch of overtly phatic small-talk in *The Bald Prima Donna* (Ionesco, 1959):

MR SMITH   Hm!
               (*Silence*)

MRS SMITH	Hm! Hm!
	(*Silence*)
MRS MARTIN	Hm! Hm! Hm!
	(*Silence*)
MR MARTIN	Hm! Hm! Hm! Hm!
	(*Silence*)
MRS MARTIN	Oh! Really!
	(*Silence*)
MR MARTIN	I think we must all have colds.
	(*Silence*)
MR SMITH	It's not cold weather though.
	(*Silence*)
MRS SMITH	There are no draughts.
	(*Silence*)

Pinter does this rather more subtly and inventively in several plays and sketches. Notice also how Stoppard exploits this feature in *Rosencrantz and Guildenstern are Dead*. He takes the following lines from *Hamlet*, act 2, scene 2:

KING Thanks, Rosencrantz and gentle Guildenstern.
QUEEN Thanks, Guildenstern and gentle Rosencrantz.

and tampers with them thus:

CLAUDIUS	Thanks, Rosencrantz (*turning to ROS who is caught unawares, while GUIL bows*) and gentle Guildenstern (*who is bent double*).
GERTRUDE	(*correcting*) Thanks Guildenstern (*turning to ROS, who bows as Guil checks upward movement to bow too — both bent double squinting at each other*) . . . and gentle Rosencrantz (*turning to GUIL, both straightening up — GUIL checks again and bows again*).

In this way, he not only reinforces notions of the way in which Ros and Guil are caught up in someone else's play, and their confusion over their loss of individual identity, but also plays on the emptiness of classic phatic communion. In this case not even the addressees are appropriately selected or recognized.

8 Focus on the phatic function in the macrocosm — orientation towards the contact aspect in the real world. Many examples are non-verbal in the sense of the curtain going up, the lights going down, 'les

trois coups', or a polite electric bell signifying the start of the interaction in the real theatre. There are also non-verbals in the punning
sense, as the audience, in response to these opening phatic moves, do
actually stop talking. I mention this here to point out that, just as the
roles of addresser and addressee switch around in the microcosm, so
they do in the macrocosm. Although the audience's potential as addresser is much less rich, it should not be forgotten. There are also
quite a few examples of specific verbal realizations of phatic function.
For example, in pantomime, where the comic says 'Hello boys and
girls' and gets the appropriate response; or in *Under Milk Wood* (Thomas, 1954), where the first voice tells us:

> Listen. It is night moving in the streets, the processional salt
> slow musical wind in Coronation Street and Cockle Row, it is the
> grass growing in Llaregyb Hill, dewfall, starfall, the sleep of the
> birds in Milk Hill.

> Listen. It is nightfall in the chill squat chapel. . .

Similarly, Ionesco's Maid in *The Bald Prima Donna* steps forward out
of the immediate action (but stays within the fictional frame) and tells
us directly:

> Elizabeth and Donald are now far too happy to be able to hear
> me. So I can tell you a secret. Elizabeth is not Elizabeth and Donald
> is not Donald. And I'll prove it to you. The child Donald talked of
> is not Elizabeth's daughter, not the same child at all. Donald's little
> girl has one red eye and one white eye just like Elizabeth's little
> girl. But whereas it's the right eye of Donald's little girl that's red
> and the left that's white, it's the left eye of Elizabeth's child that's
> red and the right eye that's white. . .

9   Focus on the referential function in the microcosm — orientation towards the context and the fictional world. 'Something is rotten
in the state of Denmark', says Marcellus in *Hamlet*, act 1, scene 4. This
function is, of course, used pretty consistently in any play — with
possible avant-garde exceptions, as usual. An interesting problem is the
whole notion of plot exposition, where details of the context that the
characters already 'know' have to be more or less subtly conveyed to
the audience. It is of course what Pinter explicitly refuses to do, and
what Stoppard (1968) parodies:

MRS DRUDGE (*into phone*)   Hello, the drawing room of Lady

Muldoon's country residence one morning in early spring? . . .
Hello! — the draw — who? Who did you wish to speak to? I'm
afraid there is no one of that name here, this is all very mysterious
and I'm sure it's leading up to something, I hope nothing is amiss
for we, that is Lady Muldoon and her houseguests, are here cut off
from the world, including Magnus, the wheelchair-ridden half-
brother of her ladyship's husband Lord Albert Muldoon who ten
years ago went out for a walk on the cliffs and was never seen
again — and all alone for they had no children.

10   Focus on the referential function in the macrocosm — orientation towards the context and the real world. The most famous examples
here are Brechtian or neo-Brechtian examples, where explicit reference
is made to the state of the real world as compared with that of the
play. The end of *The Resistible Rise of Arturo Ui* (Brecht, 1941) is one
of many such examples throughout the Lehrstücke. The reference here
is to Hitler:

> The world was almost won by such an ape!
> The nations put him where his kind belong.
> But don't rejoice too soon at your escape —
> The womb he crawled from is still going strong.

Under this category also, are explicit references to the fact of being
in a theatre — watching a play. An example here is the beginning of the
same play:

> Friends, tonight we're going to show —
> Pipe down, you boys in the back row!
> And lady your hat is in the way! —
> The great historical gangster play.

The beginning of the Robin Goodfellow speech quoted above carries
the same function:

> If we shadows have offended,
> Think but this, and all is mended,
> That you have but slumber'd here
> While these visions did appear.

11   Focus on the metalingual function in the microcosm — orientation towards the code and the fictional world. Examples are numerous
here. 'These are but wild and whirling words, my Lord' says Horatio to
Hamlet — act 1, scene 5.

12   Focus on the metalingual function in the macrocosm — orientation towards the code and the real world. This also (like 2 above) proved problematic in terms of examples. Two ideas came to mind. Firstly, the closing section of Ionesco's *The Bald Prima Donna*, in which he has the characters' talk falling into mock-proverb, clichés, letters of the alphabet and so on. So, in some sense, the meaning of this that the audience picks up is, 'all communication is meaningless gobbledegook'. In this sense the talk seems to be oriented towards a metalingual function. Notice, though, that this is only an interpretation we can put on the text — not an intrinsic feature of the text itself. Another example that came to mind was in connection with Truffaut's film *Day for Night*, when subtitled in English. Here nearly all the talk is in French, with the subtitles in English, except for about two exchanges, when some English characters have arrived on the French scene, and talk English to each other. For a joke, these exchanges are subtitled in French. Now what is happening here in terms of the code? An English-speaking audience is going to be following the English-language text, and, therefore, the subtitles for the most part, but the actual spoken dialogue for the two exchanges in English. I assume the opposite would hold for a French person watching the same artifact. What the odd sub-title choice has done is, again, to 'break frame' and draw attention to the fact that we all know, but tend to make background in our minds: that two codes are being used simultaneously. Like the Morecambe and Wise example above, in 2, we are faced with communication external to the actual fiction.

Since I was unable to find data that fitted well under function 2 and function 12, obviously I needed to rethink the model in some way. The other examples seemed to fit rather well, so I assumed a rather minor adjustment would probably be appropriate. The crucial mistake I had in fact made was to assume that a simple multiplication (two axes, multiplied by six functions, giving twelve functions) was correct. In fact, it is a fundamental point that both the addresser and the code are constant. They do not in fact differ on the two axes. In the case of the former, however many types of addressee there may be, the addresser will always be just, say, Hamlet. In the case of the latter — since the code must, by original definition, be shared by addresser and addressee(s), that, too, must always remain the same. Thus there are not twelve separate and complementary functions as I first thought, but ten. The amended diagram is show in Figure 8.4.

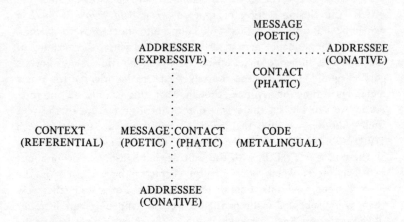

Figure 8.4.

As I mentioned briefly above, there are a number of problems associated with the basic Jakobsonian model, as there are with all functional models. The reader will have noticed a substantial amount of overlap between the different categories – particularly, say, between phatic and conative, or between poetic and metalingual. Similarly, each of the functions could be, and should be, broken down into more delicate concepts. There are substantially different realizations of, for example, phatic function (see Laver, 1974). The whole notion of code is rather vague. It is not always clear whether it refers to the abstract underlying features of a language, to a particular idiolect or to a type of talk.

There is one specific problem I want to bring out here. It is demonstrated rather neatly by Karl Popper (1965) when he discusses the richness of human language as compared with animal communication. He also expands the basic Bühler model that Jakobson adapted, albeit in a different way.

He discusses what he calls two 'lower functions' – the expressive (or symptomatic) and the conative (which he actually labels signalling or releasing) – and two 'higher functions' – the descriptive function and the argumentative function. Both of these two higher functions can be understood, in the familiar way, as the production of true or false propositions (descriptive), and valid or invalid arguments (argumentative). He argues that, whilst both animals and humans use the lower functions, only human language possesses the higher functions as well. I assume from the following quotation that elsewhere he would want to argue for other functions in human language as well: 'Human language is much richer. It has many functions and dimensions which animal languages do not have.' His concept of function is not here well defined for our purposes. We are clearly already beyond the function of the single utterance or utterance exchange (using that term loosely), since 'argumentative' presumably implies the use of a set of propositions and a notion of sequential organization and arrangement possible within one utterance, but not necessarily confined to it.

Nevertheless, Popper's 'evolutionary approach' is useful in that it makes the following important observations quite clear. If we have the four functions,

1 expressive
2 signalling
3 descriptive
4 argumentative

then, as Popper points out, we also have the following dependency relationships: the first may occur alone, but the second (by definition) cannot occur without the first. Similarly, whilst the third might occur alone, the fourth cannot occur without the third. And similarly again, he writes: 'The two lower functions are always present when any of the higher functions (which are characteristically human) are present.'

This is certainly not the place to discuss Popper's notions of human and animal communication, which are necessarily brief and truncated, but his particular observations of the hierarchical dependencies involved in the relationships between functions otherwise separated for analytical purposes is an important modification of Jakobson's rather simpler suggestion that all functions occur simultaneously, or my own loose suggestion of overlap, above.

I want now to approach Jakobson's model in this way. It would be easiest to start by numbering the six aspects on his model first, as in Figure 8.5. Clearly, in most normal interactions, the function associated with 1 is the only one that can possibly occur alone. And this, alone, would account for a minute proportion of rather uninteresting

CONTEXT[6]

MESSAGE[4]

ADDRESSER[1] . . . . ADDRESSEE[2]

CONTACT[3]

CODE[5]

Figure 8.5.

talk. In order for 2 to occur, 3, 4 and 5 are essential, whilst 3, 4 and 5 without 2 is nonsensical. Similarly, 6 cannot be used unless all other functions are available. In this sense, of course, ideation does reign supreme. Nevertheless, the simplicity of Jakobson's model is still useful for my purposes, and as long as we are clear about the inadequacies of the model itself, then it can be used with this problem taken for granted.

I have offered these problems, and the description of my developing work on adapting the basic model, with several objectives in mind. As I hope has become clear, this chapter is designed to explicate not only solutions, but problems, mistakes and similar practicalities. As Liam Hudson (1966) writes, 'Research is frequently a muddled, piratical affair, and we do no service to anyone by pretending otherwise. I have tried therefore to describe my research not as a neat experiment, but much as it happened.' Obviously, my account is highly selective, and I do not indulge in the same extremes of self-revelation that Hudson does. Nevertheless, I do believe it is useful to present the development of ideas rather than the final outcome of those ideas. In part because developmental processes are interesting *per se*, in part to make those final outcomes more easy to understand, but also to enable critics to pinpoint just where their opinions or solutions would diverge from mine.

Elsewhere (Burton, 1978), I have used the model to consider and compare a range of observations about the relationships between theatre and everyday activity from a range of sources, but focusing on the rich yet ill-organized observations in the sociology of the everyday, drawing in particular on the brilliant insights and observations in Goffman (1974). Here I would like to present just one instance of this, as it relates specifically to the correction of the model from twelve channels to ten, and I think it would be appropriate to discuss it whilst the examples are still close at hand. What my original model and later corrections have enabled me to do is to accommodate one of the ideas in Goffman's *Frame Analysis* (1974), which is one of the most exciting yet disorganized books I have ever read. It comes in the second of the categories described at the beginning of the chapter, that is, where a sociologist writes about reciprocal similarities of life to drama. In this long and immensely rich book, he amasses example after example of framed activity, framed procedure, frame violation and so on. One very interesting chapter deals particularly with framing in the theatre. Where I find the book frustrating is in the lack of formal and specific criteria which would enable me to compare and describe the different types of framed activity that are described and that I have noticed elsewhere. One conclusion my mistaken model has led me to is this: in normal theatre interaction, the expressive function only occurs in the microcosm. If it occurs in the macrocosm, either the addresser has broken frame (as when Morecambe laughs) or the audience has broken frame (as when the audience applaud the entrance of a famous actor, or the end of a well-delivered speech). What they are doing here is interacting with the figure on the stage identified as an individual person, not as the fictional part or character. Similarly, in normal theatre the metalingual function only exists in the microcosm. If it does occur in the macrocosm (as in the Truffaut example) then this is sufficient to classify the ongoing activity as frame-breaking.

R.A. Hudson (1975) 'with some hesitation' outlines a framework for a general model of communication. I include the quoted qualification as an indication that I do not intend to discuss his tentative proposal in any detail here. He suggests that hearers need three kinds of knowledge in order to make sense of conversation:

a) knowledge of the constraints on the use of sentences
b) knowledge of the contraints on conversation, or, more generally, on social interaction (Grice, 1965; Cicourel, 1973)
c) knowledge of the universe and, in particular, of the speaker and the preceding discourse

Clearly, any hearer of theatre-talk would need as specific sub-sections of (b) and (c) a knowledge of the constraints that operate in drama dialogue. Whilst there are doubtless many other observations that could be made here, I hope to have demonstrated at least a way of beginning to chart some of these constraints, and feel confident that many other useful observations could easily be charted on the model offered.

Bibliography

Abercrombie, D. (1959), 'Conversation and spoken prose', *Studies in Phonetics and Linguistics*, Oxford University Press, London, 1965, pp. 1–9.

Abrahams, R.D. (1972), 'A true and exact survey of talking black', mimeo, University of Texas, Austin.

Allwood, J., Andersson, L. and Dahl, O. (1977), *Logic in Linguistics*, Cambridge University Press, London.

Ashby, M. (1973), 'Doctor-patient interviews', *Working Papers in Discourse Analysis*, no. 1, mimeo, English Language Research, University of Birmingham.

Asimov, I. (1973), *I, Robot*, Panther, London.

Austin, J.L. (1958), 'Performative-constative', in J.R. Searle (ed.), *The Philosophy of Language*, Oxford University Press, London, pp. 1–13.

Austin, J.L. (1961), *Philosophical Papers*, ed. J.O. Urmson and G.L. Warnock, Oxford University Press, London.

Austin, J.L. (1965), *How to Do Things with Words*, ed. J.O. Urmson, Oxford University Press, London.

Bailey, R.W. and Burton, D.M. (1968), *English Stylistics: A Bibliography*, MIT, Cambridge, Mass.

Ballard, L., Conrad, R.J. and Longacre, R.E. (1971), 'The deep and surface grammar of inter-clausal relations', *Foundations of Language*, vol. 7, pp. 48–68.

Barrie, J.M. (1911), 'Peter Pan and Wendy', *The Plays of J.M. Barrie*, Hodder & Stoughton, London, 1928.

Basso, K.H. (1970), 'To give up on words: silence in western Apache culture', reprinted in P.P. Giglioli, *Language and Social Context*, Penguin, Harmondsworth, 1972, pp. 67–87.

Bauman, R. (1976), 'The development of competence in the use of solicitational routines: children's folklore and informal learning', mimeo, *University of Texas Working Papers in Sociolinguistics*, no. 34.

Bauman, R. and Sherzer, J. (eds) (1974), *The Ethnography of Speaking*, Cambridge University Press, London.

Beckett, S. (1951), *Molloy*, Minuit, Paris.

Benamou, M. (1963), 'Pour une pédagogie du style littéraire', *The French Review*, vol. XXXVII, pp. 158–68.

Bennett, A. (1969), *Forty Years On*, Faber & Faber, London.

Bergson, H. (1911), *Le Rire*, trans. Clondesley Brereton and Fred Rothwell as *Laughter: An Essay on the Meaning of the Comic*, Macmillan, London, 1913.

Bernstein, B. (1971), 'On the classification and framing of educational knowledge', in M.F.D. Young (ed.), *Knowledge and Control*, Macmillan, London, pp. 76–99.

Berry, H.M. (1976), *Introduction to Systemic Grammar*, vol. 1, Batsford, London.

Bloch, B. (1953), 'Linguistic structure and linguistic analysis', *Georgetown University Monograph Series on Language and Linguistics*, no. 4, pp. 40–4.

Brazil, D. (1975), 'Discourse intonation I', *Discourse Analysis Monographs*, no. 1, English Language Research, University of Birmingham.

Brazil, D. (1977), 'Discourse Intonation', unpublished PhD thesis, University of Birmingham.

Brazil, D. (1978), 'Discourse intonation II', *Discourse Analysis Monographs*, no. 2, English Language Research, University of Birmingham.

Brecht, B. (1937), 'The Messingkauf dialogues', in J. Willett (trans. and ed.), *Brecht on Theatre*, Methuen, London, 1964, pp. 169–79.

Brecht, B. (1941), *The Resistible Rise of Arturo Ui*, Methuen, London, 1976.

Brecht, B. (1950), 'The Street Scene', in J. Willett (trans. and ed.), *Brecht on Theatre*, Methuen, London, 1964, pp. 121–9.

Brecht, B. (1951), 'Short description of a new technique of acting', in J. Willett (trans. and ed.), *Brecht on Theatre*, Methuen, London, 1964, pp. 136–48.

Brecht, B. (1953), *Der Gute Mensch von Sezuan* (Berlin), trans. E. Bentley as 'The Good Woman of Setzuan', *Parables for the Theatre*, Penguin, Harmondsworth, 1956.

Brenneis, D. and Lein, L. (1977), ' "You fruithead": a sociolinguistic approach to a children's dispute', in S. Ervin-Tripp and C. Mitchell-Kernan (eds), *Child Discourse*, Academic Press, New York, 1977, pp. 49–67.

Brown, J.R. (1972), *Theatre Language*, Allen Lane, London.

Brown, R. and Gilman, A. (1960), 'The pronouns of power and solidarity', in T.A. Sebeok (ed.), *Style in Language*, MIT, Cambridge, Mass., pp. 253–77.

Bühler, K. (1933), 'Die Axiomatik der Sprachwissenschaft', *Kant-Studien*, vol. 38, pp. 19–90.

Burke, K. (1945), *A Grammar of Motives*, Prentice-Hall, Englewood Cliffs, NJ (republished by University of California Press, 1969).

Burns, E. (1974), *Theatricality: A Study of Convention in the Theatre and in Social Life*, Longman, London.

Burton, D. (1973), 'The exploitation of "the word" in concrete poetry', unpublished MA thesis, University of Birmingham.

Burton, D. (1977), 'Dialogue and discourse in Tom Stoppard', *Nottingham Linguistic Circular*, vol. IV, no. 2, pp. 28–49.

Burton, D. (1978), 'Dialogue and discourse', unpublished PhD thesis, University of Birmingham.

Burton, D. and Stubbs, M.W. (1976), 'On speaking terms: analysing conversational data', *Midland Association of Linguistic Studies*, vol. II, no. 2, pp. 22–44.

Carling, F. (1962), *And Yet We are Human*, Chatto and Windus, London.

Carter, R.A. (1979), 'Towards a discourse theory of stylistics', unpublished PhD thesis, University of Birmingham.

Chatman, S. and Levin, S.R. (eds) (1967), *Essays on the Language of Literature*, Boston.

Chomsky, N. (1957), *Syntactic Structures,* Mouton, The Hague.

Chomsky, N. (1968), *Language and Mind,* Harcourt Brace & World, New York.

Cicourel, A.V. (1973), *Cognitive Sociology,* Penguin, Harmondsworth.

Coulthard, R.M. (1977), *Introduction to Discourse Analysis,* Longman, London.

Coulthard, R.M. and Ashby, M. (1976), 'A linguistic description of doctor-patient interviews', in M. Wadsworth and D. Robinson (eds), *Studies in Every-day Medical Life,* Martin Robertson, London.

Coulthard, R.M., Brazil, D. and Johns, C.M. (forthcoming), *Discourse Intonation and Language Teaching,* Longman, London.

Darnell, R. (1972), 'Prolegomena to typologies of speech use', *Texas Working Papers in Sociolinguistics,* special number, March, 1972.

de Camp, D. (1976), 'The role of paradigmatic and syntagmatic contexts in variable receptive competence', mimeo, Center for Applied Linguistics, University of Texas.

Dressler, W.U. (1970), 'Towards a semantic deep structure of discourse grammar', *Papers from the Sixth Regional Meeting of the Chicago Linguistics Society,* University of Chicago, Department of Linguistics.

Duncan, S. (1972), 'Some signals and rules for taking speaking turns in conversation', *Journal of Personality and Social Psychology,* vol. 23, no. 2, pp. 283-92.

Dundes, A. (1975), 'On the structure of the proverb', *Proverbium,* vol. 25, pp. 961-73.

Duvignand, J. (1965), 'The theatre in society: society in the theatre', in *Sociologie du théâtre,* Presses Universitaires de France, Paris, pp. 7-25.

Eliot, T.S. (1935), 'Murder in the Cathedral', *The Complete Poems and Plays of T.S. Eliot,* Faber & Faber, London, 1969.

Eliot, T.S. (1949), 'The Cocktail Party', *The Complete Poems and Plays of T.S. Eliot,* Faber & Faber, London, 1969.

Enkvist, N. (1971), 'On the place of style in some linguistic theories', in Seymour Chatman (ed), *Literary Style: A Symposium,* Oxford University Press, London, pp. 47-61.

Ervin-Tripp, S. (1964), 'An analysis of the interaction of language, topic, and listener', in J.J. Gumperz and D. Hymes (eds), *Directions in Sociolinguistics,* Holt, Rinehart & Winston, New York, 1972, pp. 12-36.

Ervin-Tripp, S. (1972), 'On sociolinguistic rules: alternation and co-occurrence', in J.J. Gumperz and D. Hymes (eds), *Directions in Sociolinguistics,* Holt, Rinehart & Winston, New York, 1972, pp. 213-51.

Ervin-Tripp, S. and Mitchell-Kernan, C. (eds) (1977), *Child Discourse,* Academic Press, New York.

Fillmore, C.J. (1972), 'A grammarian looks to sociolinguistics', *Georgetown Monograph Series on Language and Linguistics,* vol. 25, pp. 273-87.

Firth, J.R. (1935), 'The techniques of semantics', *Papers in Linguistics 1934-51,* Oxford University Press, London, 1957, pp. 7-33.

Fishman, J. (1965), 'The relationship between micro- and macro-sociolinguistics in the study of who speaks what language to whom and when', in J. Pride and J. Holmes, (eds), *Sociolinguistics,* Penguin, Harmondsworth, 1972, pp. 1-15.

Fowler, R. (ed) (1971), *The Language of Literature*, Routledge & Kegan Paul, London.

Fowler, R. (1972), 'Style and the concept of deep structure', *Journal of Literary Semantics*, vol. I, pp. 5–24.

Fowler, R. (1979), 'Linguistics and, and versus, poetics', *Journal of Literary Semantics*, vol. VIII, no. 1, pp. 3–17.

Franges, I. (1961), 'Quelques remarqes sur le déviations de style', Langue et littérature: actes du VIII congrès de la Fédération internationale des langues et littératures modernes, Bibliothèque de la faculté de philosophie et lettres de l'Université de Liège, Fascicule CLXI, pp. 240–2.

Freeman, D.C. (ed) (1970), *Linguistics and Literary Style*, Holt, Rinehart & Winston, New York.

Gardner, M. (1977), 'Mathematical games', *Scientific American*, spring 1977, pp. 121–6.

Garfinkel, H. (1967), *Studies in Ethnomethodology*, Prentice-Hall, New Jersey.

Garvey, C. (1977), 'Play with language and speech', in S. Ervin-Tripp and C. Mitchell-Kernan (eds), *Child Discourse*, Academic Press, New York, 1977, pp. 27–49.

Garvin, P. (ed) (1964), *A Prague School Reader on Esthetics, Literary Structure and Style*, Georgetown University Press.

Geertz, C. (1960), 'Linguistic etiquette', in J.A. Fishman (ed), *Readings in the Sociology of Language*, Mouton, The Hague.

Giglioli, P.-P. (1972), *Language and Social Context*, Penguin, Harmondsworth.

Glaser, B.G. and Strauss, A.L. (1967), *The Discovery of Grounded Theory: Strategies for Qualitative Research*, Aldine, Chicago.

Goffman, E. (1959), *The Presentation of Self in Everyday Life*, reprinted Penguin, Harmondsworth, 1969.

Goffman, E. (1963), *Stigma: Notes on the Management of Spoiled Identity*, Prentice-Hall, Englewood Cliffs, NJ, reprinted Penguin, Harmondsworth, 1968.

Goffman, E. (1964), 'The neglected situation', *American Anthropologist*, vol. 66, no. 6, part 2.

Goffman, E. (1971), *Relations in Public: Microstudies of the Public Order*, Basic Books, New York, reprinted Penguin, Harmondsworth, 1971.

Goffman, E. (1974), *Frame Analysis*, Harper & Row, New York, reprinted Penguin, Harmondsworth, 1975.

Gorny, W. (1961), 'Text structure against the background of language structure', *Poetics*, vol. 1, pp. 25–37.

Greenfield, S.B. (1967), 'Grammar and meaning in poetry', *PMLA*, vol. LXXXII, pp. 377–87.

Grice, H. (1957), 'Meaning', *Philosophical Review*, vol. 66, pp. 377–88.

Grice, H. (1967), 'Logic and conversation', in P. Cole and J.L. Morgan (eds), *Syntax and Semantics III: Speech Acts*, Academic Press, New York, 1975, pp. 41–58.

Grimes, J. (1975), *Thread of Discourse*, Mouton, The Hague.

Gumperz, J.J. and Hymes, D. (eds) (1972), *Directions in Sociolinguistics: The Ethnography of Communication*, Holt, Rinehart & Winston, New York.

Gurvitch, G. (1956), 'The sociology of the theatre', *Les Lettres nouvelles*, vol. 35, pp. 196–210.

193

Gutwinski, W. (1976), *Cohesion in Literary Texts,* Mouton, The Hague.

Haberland, H. and Mey, J.L. (1977), 'Linguistics and pragmatics', *Journal of Pragmatics,* vol. 1, no. 1, pp. 1-12.

Halliday, M.A.K. (1961), 'Categories of the theory of grammar', *Word,* vol. 17, pp. 241-92.

Halliday, M.A.K. (1964), 'The linguistic study of literary texts', in Horace G. Lunt (ed), *Proceedings of the Ninth International Congress of Linguists,* Mouton, The Hague, pp. 302-7, reprinted in S. Chatman and S.R. Levin (eds), *Essays on the Language of Literature,* Boston, 1967.

Halliday, M.A.K. (1966), 'Descriptive linguistics and literary style', in A. McIntosh and M.A.K. Halliday (eds), *Patterns of Language,* Longman, London, pp. 56-69.

Halliday, M.A.K. (1969), 'Relevant models of language', *Educational Review,* vol. 21, no. 2, pp. 118-36.

Halliday, M.A.K. (1970), *A Course in Spoken English: Intonation,* Oxford University Press, London.

Halliday, M.A.K. (1971), 'Language in a social perspective', *Educational Review,* vol. 23, no. 3, pp. 165-88.

Halliday, M.A.K. (1973), 'Linguistic function and literary style', *Explorations in the Functions of Language,* Edward Arnold, London, pp. 103-38.

Halliday, M.A.K. and Hasan, R. (1975), *Cohesion in English,* Longman, London.

Havránek, B. (1932), 'The functional differentiation of the standard language', reprinted in P. Garvin (ed), *A Prague School Reader on Esthetics, Literary Structure and Style,* Georgetown University Press, 1964, pp. 3-17.

Hayakawa, S.I. (1952), *Language in Thought and Action,* Harcourt, Brace & World, New York.

Hendricks, W.O. (1972), 'On the notion "beyond the sentence"', *Linguistics,* vol. V, no. 1, December. pp. 38-69.

Hill, A.A. (1967), 'Some further thoughts on grammaticality and poetic language', *Style,* vol. 1, pp. 81-91.

Hirsch, E.D. (1976), 'What's the use of speech-act theory?', *Centrum,* vol. 3, no. 2, pp. 121-4.

Hudson, L. (1966), *Contrary Imaginations: A Psychological Study of the English Schoolboy,* Methuen, London, reprinted Penguin, Harmondsworth, 1967.

Hudson, R.A. (1975), 'The meaning of questions', *Language,* vol. 51, pp. 1-31.

Hymes, D. (1972a), 'Introduction: toward ethnographies of communication', in J.J. Gumperz and D. Hymes (eds), *Directions in Sociolinguistics,* Holt, Rinehart & Winston, New York, 1972, pp. 1-34.

Hymes, D. (1972b), 'Models of the interaction of language and social life', in J.J. Gumperz and D. Hymes (eds), *Directions in Sociolinguistics,* Holt, Rinehart & Winston, New York, 1972, pp. 35-72.

Hymes, D. (1977), *Foundations in Sociolinguistics: An Ethnographic Approach,* Tavistock, London.

Ionesco, E. (1950), 'La Cantatrice Chauve,' trans. Donald Watson as *The Bald Prima Donna,* Calder, London, 1959.

Ionesco, E. (1956), 'My critics and I', *Arts,* 22-8 February, reprinted in E. Ionesco, *Notes and Counternotes,* trans. Watson, Calder, London, 1964.

Jakobson, R. (1960), 'Concluding statement: linguistics and poetics', in T.A. Sebeok (ed), *Style in Language,* MIT, Cambridge, Mass., pp. 350–78.

Jakobson, R. (1968), 'Poetry of grammar and grammar of poetry', *Lingua,* vol. 21, pp. 597–608.

Jefferson, G. (1972), 'Side sequences', in D. Sudnow (ed), *Studies in Social Interaction,* The Free Press, New York, 1972, pp. 294–339.

Jones, A.R. (1972), 'Samuel Beckett's prose fiction: a comparative study of the French and English versions', unpublished PhD thesis, University of Birmingham.

Keenan, E.O. (1975), 'Conversational competence in children', *Journal of Child Language,* vol. 1, no. 2, pp. 163–83.

Keenan, E.O. (1977), 'Making it last: repetition in children's discourse', in S. Ervin-Tripp and C. Mitchell-Kernan (eds), *Child Discourse,* Academic Press, New York, 1977, pp. 125–39.

Keenan, E.O. and Klein, E. (1974), 'Coherency in children's discourse', paper presented to the summer meeting of the Linguistic Society of America, Amherst, Massachusetts, July 1974.

Keenan, E.O. and Schieffelin, B. (1976), 'Topic as a discourse notion: a study of topic in the conversation of children and adults', in C. Li (ed), *Subject and Topic,* Academic Press, New York.

Kempson, R. (1977), *Semantic Theory,* Cambridge University Press, London.

Kirschenblatt-Gimblett, B. (1974), 'The concept and varieties of narrative performance in east european Jewish culture', in R. Bauman and J. Sherzer (eds), *The Ethnography of Speaking,* Cambridge University Press, London, pp. 283–311.

Kirschenblatt-Gimblett, B. (1976), *Speech Play,* University of Pennsylvania Press, Philadelphia.

Krumm, H.J. (trans. and ed.) (1977), *Analyse der Unterrichtssprache* (see Sinclair and Coulthard, 1975), Quelle & Mayer, Heidelberg.

Kuhn, T.S. (1962), *The Structure of Scientific Revolutions,* University of Chicago Press, revised 1970.

Kuusi, M.I. (1972), 'Towards an international type-system of proverbs', *Folklore Fellows Communications,* no. 211, Helsinki, Suomalainen Tiedeakatemia.

Labov, W. (1969), 'Contradiction, deletion, and inherent variability of the copula', *Language,* vol. 45, no. 4, pp. 715–62.

Labov, W. (1970), 'The study of language in its social context', *Studium Generale,* vol. 23, pp. 66–84.

Labov, W. (1972a), 'Rules for ritual insults', in D. Sudnow (ed), *Studies in Social Interaction,* The Free Press, New York, 1972, pp. 120–69.

Labov, W. (1972b), *Language in the Inner City,* University of Pennsylvania Press, Philadelphia.

Labov, W. and Waletzky, J. (1967), 'Narrative analysis', in J. Helm (ed), *Essays on the Verbal and Visual Arts,* University of Washington Press, Seattle, pp. 12–44.

Lakoff, G. (1971a), 'Linguistics and natural logic', *Synthese,* vol. 22, pp. 151–271.

Lakoff, G. (1971b), 'On generative semantics', in D. Steinberg and L.A. Jakobivits (eds), *Semantics: An Interdisciplinary Reader in Philosophy,* Cambridge University Press, London, pp. 370–92.

Lakoff, R. (1972), 'Language in Context', *Language,* vol. 48, pp. 907–27.

Lakoff, R. (1973), 'The language of politeness', *Papers from the Ninth Regional Meeting of the Chicago Linguistic Society*, Department of Linguistics, University of Chicago, pp. 292–305.

Larthomas, P. (1972), *Le Langage dramatique: sa nature, ses procédés*, Libraire Armand Colin, Paris.

Laver, J. (1970), 'The production of speech', in J. Lyons (ed), *New Horizons in Linguistics*, Penguin, Harmondsworth, pp. 53–76.

Laver, J. (1974), 'Communicative functions in phatic communion', *Work in Progress*, no. 7, Department of Linguistics, University of Edinburgh, pp. 1–18, also in A. Kendon, R.N. Harris and M.R. Key (eds), *The Organisation of Behaviour in Face-to-Face Interaction*, Mouton, The Hague, 1974 (a volume of World Anthropology, the proceedings of the IXth International Congress of Anthropological and Ethnological Sciences, Chicago, 1973).

Laver, J. and Hutcheson, S. (1972), *Communication in Face-to-Face Interaction*, Penguin, Harmondsworth.

Leitner, G., Kläge, H., Mundt, H.-H., Olejniczak, V. (1977), 'Sprachgebrauch im Rundfunk: Die Analyse von Phone-in Programmes. Ein Beitrag zur Gesprachsanalyse', mimeo, Technische Universität Hammover.

Levin, S.R. (1963), 'Deviation – statistical and determinate – in poetic language', *Lingua*, vol. XII, pp. 276–90.

Levin, S.R. (1964), 'Poetry and grammaticalness', in Horace G. Lunt (ed), *Proceedings of the Ninth International Congress of Linguists*, Mouton, The Hague, pp. 308–14, reprinted in S. Chatman and S.R. Levin (eds), *Essays on the Language of Literature*, Boston, 1967, pp. 224–30.

Levin, S.R. (1965), 'Two grammatical approaches to poetic analysis', *College Composition and Communication*, vol. XVI, pp. 256–60.

Levinson, S. and Brown, P. (1974), 'Some universals in language usage: politeness phenomena', mimeo, University of Texas.

Lewis, D. (1969), *Convention*, Harvard University Press, Cambridge, Mass.

Lodge, D. (1977), *Metaphor and Metonymy: The Modes of Modern Writing*, Edward Arnold, London.

Longacre, R.G. (1976), Review of Teun A. van Dijk, 'Some Aspects of Text Grammars', *Journal of Linguistics*, vol. 12, no. 1, pp. 169–97.

Lyman, S.M. and Scott, M.N. (1975), *The Drama of Social Reality*, Oxford University Press, London.

Lyons, J. (1968), *Introduction to Theoretical Linguistics*, Cambridge University Press, London.

Lyons, J. (1977), *Semantics*, Cambridge University Press, London.

McGranahan, D. and Wayne, T. (1948), 'Germanic and American traits reflected in popular drama', *Human Relations*, no. 1, 1948, pp. 429–55.

McIntosh, A. (1961), 'Patterns and ranges', in *Language*, vol. XXXVII, pp. 325–37.

McIntosh, A. (1966), 'Some thoughts on style', in A. McIntosh and M.A.K. Halliday (eds), *Patterns of Language*, Longman, London, pp. 83–97.

McIntosh, A. and Halliday, M.A.K. (eds) (1966), *Patterns of Language: Papers in General Descriptive and Applied Linguistics*, Longman, London.

McKnight, A. (1976), 'Large group conversation: problems for discourse analysis', unpublished MA dissertation, University of Lancaster.

McTear, M.F. (1975), 'Cos', paper read to the Child Language Conference, School of Education, University of Bristol, April 1975.

McTear, M.F. (1976), 'Repetition in child language: initiation or creation?', paper read at NATE conference 'Psychology of Language', Stirling University, June 1976.

McTear, M.F. (1977), 'Starting to talk: how pre-school children initiate conversational exchanges', mimeo, School of Communication Studies, N. Ireland Polytechnic.

Mead, R. (1976), 'The discourse of small-group teaching', mimeo, English Language Research, University of Birmingham.

Mead, R. (forthcoming), 'The discourse analysis of seminar discussion', unpublished PhD thesis, University of Birmingham.

Middleton, R. (1960), 'Fertility values in American magazine fiction', *Public Opinion Quarterly*, no. 24, 1960, pp. 139–43.

Milner, G.B. (1971), 'The quartered shield: outline of a semantic taxonomy', in E. Ardener (ed), *Social Anthropology and Language*, Tavistock, New York, pp. 243–69.

Mitchell-Kernan, C. (1972), 'Signifying and marking: two Afro-American speech acts', in J.J. Gumperz and D. Hymes (eds), *Directions in Sociolinguistics*, Holt, Rinehart & Winston, New York, pp. 161–80.

Montague, R. (1968), 'Pragmatics', in R. Klibansky (ed), *La Philosophie contemporaire*, La Nuova Italia Editrice, Firenze.

Montgomery, M.M. (1976), 'The discourse structure of lectures', mimeo, English Language Research, University of Birmingham.

Montgomery, M.M. (1977), 'The discourse structure of lectures', unpublished MA thesis, University of Birmingham.

Mowrer, P. (1970), 'Notes on Navajo silence behaviour', unpublished MS, University of Arizona.

Mukařovský, J. (1932), 'Standard language and poetic language', reprinted (abridged) in P. Garvin (ed), *A Prague School Reader on Esthetics, Literary Structure and Style*, Georgetown University Press, 1964, pp. 48–61.

Ogden, C.K. and Richards, I.A. (1923), *The Meaning of Meaning*, Routledge & Kegan Paul, London.

Ohmann, R. (1964), 'Generative grammars and the concept of literary style', *Word*, vol. 20, pp. 424–39.

Orton, J. (1967), *Loot*, Methuen, London.

Osborne, J. (1957), *The Entertainer*, Faber & Faber, London.

Page, N. (1973), *Speech in the English Novel*, Longman, London.

Parrett, H. (1976), 'Conventional implications and conversational implicatures', mimeo, Katholicke Universiteit Leuven, Department Linguistiek.

Pearce, R. (1973), 'The structure of discourse in broadcast interviews', unpublished MA thesis, University of Birmingham.

Pearce, R.D. (1974), 'Discourse analysis of the T.V. discussion programme', mimeo, English Language Research, University of Birmingham.

Pearce, R.D. (1977), 'A stylistic analysis of James Joyce's "A Portrait of the Artist as a Young Man"', unpublished PhD thesis, University of Birmingham.

Pike, K. (1964), 'Discourse analysis and tagmemic matrices', *Oceanic Linguistics*, vol. 3.

Pinter, H. (1957), *The Room and the Dumb Waiter*, Methuen, London.

Pinter, H. (1960), *The Birthday Party*, Methuen, London.

Pinter, H. (1961a), 'Last to go', in *A Slight Ache and Other Plays*, Methuen, London, 1972, pp. 29–32.

Pinter, H. (1961b), *A Slight Ache*, Methuen, London.

Pinter, H. (1961c), 'Trouble at the Works', in *A Slight Ache and Other Plays*, Methuen, London, 1972, pp. 33–4.

Pinter, H. (1967), *The Basement*, Methuen, London.

Pirandello, L. (1922), *Six Characters in Search of an Author*, trans. F. May, Methuen, London, 1954.

Pittenger, R.E., Hockett, C.F. and Daneby, J.J. (1960), *The First Five Minutes: A Sample of Microscopic Analysis*, Paul Martineau, New York.

Popper, K. (1965), 'Of clocks and cuckoos', 2nd Arthur Holly Compton memorial lecture, Washington University, 21 April 1965, reprinted in K. Popper, *Objective Knowledge: An Evolutionary Approach*, Routledge & Kegan Paul, London, 1972.

Pride, J. and Holmes, J. (eds) (1972), *Sociolinguistics*, Penguin, Harmondsworth.

Propp, V. (1928), *Morphology of the Folk-Tale*, trans. L. Scott, Indiana University Press, Bloomington, 1958.

Quigley, A. (1969), 'A stylistic analysis of H. Pinter's "The Dwarfs"', unpublished MA thesis, University of Birmingham.

Quigley, A. (1976), *The Pinter Problem*, Princeton University Press, New Jersey.

Quirk, R. (1972), *Linguistics and the Teacher of English*, Longman, London.

Ray, M.L. (1965), 'Cross-cultural content analysis: its promise and its problems', unpublished MS, Northwestern University.

Reisman, K. (1974), 'Contrapuntal conversations in an Antiguan village', in R. Bauman and J. Sherzer (eds), *The Ethnography of Speaking*, Cambridge University Press, London, pp. 110–25.

Rifaterre, M. (1959), 'Criteria for style analysis', in *Word*, vol. XV, pp. 154–74, reprinted in S. Chatman and S.R. Levin (eds), *Essays on the Language of Literature*, Boston, 1967, pp. 412–30.

Rifaterre, M. (1960), 'Stylistic Context', in *Word*, vol. XVI, pp. 207–18, reprinted in S. Chatman and S.R. Levin (eds), *Essays on the Language of Literature*, Boston, 1967, pp. 223–336.

Rifaterre, M. (1964), 'The stylistic function', in Horace G. Lunt (ed), *Proceedings of the Ninth International Congress of Linguists*, Mouton, The Hague, pp. 316–22.

Rockwell, J. (1974), *Fact in Fiction: The Use of Literature in the Systematic Study of Society*, Routledge & Kegan Paul, London.

Rothstein, R.A. (1968), 'The poetics of proverbs', in C.E. Gribble (ed), *Studies Presented to Professor Roman Jakobson by his Students*, Slavia Publications, Cambridge, Mass., pp. 265–74.

Sacks, H. (1968–70), lecture notes, mimeo, UCLA and Irvine.

Sacks, H. (1972), 'On the analysability of stories by children', in J.J. Gumperz and D. Hymes (eds), *Directions in Sociolinguistics*, Holt, Rinehart & Winston, New York, pp. 325–46.

Sacks, H. (1974), 'An analysis of the course of a joke's telling in conversation', in R. Bauman and J. Sherzer (eds), *The Ethnography of Speaking*, Cambridge University Press, London, pp. 337–54.

Sacks, H., Schegloff, E.A. and Jefferson, G. (1974), 'A simplest systematics for the organisation of turn-taking in conversation', *Language*, vol. 50, no. 4, pp. 696–735.

Saporta, S. (1960), 'The application of linguistics to the study of poetic language', in T.A. Sebeok, (ed), *Style in Language*, MIT, Cambridge, Mass., pp. 82–93.

Schaffer, A. (1973), *Sleuth*, Methuen, London.

Schegloff, E.A. (1968), 'Sequencing in conversational openings', *American Anthropologist*, vol. 70, no. 6, pp. 1075–95.

Schegloff, E.A. (1972), 'Notes on a conversational practice: formulating place', in D. Sudnow (ed), *Studies in Social Interaction*, The Free Press, New York, pp. 75–119.

Schegloff, E.A. and Sacks, H. (1973), 'Opening up closings', *Semiotica*, vol. 8, no. 4, pp. 289–327.

Searle, J.R. (1969), *Speech Acts: An Essay in the Philosophy of Language*, Cambridge University Press, London.

Sebeok, T.A. (ed) (1960), *Style in Language*, MIT, Cambridge, Mass.

Seitel, F. (1969), 'Proverbs: a social use of metaphor', *Genre*, vol. 2, pp. 143–61.

Sherzer, D. (1976), 'Gnomic utterances in Samuel Beckett's *Molloy*', in B. Kirschenblatt-Gimblett (ed), *Speech Play*, University of Pennsylvania Press, Philadelphia, pp. 204–26.

Short, M.H. (1970), 'A stylistic analysis of John Steinbeck's *Of Mice and Men*', unpublished MA thesis, University of Birmingham.

Short, M.H. (forthcoming), '*An Introduction to the Stylistic Analysis of Drama*', Allen & Unwin, London.

Simnel, G. (1898), 'Zur Philosophie der Schauspielers', in *Das Individuelle Gesetz*, Suhrkamp, 1968, pp. 75–95.

Simpson, N.F. (1957), *A Resounding Tinkle*, Penguin, Harmondsworth.

Sinclair, J. McH. (1966a), 'Taking a poem to pieces', in R. Fowler (ed), *Essays on Style and Language*, Routledge & Kegan Paul, London, 1968, pp. 68–72.

Sinclair, J. McH. (1966b), 'Indescribable English', inaugural lecture, University of Birmingham, unpublished.

Sinclair, J. McH. (1968), 'A technique of stylistic description', *Language and Style*, vol. 1, no. 4, pp. 27–41.

Sinclair, J. McH. (1972), *A Course in Spoken English: Grammar*, Oxford University Press, London.

Sinclair, J. McH. (1973), 'Linguistics in colleges of education', *Dudley Educational Journal*, vol. 1, no. 3, pp. 12–20.

Sinclair, J. McH. (1975), 'Discourse in relation to language structure and semiotics', paper prepared for the Burg Wartenstein Symposium on the Semiotics of Culture and Language, no. 66, August, 1975.

Sinclair, J. McH. (1977), 'Discourse in relation to language structure and semiotics', mimeo, paper given at the Burg Wartenstein Symposium on the Semiotics of Culture and Language.

Sinclair, J. McH., Coulthard, R.M., Forsyth, I.J. and Ashby, M. (1972), *The English Used by Teachers and Pupils*, report to the SSRC, mimeo, University of Birmingham.

Sinclair, J. McH. and Coulthard, R.M. (1975), *Towards an Analysis of Discourse: The English used by teachers and pupils*, Oxford University Press, London.

Soskin, W.F. and John, V. (1963), 'The study of spontaneous talk', in R.G. Barker (ed), *The Stream of Behaviour,* Appleton, New York.

Stankiewicz, E. (1960), 'Linguistics and the study of poetic language', in T.A. Sebeok (ed), *Style in Language,* MIT, Cambridge, Mass., pp. 69–81.

Stern, W. (1974), 'Mother and infant at play: the dyadic interaction involving facial, vocal and gaze behaviour', in M. Lewis (ed), *The Effect of the Infant on its Caregiver,* Wiley, New York.

Stewart, W.A. (1967), 'Sociolinguistic factors in the history of American negro dialects', *The Florida F L Reporter,* vol. 5, no. 2.

Stocker-Edel, A. (1976), 'Gesprachsanalyse in einer bestimmten Interview-situation', in W. Vierech (ed), *Sprachliches Handeln Soziales Verhalten: Ein Reader zur Pragmalinguistik und Soziolinguistik,* Wilhelm Funk Verlag, Munich.

Stoppard, T. (1967), *Rosencrantz and Guildenstern are Dead,* Faber & Faber, London.

Stoppard, T. (1968), *The Real Inspector Hound,* Faber & Faber, London.

Stoppard, T. (1969), *If You're Glad I'll be Frank,* Faber & Faber, London.

Stoppard, T. (1975), *Travesties,* Faber & Faber, London.

Strawson, P.F. (1974), 'Intention and convention in speech acts', *Philosophical Review,* vol. 73, pp. 439–60.

Stubbs, M. (1973), 'Some structural complexities of talk in meetings', *Working Papers in Discourse Analysis,* no. 5, mimeo, English Language Research, University of Birmingham.

Stubbs, M. (1974a), 'Discourse analysis of informal committee-talk', unpublished paper, English Language Research, University of Birmingham.

Stubbs, M. (1974b), 'Organising classroom talk', in *Occasional Paper 19,* Centre for Research in the Educational Sciences, University of Edinburgh.

Stubbs, M. (1976a), 'Keeping in touch: some functions of teacher-talk', in M. Stubbs and S. Delamont (eds), *Explorations in Classroom Observation,* Wiley, London.

Stubbs, M. (1976b), *Language, Schools and Classrooms,* Methuen, London.

Sudnow, D. (ed) (1972), *Studies in Social Interaction,* The Free Press, New York.

Tadros, A. (forthcoming), 'The structure of economics text', unpublished PhD thesis, University of Birmingham.

Thomas, D. (1954), *Under Milk Wood,* Penguin, Harmondsworth, 1965.

Thorne, J.P. (1965), 'Stylistics and generative grammars', *Journal of Linguistics,* vol. 1, pp. 49–59.

Thorne, J.P. (1969), 'Poetry, stylistics and imaginary grammars', *Journal of Linguistics,* vol. 5, pp. 17–50.

Turner, R. (1970), 'Words, utterances and activities', in J. Douglas (ed), *Understanding Everyday Life,* Aldine, Chicago, pp. 165–87, reprinted in R. Turner (ed), *Ethnomethodology,* Penguin, Harmondsworth, 1974, pp. 197–215.

Turner, R. (1972), 'Some formal properties of pre-therapy talk', in D. Sudnow (ed), *Studies in Social Interaction,* The Free Press, New York, pp. 367–97.

Turner, R. (1974), 'Utterance positioning as an inter-actional resource', in Robert J. Wilson (ed), *Ethnomethodology, Labelling Theory and Deviant Behaviour,* Routledge & Kegan Paul, London.

Tynan, K. (1958), 'Ionesco: man of destiny', *Observer,* 15 June, p. 18.

Uitti, L.D. (1969), *Linguistics and Literary Theory*, Prentice-Hall, Englewood Cliffs, NJ.

Van Dijk, T.A. (1970), 'Sémantique générale et théorie des textes', *Linguistics*, vol. 62.

Van Dijk, T.A. (1972), *Some Aspects of Text Grammars: A Study in Theoretical Linguistics and Poetics*, Mouton, The Hague.

Veltruský, J. (1940), 'Man and object in the theater', reprinted (abridged) in P. Garvin (ed), *A Prague School Reader on Esthetics, Literary Structure and Style*, Georgetown University Press, pp. 83–93.

Walker, R.C.S. (1975), 'Conversational implicatures', in S. Blackburn (ed), *Meaning, Reference and Necessity*, Cambridge University Press, London, pp. 131–81.

Ward, M.C. (1971), *Them Children: A Study in Language Learning*, Holt, Rinehart & Winston, New York.

Webb, E.J., Campbell, D.T., Schwartz, R.D. and Sechrest, L. (1966), *Unobtrusive Measures: Non-reactive Measures in the Social Sciences*, Rand McNally & Co., Chicago.

Weinreich, U. (1966), 'Explorations in semantic theory', in T.A. Sebeok (ed), *Theoretical Foundations*, vol. 3 of Current Trends in Linguistics, Mouton, The Hague.

Widdowson, H.G. (1972), 'On the deviance of literary discourse', *Style*, vol. 6, no. 2, pp. 294–305.

Widdowson, H.G. (1973), 'Directions in the teaching of discourse', *Theoretical Models in Applied Linguistics*, papers from the 3rd AIMAV seminar, in collaboration with AILA, CILA, and the Council of Europe, Neuchâtel, 5–6 May 1972, Didier, Paris, pp. 65–76.

Widdowson, H.G. (1974), 'An applied linguistic approach to discourse analysis', unpublished PhD thesis, University of Edinburgh.

Widdowson, H.G. (1975), *Stylistics and the Teaching of Literature*, Longman, London.

Widdowson, H.G. (1976), 'Approaches to discourse', in C. Gutknecht (ed), *Grundbegriffe und Hauptströmungen der Linguistik*, Hoffman und Campe, pp. 236–60.

Widdowson, H.G. (1979), 'Othello in person', mimeo, London Institute of Education.

Wilde, O. (1895), *The Importance of Being Ernest*, reprinted in Penguin Plays, Penguin, Harmondsworth, 1966.

Willes, M. (1975), 'Early Lessons learned too well', paper read to SSRC-funded conference on Collecting, Using and Reporting Talk for Research in Education, September 1975, University of Nottingham.

Willes, M. (1976), 'Sounding in King Lear', *MALS* journal, new series, no. 2, pp. 14–20.

Willett, J. (trans. and ed) (1964), *Brecht on Theatre*, Methuen, London.

Williams, R. (1968), *Drama from Ibsen to Brecht*, Chatto & Windus, London.

Williams, S. (1974), 'A sociolinguistic analysis of the general practice interview', unpublished MA thesis, University of Birmingham.

Winograd, T. (1972), *Understanding Natural Language*, The University Press, Edinburgh.

Winter, E.O. (1977), 'A clause-relational approach to English texts: a study of some predictive lexical stems in written discourse', *Instructional Science*, special issue, vol. 6, no. 1.

Wolfram, R.A. (1969), *A Sociolinguistic Description of Detroit negro speech*, Center for Applied Linguistics, Washington, DC.

Wooton, A. (1975), *Dilemmas in Discourse*, Routledge & Kegan Paul, London.

Yngve, M. (1970), 'On getting a word in edgewise', *Papers for the VIth Regional Meeting of the Chicago Linguistic Society*, pp. 567–77.

Index of names and titles

Index of subjects

AB-events, 13
Abstract, 57–8; *see also* Narrative
Absurdity, 26, 68, 112
Accepts, *see* Acts
Accuse, *see* Acts
Acknowledge, *see* Acts
Acts, 124, 126, 130; accept, 126, 137, 143, 145, 158; accuse, 143, 145, 157; acknowledge, 135, 158; aside, 120, 138; bid, 133; check, 132; clue, 133; comment, 136, 143, 146, 158; conclusion, 157; cue, 133; directive, 80–2, 91, 132, 157; elicitation, 97, 122, 126, 131, 157; engage, 134; evaluate, 126, 137, 159; excuse, 143, 145, 158; informative, 133, 143, 146, 157; loop, 138; marker, 130, 143, 156; metastatement, 138, 157; nomination, 126, 135; preface, 143, 146, 158; prompt, 133, 159; react, 80, 136, 158; reply, 126, 136, 158; silent stress, 137, 157; starter, 122, 131, 157; summons, 143–4, 156
Additive clauses, 146
Addressee, 175 f.
Addresser, 175 f.
Address terms, 48–9
Adjacency pairs, 59

Adult–child talk, 70, 71, 75, 78, 89, 97
Alienation devices and effects, 101 f.
Analysis, 68, 92 f., 119; *see also* Comparative analysis

Babbling, 66
Backchannelling, 32–3
Background expectancies, 106 f.
Bid; *see* Acts
Black American English, 58, 71
Boundary, *see* Exchange
Bound and free units, 124
Bound-Opening, *see* Move
Bourgeois theatre, 111, 173 f.
Breach of commitment, 43; *see also* Speech act theory, Philosophy of language
Breaking frame, 180

Category-bound activity, 40
Challenging, *see* Move
Check, *see* Acts
Childlike talk, 70–1, 75, 85
Children's talk, 16, 40, 41, 58, 60, 66–7, 76, 86–7
Claiming the floor, 54, 57
Clarity, 119
Classroom discourse, 109, 120
Close analysis, 119
Closings, 22–3, 58–9